COMMUNITY ACROSS TIME

COMMUNITY

ACROSS

TIME

ROBERT MORGAN'S
WORDS FOR
HOME

REBECCA GODWIN

WEST VIRGINIA UNIVERSITY PRESS / MORGANTOWN

ISBN 978-1-952271-82-3 (paperback) / 978-1-952271-83-0 (ebook)

Library of Congress Control Number: 2022049955

Cover design by Than Saffel / WVU Press
Cover image by Randi Anglin

He realized that he needed both kinds of perception to be who he was. He could draw and paint the isolated, tattered cornstalks, the hidden alcove in the pines, but in doing so he had to be conscious of the world in general, all kinds of people, even the course of history. He could not have one without the other.

—Robert Morgan, "Murals,"
The Balm of Gilead Tree: New and Selected Stories

Contents

Preface

When Robert Morgan received the North Carolina Literary and Historical Association's 2007 R. Hunt Parker Memorial Award for significant contributions to the literature of North Carolina, his biography of Daniel Boone had just appeared, joining volumes of poetry and fiction that bring the western part of the state's landscape, culture, and history alive. Delivering the keynote address that evening in Asheville, he spoke passionately about his new book, clearly enjoying the discoveries that deepened his understanding of westward expansion and the man behind the frontier myth. He described complexities and connections key to his vision of history, a vision informed by his home soil as well as the people who dwelt on it earlier than he. Discovering much to say about his southern Appalachian home, he has become its historian, cultivating memory and community through an examination of his "mother world"—as he calls the forest where Boone summered as a boy with his mother—a place of vast mystery to be explored.

Accepting membership in the North Carolina Literary Hall of Fame in October 2010 in Southern Pines, Morgan made clear that he had no choice but to follow a call to mine not just the square mile of land on which he grew up in the Blue Ridge Mountains but also the landscape of language. In remarks recorded that induction day, he relates North Carolina's literary richness to the Southern Renaissance, to Thomas Wolfe, and then to the flourishing literary scene in southern Appalachia, "a region discovering itself," with mountain music and Bible-reading inspiring a love of language, motivating writers to explore the place and "to never let the truth stand in the way of a good story."[1] An earlier interview with Jeff Daniel Marion, published in *The Small Farm* in 1976, reveals that one of Morgan's truths is the sense of isolation from and inferiority to the rest of the country that he felt growing up in southern Appalachia. He embraces and challenges these early feelings, revealing in poetry and prose the wisdom, survival skills, and deep, imperfect humanity of ordinary Appalachian people while using language to excavate the treasures of the Blue Ridge's natural world.

After introducing Morgan's place, influences, and literary context, I offer an extended biographical essay going back several generations, to the ancestors who were especially important for his fiction but also much of his poetry. These earlier generations gave Morgan stories that he shapes into a narrative of the Appalachian South, a region playing its part in United States history. Some of this material appears in condensed form in later chapters that analyze the literature, providing immediate context for characters, plots, or themes, particularly for readers going straight to discussions of particular books or stories. Chapters three through five focus on the fiction but integrate poetry to illustrate Morgan's whole-cloth approach to his writing. I separate the historical fiction from the family novels, although these categories often overlap, and I analyze the short fiction relating closely to the longer narratives according to chronology or subject matter in the chapters devoted mainly to the novels. Chapter five analyzes short stories not previously discussed. Chapter six, a brief exploration of the poetry, introduces readers to Morgan's study of subjects in different genres, with a glance at the development of his poetic style and his achievements in classical forms.

I owe a great debt to Robert Morgan for his openness during in-person and e-mail interviews over a decade. Forming the biographical essay, details he shared unveil his respect for his relatives, the land he knew growing up, the natural world, science, history, and knowledge of all kinds. Studying Morgan's work, I have enjoyed meeting many others who admire it, and I thank them for their scholarship, much but not all of it cited in this study. Finally, I share that Robert Morgan's stories and poems resonate with my upbringing on a small family farm in eastern North Carolina among a large extended family. My own storytelling relatives, along with memories of chopping corn and feeding chickens, have become even dearer because of his authentic, learned portrayal of the Morgan land at the opposite end of the state.

Rebecca Godwin
August 21, 2021

Influences and Context: Robert Morgan in Literary Community

O nce, an interviewer meeting Robert Morgan at his childhood home in North Carolina's Blue Ridge Mountains asked how Morgan possibly could have gotten from that modest farm to Cornell University. Morgan understood the difficulty of connecting an accomplished writer to cornfields and an old barn, especially given stereotypes about rural Appalachia. Yet he credits being born and raised in this state, on this hardscrabble farm, with making him the writer he became.[1] He believes that these southern highlands were given to him as his subject: "stories told me by members of my family, or just the history of the area, the geology and geography."[2] With few American writers focusing on the region, he saw an opportunity that he seized, exploring difficult national narratives as they played out in this particular locale: economic hardship, the ravaging of Indian tribes during settlement, divisions and griefs shaped by wars and religious differences, worrisome social class distinctions, slavery, and environmental destruction. The physical terrain, storytellers, and rich literary landscape of his home state created the sense of place that allowed his imagination to soar into and beyond the confines of his childhood community.

The western North Carolina mountain range where he sets most of his work, a place of high elevations and astounding biodiversity, presents a backdrop for the history that Morgan's relatives highlighted through stories of generations past. Rambling through woods and working fields on his family's farm near Zirconia—roughly seventy miles southwest of Mount Mitchell, the highest peak in the eastern United States—as a child, Morgan learned to distinguish soils, weeds, trees, insects, and birdsong. He found Indian arrowheads and imagined those who preceded him on this spot of earth. He dug in the zircon pits that gave his community its name when mineralogist William Hidden, a Thomas Edison associate who discovered that zirconium could be used in light bulb filaments, opened a zircon mine in the 1890s, giving jobs to locals, including Morgan's relatives.[3] His surroundings thus taught Morgan to explore history and science from a personal perspective, as revealed in his poem "Zircon," published in *Dark Energy*. Here, we see his typical interweaving of place, time, family, and history, with science completing the field, as it does in many poems: "When my great-uncles dug for zircons on / the mountain-side and on the pasture hill / a hundred years ago they'd no idea / the little crystal bit they sought would be / a token from the planet's fiery birth."[4] Early intimacy with the landscape joined with family stories to give him constant lessons in nature's workings as well as time's steady movement, leading him to understand "community across time," a phrase he offers in a 2001 *Appalachian Journal* interview to describe his fictional writing about the past.[5] His non-fiction and poetry share that thematic thread, with his sense of community extending to the physical universe providing people's home.

The range of Morgan's literary achievements—poetry, novels, short fiction, biography, historical vignettes, and drama—marks the artistic distinction with which he has mined the history of his Mountain South. As of 2021, he has published four short story collections, sixteen poetry volumes, seven novels, and three books of nonfiction. *Good Measure* assembles some of his interviews and essays on poetry. His biography *Boone* and his biographical sketches of ten Americans important to the country's westward expansion, *Lions of the West: Heroes and Villains of the Westward Expansion*, both received praise from historians such as David Brinkley and the Pulitzer Prize-winning Michael Kammen. Author Richard Bausch's *Boone* cover blurb, "I wish more first-rate novelist-poets wrote biography," attests to Morgan's flair for language that makes the *story* in *history* come alive. His narrative skills and poetic concision obviously transfer well to script writing, too. The University of Tennessee, Knoxville staged his play *Homemade Yankees* when it won the John Cullum Civil War Playwriting Contest sponsored by the Clarence Brown Theatre and the East Tennessee Civil War Alliance in 2014. This play, like much of Morgan's fiction, is based upon family history, a Home Guard assault of a young girl. Morgan connects the specific family story to universal truths that emanate through all his writing, no matter the genre: human frailty and endurance, moral ambiguities that complicate human struggle, and the divinity of the natural world that humans ignore at their own peril.

Relating to Appalachian Writers

Several writers helped Morgan see his Southern mountain homeland as a worthy subject for literature. When he read *Look Homeward, Angel* by Thomas Wolfe (1900–1938) at age sixteen, he recognized its setting of nearby Asheville and also felt that protagonist Eugene Gant embodied his own anxieties and aspirations. Wolfe's rich language thrilled him even though it described a town life that the farm boy had never known. Later, the rural landscapes of another fine novelist born in Asheville, John Ehle (1925–2018), also triggered Morgan's imaginative view of his home. Critic and Appalachian novelist Terry Roberts argues that Ehle's national reputation remains limited precisely because he set his best-known work, a seven-novel series recounting North Carolina mountain settlement from the late eighteenth century through the Great Depression, in Appalachia, a region that many outsiders continue to stereotype as "backward."[6] Ehle published *The Landbreakers* in 1964, decades before Morgan's first story collection appeared. In it, he begins a family lineage that continues through *Last One Home*, published twenty years later, his "little postage stamp of native soil"—like Faulkner's and, later, Morgan's—holding a world of kin living the American story.[7] European settlement, the building of railroads, the Civil War in Appalachian communities, and agricultural as well as urban landscapes mark Ehle's description of regional development. Morgan acknowledges that Ehle inspired him, noting the influence of *The Land Breakers* and *The Road*, especially: "I was caught up in the sweep of history, the precise and accurate detail, the sheer beauty of the description of the mountains themselves." For his generation, Morgan attests, "writers such as John Ehle . . . encouraged us to imagine that we might one day write stories of the region and its history and people and get them published."[8] Like Ehle, Morgan avoids stereotyping, never presenting mountain people as heroes or hillbillies but as working-class people simply confronting life's challenges.

Morgan also credits as an important influence Asheville native Wilma Dykeman, whose first book, *The French Broad*, appeared in 1955 as part of the Rivers of America series. With narrative flair, Dykeman (1920–2006) tells this western North Carolina–Tennessee river country's history, including the settlers' cheating of the Cherokees, Civil War massacres, hog drives, religion, and industrialization, bringing daily work to life and connecting human endeavors to indiscriminate environmental desecration. Reading Dykeman in the early 1970s, Morgan found *The French Broad* inspiring him "to think about the mountains and history in new ways."[9] His remarks at her memorial service, printed in *Appalachian Journal*, explain that she showed him that fiction about this region must center on "the land and the seasons, and the strong women who struggled on the land . . . to keep families together over the generations," a lesson he applied in his work.[10] Morgan wrote the introduction for Dykeman's posthumously published memoir, *Family of Earth* (UNC Press, 2016), and in April 2016, he delivered the keynote address at the Wilma Dykeman Festival at the University of Tennessee, Knoxville. Giving back to the literary community that helped him find his own place in it has been a defining trait of his career.

Morgan recognizes another woman who taught him to appreciate the speech of his mountain people, an important step in finding his own fictional voice. In the 2001 *Pembroke Magazine* issue honoring a writer born the same year as he, Morgan contributes a short essay called "Writing the Living Voice: The Achievement of Lee Smith":

> I will never forget the excitement of discovery when I first read Lee Smith's *Oral History* in the 1980s. I was working my way back into fiction, after years of writing only poetry, and I was looking for books to teach me how to make a story come alive. As I began *Oral History*, I saw how dead-on the voices were, how Smith had caught the living idiom of the Appalachian region. . . . It is exhilarating to see how she gets a complex story of families and communities underway and lets it unfold across the years. . . . She writes the living voices. . . . Reading her work showed me the possibilities of contemporary fiction, and of Appalachian fiction.[11]

Notably, Smith's voices in this 1983 novel reflect a century of changing Appalachian idiom, with Granny Younger's late nineteenth-century vernacular giving way to less metaphoric, more educated speech as narrators live in later decades. Language reflects history here, as Morgan understands.

Morgan's fellow writers Fred Chappell and Ron Rash, like him award-winners in both prose and poetry, also probe their southern Appalachian roots in major contributions to America's literary tradition. Chappell, who is especially adept at integrating mythology and allusion with regional elements, modeled for Morgan the marriage of mountain voice and remarkable intellect when he encouraged him in the graduate program at the University of North Carolina at Greensboro in the 1960s. In a 1982 essay on Chappell's four-volume poetry work *Midquest*, Morgan acknowledges his teacher's talents for poetry, novels, and short stories—an ironic lauding of the versatility that he himself achieved within a decade. "There is a wholeness about the work of Fred Chappell," Morgan declares. "Everything he does seems a piece of the same cloth. . . . It is the voice that dominates and is recognizable . . . speaking with great richness of mind and language, deeply learned."[12] Chappell establishes the community through time that Morgan also portrays, and Morgan weaves the same "whole cloth" magic into his own work, creating poetry from tidbits of historical research or sharpening a family member's fictional portrayal in poetic lines. As Chappell inspired Morgan, Morgan in turn has influenced the slightly younger Ron Rash. Morgan's work correlates to Rash's, particularly in their portrayals of agrarian landscapes, their fictionalizing of southern Appalachian history, and their calling attention to environmental destruction, a key theme in Rash's *Serena*. Rash dedicates his story collection *Nothing Gold Can Stay* to Morgan, and its settings range from the Civil War to contemporary periods, reminiscent of the time spans in all of Morgan's story collections.

Hemingway and the Romantics

Robert Morgan's influences and his place in the literary canon do move beyond Appalachia. As he began to develop as a writer, he consciously chose Ernest Hemingway's concise prose style as a model, finding its directness and clarity just as powerful as Thomas Wolfe's rhetorical sentences. Morgan first read Hemingway as a teenager, a few weeks before that writer's July 3, 1961, death and months after he had discovered Wolfe's lavish prose. He observed that "Hemingway's diction was plain and spare, his sentences stripped down," creating a "quiet language." Morgan compares the two writers: "Where Wolfe had celebrated emotion through overstatement and explicitness, Hemingway drove home the emotions by suggestion, by implicitness" that "evokes emotional and spiritual depth under a surface of fact and control, even nonchalance." He saw Hemingway's style as implying "a rigor similar to science,"[13] a comparison reflecting his college training in mathematics and aerospace engineering. Morgan adopted Hemingway's controlled diction and indirectness, and the precise, succinct language that Morgan honed through poetry carried over to the plain-style voice of his fictional narrators.

Morgan's language and sensibilities also reflect his attraction to the American Romantics and Transcendentalists, an affinity that grew when he taught these literary giants at Cornell University. He explains that as he struggled to come to terms with his parents' Southern Baptist and Pentecostal Holiness religions, both emphasizing otherworldliness rather than this-worldliness, writers such as Emerson, Whitman, Thoreau, and Dickinson guided his "coming out from under Calvinism."[14] Emerson's clear language and philosophical stance on nature profoundly affected Morgan's articulation of the unity of all creation. In chapter IV of his essay "Nature," Emerson explains nature as the source of all language, and language as the connector between the physical and spiritual worlds. Morgan's hours spent alone in fields and woods showed him the truth of this paradigm. On the cover of *Sigodlin*, Sandra McPherson observes that Morgan's poetry "has more *touchable* things per line than one would think the world offers; but that is exactly how he gets us to stop ignoring our world." Morgan sees, in the tradition of these American literary forebears, resurrection in this observable world: "physical regeneration within nature, moral and spiritual renewal within the human community."[15] His focus on this capacity for rebirth helped him to overcome the poverty and occasional gloominess that his childhood world presented, particularly in his father's fatalistic attitude toward his own failed farming endeavors. Morgan mines language's possibilities for validating this world's value, in poetry and prose celebrating nature's and people's energy for movement and change.

Belief in possibility is evident in the motif of work that permeates Morgan's writing. He plowed behind a horse the day before leaving for college at age sixteen and maintained his respect for physical labor as he moved to more intellectual endeavors. In an unpublished memoir titled *Mountains, Machines, and Memory*, he shares that he started hoeing corn at age five and describes his early zeal for clearing away weeds, no doubt imitating his father's passion for mowing ditch banks in order to ignore money troubles or church quarrels. In the memoir, Morgan invokes a metaphor that appears in many of his poems, a comparison erasing the distinction between physical and cerebral labor, particularly the art of writing. He remembers seeing weeds as a weakness disrupting life's tidiness. To weed is to "edit the soil," he says, so that only the desired plants flourish.[16] Ordering plants through weeding is much like lining up just the right words to contain life's chaos. He also explains in the memoir that he saw his building of a dam and pond when he was eleven as the "essence of art," in that it imposed his idea on the natural world.[17] His understanding of physical work as art, and verbal art as labor—reminiscent of Seamus Heaney's parallel of the two in his poem "Digging"—helped Morgan see, as an adult, that his father's manual toil, although it brought little income, nevertheless had a "grandeur" that "belonged not just to him, but to the work itself."[18] In prose and poetry, he elevates physical work as well as nature's communication that agricultural labor helps people see firsthand.

Finding His Own Literary Place

When Morgan turned to fiction in the 1980s, after eight volumes of poetry, he did so because his emotional connection to the North Carolina farm kept pulling his imagination. His attachment to home often literally pulled him back to the South after he moved to New York in 1971. When his parents were alive (his father died in 1991 and his mother in 2010), he visited numerous times each year, and more often than planned when he was called upon to help with their care. Since his parents' deaths, he returns to Green River to maintain the homeplace and visit relatives. With that home base, he gives of his time to advance Appalachian writing and storytelling. In 2010, for instance, he helped poet Keith Flynn, founder and editor of *Asheville Poetry Review*, to plan an Asheville Wordfest fundraiser.[19] September 2012 found him at the annual Carolina Mountains Literary Festival in Burnsville, speaking on the theme of "Landscapes of the Imagination." That same fall, he spoke at a Western Carolina Community Action fundraiser in Hendersonville, raising money to assist literacy programs, the homeless, and battered women. He lectured at Hindman Settlement School in Kentucky in the fall of 2012 and addressed the Fellowship of Southern Writers, of which he is a member, on writing about warfare at its April 2011 meeting in Chattanooga, Tennessee.[20] These events exemplify Morgan's efforts to create community with neighbors, readers, and fellow writers in southern Appalachia, giving back to the place that helped him find his voice.

His reading community has in turn paid tribute to Morgan's literary excellence. Emory & Henry College in Virginia featured Morgan at its annual festival honoring a single Appalachian writer and published conference assessments of his work in its 1990 *Iron Mountain Review*. Pembroke University, in southeastern North Carolina, later organized a Robert Morgan symposium and published papers in the 2003 issue of *Pembroke Magazine*. The 2004 *Appalachian Heritage* is devoted to his work, and the *Southern Quarterly* offered in the spring of 2010 the *Robert Morgan Special Issue: A Community across Time*. He has appeared several times at the University of South Carolina Union's Upcountry Literary Festival. While he was there in 2013, he received the Singing Billy Walker Award and paid homage to this song composer, whose *Southern Harmony* shape note singing hymnbook became a nineteenth-century regional cultural treasure. And of course, his renown extends to the country as a whole, as signified by his 2007 Academy Award in Literature from the American Academy of Arts and Letters.

As Morgan reflects on his acclaimed work in prose and poetry, he explains a change in his thinking about himself as a writer. His initial goal, in his late teens, was to be a novelist. Then he turned to poetry in college, with early publications making that genre seem to be his forte. In his midthirties, he again started writing fiction, giving way to the joy of losing himself in the voice of characters. When the Oprah Book Club selection of *Gap Creek* brought him "hundreds of thousands of readers," dwarfing his poetry audience, Morgan realized that he liked writing "human stories that almost anybody can understand," that he had "all along . . . wanted to write the kind of fiction that would *really mean* something to a large number of people."[21] Although he continued a prolific schedule of writing and publishing poetry, he began to devote equal time to prose. His resulting novels focus mainly on agrarian southern

Appalachia, while his short fiction also incorporates the industrialized South. These two aspects of his exploration echo other double visions that mark his literary production.

When Morgan moved to the Appalachian North to teach at Cornell, he was surprised that his thoughts kept returning to Green River and the farm he had wanted to escape. He found himself scouring shelves in the university library for books on the history and geography of his Appalachian South. He offers the Welsh word *hiraeth*, meaning "intense longing for home," to explain the "repulsion and attraction" that led family members to leave the mountains and then return, an explanation for the many words he has published about the southern Appalachian homeland he left physically.[22] Speaking of his up-bringing on the square mile of land that his great-great-grandfather bought, he says, "Since moving away, I have found myself comparing everything I've seen to that archetypal acreage, soil, plants, climate, stream beds, as well as people."[23] That place in Green River holds tensions that feed Morgan's imagination. Like other writers from the South, Morgan points to childhood church services as one source of his love of language. Oral biblical reading, hymns, and preaching let him know that he had to get to that place of language, although he eschewed institutionalized religion as an adult. And while his characters seem integrated with the natural landscape of their place, journeying is also a recurring theme in his work. In *The Hinterlands*, *Gap Creek*, *Brave Enemies*, and *Chasing the North Star*, as well as in the biography *Boone*, characters travel, sometimes going out and returning to a homeplace, as does Muir in *This Rock* and *The Road from Gap Creek*. Their explorations reflect not only Morgan's own leaving and frequent return to Green River but also America's movement westward and, for African Americans, northward. As Jim Wayne Miller says of James Still's characters, journeying outward "heighten[s] the sense of belonging to one familiar spot of earth." Morgan's characters, too, are rooted yet "journeying through the world."[24]

This paradox resonates with the dual vision in one of Morgan's early poems. In "Double Springs," published in his 1976 collection *Land Diving*, he describes two underground springs that surface close together, one flowing from a southern direction, with "sweeter" but "slow" water, the other from the north, "icy." Despite its sediment, the speaker drinks last from the southern flow, saying its "ungodly taste" is the one he would "carry home."[25] These two springs mirror Morgan's own double vision and represent Appalachia as a border country within the United States. His sense of the past and its impact on our current world, his rural upbringing and his urbanity, his scientific and mathematical knowledge and his devotion to the humanities, his fitting into both Northern and Southern cultures—all these dichotomies define the man and help to explain his literary work that makes us appreciate the large sweep of history, the tiny dahlia, and the significance of everyday persons' views of each.

Morgan's final poem in *At the Edge of the Orchard Country*, "Field Theory," ends with these lines: "when I woke / . . . in the non-euclidean mountains / recovering pieces of the morgenland." The German word *morgenland*, meaning "morning land," provides a positive pun for Morgan's Welsh name as it announces his desire to bring to light that section of America he knew as a child, those relatives and mountain people who "didn't care . . . to step on horizons."[26] *Non-euclidean* evokes the mountains' curved surfaces as well as the fact that parallel lines can meet in non-euclidean geometry, an image relating to the community across time that Morgan's work establishes, the meeting of the past and the present. And if we consider that *euclidian* denotes the geometry of ordinary experience, *non-euclidian* seems to be a paradox, given that Morgan's poetry and fiction most often describe the everyday. Perhaps he hints that the Blue Ridge's landscape and working-class people are not ordinary at all.

Chapter 2

Roots of a Writing Life: His Appalachian Homes, South and North

When Robert Morgan was born one year before the end of World War II, his home in the Blue Ridge chain of the Southern Appalachians was on the verge of change. The economic boom following the war brought needed jobs to rural communities and small towns there as it did to the rest of the country, beginning a transformation whose pace escalated as the twentieth century progressed. Morgan's family both embraced and resisted this modern world, creating a tension mirrored in cultural shifts and, ultimately, in his own transition from hardscrabble farm boy to Ivy League university professor and writer. He left North Carolina in 1971 to teach at Cornell University, but during frequent visits home, he witnessed the demise of the agricultural life he knew in childhood, fields replaced with strip malls or gated communities and increasing numbers of summer tourists. A culture in transition often prompts writers to examine what is disappearing, and although Morgan felt at home in northern Appalachia in many ways, his homesickness for his Blue Ridge community also drew him to that landscape and his own family history. As Eudora Welty contends in her essay "Place in Fiction," "One place comprehended can make us understand other places better," and "How can you go out on a limb if you do not know your own tree?"[1] Sharing Welty's understanding that writers bring a new vision to heritage and place, Morgan began to look closely at the work, the speech, and the religion of his people, preserving the past by turning familial history into art representing America's story.

As his poetry and fiction, as well as his essays and interviews, make clear, Morgan believes that place goes beyond geography to language itself—and not just the mountain vernacular. "The landscape I'm interested in is as much the landscape of language as the literal terrain," he says in an interview concentrating on his poetry, adding, "We live and speak in a landscape of symbols and references and cultural images and conditioning, as well as a world of trees and windy fields."[2] Morgan connects the metaphoric landscape of language directly to the natural world that records its own history: "the continent has been written on by glaciers, earthquakes, floods, buffalo, Indians, and hunters," he declares.[3] His Emersonian view that nature's language connects the physical world with spiritual truths reflects his sense of unity, of humans' connections over time and their elemental bond with the natural world. Alertness to vivid physical place as well as to the cerebral world of language and metaphor has led Morgan to live with a foot in two worlds, as he believes all writers do. Binaries and oppositions were there to be reconciled as he grew, left home yet retained ties to his birthplace, shifted his study from science and mathematics to literature, and became a serious writer.

Ancestors: Great-Great-Grandparents through Grandparents

Robert Morgan's birth in Hendersonville's Patton Memorial Hospital on October 3, 1944, brought him into a family that knew its heritage and passed it down. Although he has just one sibling, his sense of direct kinship includes four generations that shaped the earliest setting he knew. His Welsh ancestors, probably sheepherders around Bala, left North Wales in the eighteenth century, searching for free land in America.[4] From Philadelphia, they spread south along the Appalachian Mountains, and since Blue Ridge land was available and looked like their Welsh hills, many settled in western South Carolina and North Carolina. In fact, Morgan's home area was at one time called the Morgan District. He acknowledges that the focus on land in his work stems from his sense that these ancestors became obsessed with owning family land.[5] These generations of kin shape both his poetry and prose.

Great-great-grandfathers on both parents' sides owned tracts in Henderson County. Morgan's maternal great-great-grandfather, John Levi (1798–1873), received a land grant on Painter Mountain, the local name for Panther Mountain, for his youthful service in the War of 1812. An adventurous, gambling man born in Pickens County, South Carolina, Levi claimed to be a Jew from London, and London Jews did settle in the early eighteenth century just a few counties away from Morgan's birthplace. Not far from Painter Mountain, Morgan's paternal great-great-grandfather, Daniel Pace (1791–1871), moved from the Mountain Page area near Saluda to buy one square mile of land, 640 acres, for $500 in 1838, settling there with his wife, Sarah Revis Pace (1793–1877). The tract runs from Green River to the rim of Mount Olivet, a place often referenced in Morgan's fiction. Both Levis and Paces form family lines important to his fiction.

The son born to Daniel and Sarah Pace the year they put down roots, John

Benjamin Franklin Pace (1838–1918), came vividly to life for Morgan through stories he told his grandson, Morgan's father. With straight, black hair and dark coloring evidenced in his Confederate photograph, Frank Pace almost surely had Cherokee blood according to Morgan, although family explained his coloring as deriving from "some Italian way back there." In his later years, when Frank's neighbors were suffering from ailments, he provided herbal remedies, some his ancestors learned from Catawba and Cherokee Indians. He once took his ill teenaged daughter Sarah to an Indian doctor in South Carolina for a successful cure. Frank Pace, this "colorful storyteller," went to Washington, DC, around 1900 to tell the Bureau of Indian Affairs what he knew about the 1785 Treaty of Hopewell, an agreement between the Confederation Congress of the United States of America and Cherokees. This treaty, signed in northwestern South Carolina, set a western boundary for American settlement. Pace shared with government officials his knowledge of the Ninety-Six Line that colonial Governor Tryon established with Attakullakulla, a Cherokee chief.[6] Morgan explores this history in his poems "Attakullakulla Goes to London" and "Ninety-Six Line," where he clarifies that white settlers did not stay on their side of the line that intersected the land "where / [he] grew up many treaties later / with one foot in the English / country, one in the high dark / hunting ranges."[7] In his Daniel Boone biography and other work, Morgan redresses the disparaging attitude toward Indians reflected in his family's refusal to acknowledge Cherokee blood in their own.

For Morgan, Frank Pace became an emblem of history, especially of the Civil War, for he was one of two paternal great-grandfathers who were taken prisoner while fighting for the Confederacy. Morgan commemorates John Morgan (1836–1863), who died at Camp Douglas in Chicago, in his short story "A Brightness New and Welcoming." Frank Pace joined the Confederate Army in 1861, being falsely promised one year's service if he volunteered.[8] After fighting with Longstreet at Chickamauga, he was captured at Petersburg in 1864 and hauled to the Elmira, New York, prison camp, called "Hell-mira" by detainees. When the war ended in April 1865, he rode a Union train to Greenville, South Carolina, and walked back to Green River. Morgan immortalizes Frank Pace's experiences in the poems "The Road from Elmira," which appeared in *Sigodlin*, and "Confederate Graves at Elmira," published in *Terroir*, as well as in the short story "Martha Sue." This story also includes Pace's marriage to a Union soldier's daughter, Mary Ann Jones (1838–1880). Her father, John Jones (1815–1864), from nearby Upward, crossed the mountains to Tennessee to join Union forces and died at Cumberland Gap. Pro-Union sentiment ran strong in North Carolina's western mountain region, but although much violence ensued between Unionists and Confederate sympathizers, Morgan's great-grandfather chose to move past all animosities once the conflict ended. In his fiction, Morgan follows the historical reality that political differences did not cause a problem in the Pace-Jones marriage. Religion caused the trouble, as it did for generations to come.

The religious rifts appearing in "Martha Sue," as in Morgan's novels *The Truest Pleasure* and *This Rock*, have roots in America's Second Great Awakening, a period of religious revival that began in the late eighteenth century and reached its zenith in the second half of the nineteenth. This movement swept the Southern armies during the Civil War and continued afterward, with traveling charismatic preachers holding revival camp meetings all over the country. These revivals emphasized the direct experience of God through baptism with the Holy Spirit, evidenced in speaking in tongues or dancing. Prisoners at the Elmira prison camp found gospel singing and emotional worship helped them to survive the camp's gruesome conditions, and Frank Pace returned to Green River experienced in these Holiness practices that led to the emergence of Pentecostalism in the early twentieth century. After going to one camp meeting with him, his Hard-Shell Baptist wife refused to attend another. Morgan's great-grandmother Mary Ann disapproved so vehemently of speaking in tongues and dancing that she insisted she not be buried in the Pace cemetery, where her husband Frank rests. Her grave lies at Upward Refuge Baptist Church in the nearby Dana community. Interestingly, in 1890, Frank Pace gave land for the Green River Baptist Church, built at the center of a community that came to be known as Meeting House Mountain,[9] and when that congregation "churched" him for attending brush arbor meetings, throwing him out of the church, he simply ignored the decree and remained an active member. Such conflict within an institution that purportedly brought solace to humans, a conflict Morgan saw firsthand in ensuing generations, presented one of the paradoxes forming his perception of the world's ironies and contradictions.

Morgan's mother's family appears as often as his father's in his work, their stories presenting equally intriguing visions of history and human strife. His dark and French-looking great-great-grandmother, Rebecca Ann Blocker Johnson (1832–1924), born to Huguenots on a South Carolina plantation near Walterboro, came to Flat Rock, North Carolina, for her health at age sixteen. Her plantation connection brought pretensions to blue blood into the family, although some relatives think her father may have managed, not owned, the plantation. When Rebecca married George Johnson, a cabinetmaker who did carpentry work for summer homeowners in Flat Rock, her family disowned her. They left her no inheritance but evidently welcomed her and her children to Walterboro during the Civil War. George Johnson had been drafted into the Confederacy, and Rebecca feared the Home Guard, whose brigades sometimes treated civilians brutally, as Charles Frazier depicts in his novel *Cold Mountain* (1998). Rebecca and her children arrived in South Carolina shortly before General Sherman marched through the state. Morgan's great-grandmother Delia Johnson Capps (1860–1953), pictured at age fourteen on the cover of his poetry collection *The Strange Attractor*, remembered seeing bodies stacked on porches and dogs licking the blood during this time.[10]

Knowing someone with memories of the Civil War deepened Morgan's grasp of history. In his unpublished memoir, *Mountains, Machines, and Memory*, Morgan describes Sunday afternoon visits with Delia, whom he called Grandmother as his mother did. "Grandmother's place stirred an intimate sense of connection to the past," he explains. Layers of pine needles in the deep woods and old walls where paths had been many decades earlier, as well as skeletons of chestnut trees killed during the 1924 blight, made him know that the place had existed for a long while.[11] Adventures inside her house also enhanced his connection to bygone times. His great-aunt Corola, for instance, once showed him Great-Great-Grandpa George's hat among the dusty trunks and old furniture in the attic. Great-Grandmother Delia connected him, too, to her husband Fidelie (Dele) Capps (1850–1933), left at home with his sister after his mother died and his father was drafted for Confederate service. Great-Grandpa Fidelie's efforts to fend off Home Guard raiders finds its way into Morgan's play *Homegrown Yankees*. At the death of his father-in-law, George Johnson, who helped found Hendersonville along with an ancestor of the poet Jonathan Williams, Fidelie, who had grown up on Mount Olivet, agreed to move with his wife Delia into her mother Rebecca Blocker Johnson's home on Pleasant Hill, caring for her and her afflicted daughter Alice in exchange for the Johnson house and land. Alice becomes the subject of Morgan's poem and story called "Death Crown," while Great-Grandmother Delia is the beloved matriarch in the poem "White Autumn," finding deserved rest in the "river of books" she reads late into the night in her twilight years.[12]

The daughter of Delia and Fidelie Capps, who would become Robert Morgan's maternal grandmother, played a major role in his success as a fiction writer. Julia Capps Levi (1883–1948) is the model for Julie in *Gap Creek* and *The Road from Gap Creek*. When Julia Capps married a man born to a Civil War veteran, she brought another direct connection to that conflict to the future writer. In 1862, at age fourteen, Lafayette (Fate) Levi joined the Confederacy with his three brothers (John Jr., Calvin, and David), all serving in Virginia. All four brothers survived the battles, but the oldest, John Jr., died from illness as they walked home at the war's end. His brothers buried him beside a road. Fate later named his son for Confederate generals Robert E. Lee and Wade Hampton III. Robert Hampton Levi (1877–1955), Morgan's Grandpa Hamp, became the model for Hank Richards in the Gap Creek novels. When Julia and Hamp left Gap Creek after their first years of marriage, they bought land from a descendent of Daniel Pace, thus bringing Robert Morgan's maternal family to the land his paternal great-great-grandfather had purchased in 1838.

The story of this tract reflects America's twentieth century. As one of three children, Frank Pace had received one-third of Daniel Pace's one square mile, and he later divided his portion among his two sons and two daughters, including Sarah. Her marriage to John Morgan turned the house Frank Pace built in 1867 into the Morgan house that was Robert Morgan's first residence. Frank's son Volney Pace, the model for Locke in *The Truest Pleasure*, built a house on his parcel after serving as a nurse in the Spanish-American War of 1898. But when his wife died in childbirth, as many women of that era did, Volney gave the baby to his sister Rose, the model for Florrie in *The Truest Pleasure*, and went back into the army, putting his land up for sale. Morgan's grandfather Hamp Levi, who was living in poverty on Gap Creek when he learned that Volney Pace's land was available, convinced a brother to send him money for a down payment. Wasenura Levi carried an Indian name that the family shortened to Wass (and that Morgan makes Russ in some short fiction). He worked in an automobile factory in Detroit, America's Motor City that boasted more than one hundred automobile companies in the early twentieth century. Ford took the lead when it introduced the Model T in 1908, and the five-dollars-per-day salary the company began offering in 1914 drew workers from across the United States. Wass sent his brother money, and by the time the Great Depression hit, Grandpa Hamp had paid off his mortgage. He also added rooms to the tiny house that Volney Pace had built, turning it into the Levi house that provides the setting for *The Road from Gap Creek*. When Robert Morgan's parents married in 1939, they united by blood the Pace and Levi families who both already inhabited that square mile Morgan describes as his touchstone for the local, for place.

His Parents, Clyde Ray and Fannie Levi Morgan

Morgan notes his parents' influences on his becoming a writer, particularly his father's reading of history and both parents' storytelling. Details of his mother's and father's lives appear in various works. But it is his father who appears most vividly, particularly in the poetry. Morgan acknowledges that he fits into the tradition of male writers who were orphaned or who had weak fathers: Dylan Thomas, Ernest Hemingway, William Faulkner, Robert Lowell, William Shakespeare, John Keats, Samuel Taylor Coleridge, Walt Whitman.[13] In a *Southern Review* essay titled "Work and Poetry, the Father Tongue," published four years after his father's 1991 death, Morgan reflects on poems he had written about his father in earlier decades. At age fifty-one, the poet saw that he had revealed to himself, through poetry's elevated language and form, the admirable dimensions of his father's exasperating personality, the dignity of his physical labor that in fact did little to provide a decent living for his wife and children. It seems clear that the contradictions and frustrations paralyzing his father influenced Morgan's efforts to achieve what his father never did.

In a sense, Clyde Ray Morgan (1905–1991) inherited unease, from generations split by religious discord in a community where church played a dominant role. He was the second of four children born to John Morgan (1863–1941), a farmer and mason's helper who helped build Biltmore Estate in Asheville in the early 1890s and who served as the model for Tom Powell in *The Truest Pleasure*, and Sarah Pace Morgan (1871–1912), the model for Ginny in that novel as well as in *This Rock* and *The Road from Gap Creek*. Sarah, the daughter of Civil War veteran Frank Pace, gave herself to the emotionalism of camp meetings she attended with her father, performing holy dances and speaking in tongues. Her husband disapproved vociferously. Sarah's death from measles when Clyde was seven years old no doubt intensified his sympathy for his mother's side in this religious argument. As a teenager, he began going to Pentecostal Holiness services and participating in glossolalia. Like his grandfather Frank Pace, he continued to attend the Baptist church as well, despite fellow congregants' hostility toward his Pentecostal ties. Clyde Morgan spent his life frustrated by church quarrels that deepened his confusion about life.

Dichotomies seemed to define Morgan's father's personality. He stopped school after the sixth grade, not unusual for his time and place, yet remained bookish, like the Pace men who preceded him, including his grandfather Frank. Clyde bought his first history volume at twelve years of age and throughout his life read daily, mostly *National Geographic*, books of history or biography, and the Bible. Titles in his library include *America's War for Humanity: A Pictorial History of the World War for Liberty*, published by L. H. Walter in 1919, a book he bought that year from a teacher for two dollars; *A History of Germany, from the Earliest Times* by Charleton T. Lewis, published in 1902; *The Winston Encyclopedia: A Compendium of Information and Instruction on All Subjects*, edited by Logan Marshall, published in 1920 and inscribed by Clyde Morgan in 1922, when he was seventeen. Clyde's father and siblings ridiculed him for his bookishness, perhaps believing that it kept him from participating fully in the world around him. Throughout his life, as Morgan writes, his father seemed to live in the past, to be an "anachronism," to belong "to a world of hunting and trapping, of storytelling."[14] Perhaps one of Morgan's reasons for exploring Daniel Boone's frontier world in his 2007 biography of this eighteenth-century American pioneer was to immerse himself in the wilderness his father loved. In *This Rock*, he fictionalizes his father's thwarted attempts to escape his frustrations. When gangsters stopped his car near Lima, Ohio, assuming he was running moonshine, Clyde aborted his 1927 trek to Canada to trap. Bad luck met him each time he left, and Clyde Morgan always returned to Green River. His lofty dreams and lack of nerve to achieve them seemed the essential extremes of his personality. The painting he commissioned of himself, sitting with his dog Prince before an image of the castle he longed to erect in the meadow behind the house he built when his children were small, illustrates the mismatch between his aspirations and the reality of his life.

When he married Fannie Geneva Levi in 1939, Clyde Morgan was thirty-four years old and living, along with his father, John, at the home of his married sister Mae. Like Annie and Muir Powell in *The Road from Gap Creek*, the couple married secretly and, at Fannie's insistence, did not live together for several months, until she worked up the courage to tell her parents that she had eloped. Then she moved with Clyde into the Morgan house, built by Frank Pace in 1867 and coming to John through his marriage to Sarah Pace. John Morgan improved the farm and made a good living from it, making his son Clyde's inability to turn the land to profit even clearer. Although Clyde worked hard physically, as Morgan describes in poems such as "Mowing," published in *Topsoil Road*, his father's favored labors of cutting weeds or cleaning off cemeteries earned no income. Morgan suggests that his mother, twenty-seven years old when she married Clyde, perhaps unconsciously chose him over numerous other suitors because she knew he was so feckless that she could control the family's purse strings. Indeed, she did find herself managing the family's finances, no doubt to an extent she did not foresee.

Fannie Levi Morgan (1912–2010), the second-youngest of six children born to Julia and Hampton Levi, was five years old when her family traveled by wagon from Gap Creek, South Carolina, to Green River, North Carolina, when Hampton bought Volney Pace's house. Morgan says that trip of four or five miles began his mother's decades-long frustration over transportation,[15] for Fannie walked most of the way so that the horse could pull the already overloaded wagon up the steep hill. In high school, Fannie entertained thoughts of being an actress, but the Great Depression, impacting her family's already meager finances, squelched such dreams. A pretty girl, Fannie could talk her way into a job, Morgan claims. After high school, she worked to support her family, first at a Hendersonville dime store, where six days' work at $1.50 a day earned her nine dollars a week, and later at a Jewish clothing store and cotton mill. Her brother William Velmer Levi, one of the models for Velmer in *The Road from Gap Creek*, trapped muskrats and sold the furs to a Mount Airy trader and also harvested and sold ginseng. Her youngest brother, Robert, the model for Troy in *The Road from Gap Creek* and "The Mountains Won't Remember Us," contributed to the family's income by joining the Civilian Conservation Corps (CCC), created in 1933 by the United States Congress to give young men jobs during the Great Depression. In western North Carolina, CCC workers restored land wasted by overfarming, clear-cut timbering, and erosion. They also helped build the Great Smoky Mountains National Park. Robert Levi became a CCC "powder man," dynamiting rock to build the Blue Ridge Parkway.

Morgan's mother continued to supplement farm income after she married, working at a cigarette-paper-rolling plant until she conceived her first child, Evangeline, who was born in 1941. Fannie told Morgan that the cemetery on the Hendersonville-to-Brevard Highway, once a field where older family members grew pole beans, held the graves of many cigarette plant workers who died from ingesting chemicals. But she did not leave the factory for her health. She left because at that time, women could not work any kind of public job when pregnant. So Fannie sold eggs and butter, from chickens and cows they kept, and the family depended upon pole beans as their main cash crop.

But having no transportation to get those beans to a marketplace compromised profits, just one of the hardships that not having machines in a modernizing world caused the Morgan family. Clyde Morgan continued the farming practices of his youth, working the land with his father-in-law's horses after a neighbor with a tractor plowed the fields in the spring. During harvest, Clyde asked a brother or brother-in-law to take his beans to market. If the relative's truck had no room, Clyde's hampers sat by the road, beans wilting and losing value. In Morgan's unpublished memoir, he describes going with his dad and uncle to the Hendersonville market when he was six years old and feeling embarrassed when his dad said "no sale" to the $2.25 per bushel that a buyer offered for his beans. The family needed money, and, in fact, they had picked the beans a day beyond their prime to coincide with the uncle's trip to sell his own beans. But Morgan's father refused to admit his crop's true worth or the need for his own truck. He had owned a Model T Ford in the 1920s with his brother Dwight, but he lost that vehicle during the Depression and had no interest in getting another. His wife relied on neighbors and relatives to get to the grocery store, to town to pay bills, and to a doctor when the children were sick or needed inoculations. That dependence brought Fannie considerable grief. She never forgot the time her father and brothers refused to drive her to a Hendersonville doctor's office when young Evangeline was running a high fever. Fannie walked, carrying the sick child and seething over the men's belittling of her concern about a temperature that turned out to signal pneumonia.

These scenes formed the basis of Morgan's short story "The Dulcimer Maker," published in *As Rain Turns to Snow*. When Morgan was a toddler, his mother returned to work at the Tuxedo cotton mill, hitching a ride every day after leaving her children with her parents.

Morgan's mother worked persistently to keep the family going and in fact did have the business sense in this marriage, in a time when women had few rights to conduct legal affairs. She desperately wanted transportation to provide her children with more opportunities, such as traveling to school events or music lessons, and so in 1953, she asked her brother Charlie, who ran a roofing business in Fayetteville, North Carolina, to find her a vehicle. She sent him $300 she had saved, and he soon delivered a 1946 Chevrolet truck, making nine-year-old Morgan feel connected to his community for the first time.[16] His father got his driver's license, proud to have the truck once his wife had bought it. Three years later, Fannie took the initiative to replace the old Chevrolet that spent much time in a repair shop, purchasing a Studebaker pickup that took the family to Double Springs Church every Sunday and to Asheville each Saturday for Evangeline's organ lessons. Morgan says in his unpublished memoir that his mother let her husband pretend the new truck was his idea.[17] Fannie continued public work, at a hosiery mill in East Flat Rock and at a cotton mill where she witnessed fights between pro-union and anti-union workers before a strike closed the plant. She then trained for a beautician's license and worked at a Hendersonville beauty parlor until permanent wave chemicals poisoned her. She gave up salon work and eventually gained employment at a General Electric plant.

Fannie Morgan also initiated business ventures at home. During the Cold War years, a county extension agent convinced her to invest in chickens to sell eggs to new grocery chains coming into the area, Winn-Dixie and A&P. Morgan's father built houses for three hundred leghorn chicks, and young Robert, feeding and watering them daily, grew to despise their stench. The flock contracted a digestive tract infection that necessitated the killing of every bird, as Morgan remembers in his poem "Coccidiosis": "we chopped off every head and filled / a pit in the garden with our / white investment."[18] His mother then began growing boxwoods to sell to landscapers, her husband making a sand bed for cuttings that her children watered and helped to set in cans and then in rows. Someone stole the shrubs, "the work of three or four years gone," Morgan laments in his memoir.[19] Years later, Fannie Morgan's investment efforts met frustration not from sheer bad luck but from her gender. She twice wanted to buy land that a relative was selling cheaply. But a married woman could not get credit without her husband's signature, and Clyde would not sign the papers. Her father would not loan her the money, either. Fannie had to give up her dream of expanding the farm beyond the ten arable acres the family planted each year, five the Pace-Morgan land and five her Levi inheritance.

Not surprisingly, Morgan's mother took the lead in building a house she could call her own. The family had lived in the Pace-Morgan house until they moved in with Julia and Hampton Levi to care for Julia when she became ill. After her mother's death from a brain tumor in 1948, Fannie refused to move back into the Morgan house, saying that she would not keep walking through wet pasture to get to the road. She drew plans for a house and selected for its construction the spot where her brother Robert Levi, killed in East Anglia in 1943, had napped and painted. Her father had deeded this land to her when he had divided the land among his children after his wife's death. By 1949, Fannie had $1,700 in a post office savings account, money she had earned from working at the cotton mill and selling eggs, butter, cows, and chickens. When the Great Depression started, both of Morgan's grandfathers had lost all the money they had in a bank. "Nobody in my family used banks again until the late fifties," instead keeping money in a shoebox or the post office, he says.[20] Morgan's father agreed to add the money he made from selling beans so that they could start building. But rather than depositing his profits, Clyde spent his $500 on a Winchester rifle. Morgan remembers being frightened as his parents fought for days. While he later determined that his father could not help buying this longed-for gun rather than continuing to borrow a rifle during deer hunting season, it seems clear that the incident joins others in triggering Morgan's sympathy for his mother's frustrations, sympathy evident in his eventual portrayal of the woman's point of view in much of his fiction. His parents' differences continued to occupy Morgan's mind as he aged: "I've been thinking about how different my parents' attitudes were toward hospitality. My dad loved to talk and would invite people, even strangers sometimes, to dine, or even stay the night. My mother cringed at strangers in her house, but had to do the work of cooking and entertaining. A real mismatch." [21]

Clyde Morgan did work hard on the house construction when it finally got underway, enjoying the physical labor. As he built, he taught his young son mathematical precision, the language of construction, and the joy of building. Five-year-old Morgan mixed cement for the footing that his father and Uncle Abram, an experienced carpenter, poured. He watched his father place rocks he dug from Rock Creek over boards sawed from trees felled on family land, and he eventually helped lay rocks for the porch wall. With the tool kit he got for Christmas, Morgan spent the next several years building objects from wood scraps: bows and arrows, bulldozers, and helicopters he saw in *National Geographic*. The art of building as well as a respect for his father's skills stuck in the young Morgan's mind. In poems such as "Sigodlin," he honors those local carpenters who "made as they were," sturdily yoking studs and joists to last: "And what they fitted / and nailed or mortised into place, downright / and up-standing, straight up and down and flat / as water, established the coordinates / forever of their place in creation's / fabric." In lines informed by his training in mathematics and quantum physics, Morgan builds an ironic comment on his father's complicated imperfection: "everything in the real may lean just / the slightest bit sigodlin or oblique."[22] The family moved into the rock house in 1951 but had to save money for a few more years to put in a bathroom.[23]

As he observed his parents' oppositions, young Morgan balanced economic hardship with the comforts of place, work, and extended family. He learned to make and to make-do. In his unpublished memoir, he describes using a polished board to slide on leaves down Meetinghouse Mountain. On this homemade sled, he zigzagged to keep from running into trees, learning to steer by leaning left or right, learning to make his way. The glow of nature, reflecting possibilities in the changes inherent in seasonal cycles, countered any tinge of sadness occasioned by the family's limited finances. Experiences such as spending an idyllic Sunday afternoon with his cousin Harold in Aunt Ida's Golden Delicious tree, eating apples as well as red grapes from the vine threading through the tree limbs,[24] planted seeds of a romanticism that drew him later to Emerson and Wordsworth. Enjoying his father's occasional poetry recitations—Clyde took particular pleasure in declaiming Tennyson's "Crossing the Bar" and John Burrough's "Waiting"[25]—Morgan learned to accept his father's eccentricities, following the lead of his mother's family, who seemed less judgmental of Clyde than his own relatives. Although admitting that in his teens and twenties he saw the older man as a failure, a sentiment evidenced by calling him the "old man" in letters to Russell Banks and William Matthews,[26] his practice in accommodating disappointments and people's different personalities prepared him for life, as well as fiction writing, later on. And reading before he started school, thanks to his mother's instruction, this future writer early became aware that attending to the inner life as well as the outer world created the rich existence that he craved.

Morgan's Teenage Years and Burgeoning Attraction to the Arts

Morgan's vision of his future began to extend beyond the Blue Ridge farm as he approached his teen years and felt more palpably the world beyond his small community. He says that he feels lucky to have grown up in a world before television, a world where listening to older family members tell stories was the norm. While several Green River neighbors did own a television by 1956, his parents did not want one, saying it broadcast "sinful things."

However, they did allow Morgan to watch *The Roy Rogers Show* and *Hopalong Cassidy* on Saturday mornings at a cousin's house. Mesmerized by the action, he had to readjust back at home, feeling that the real world moved more slowly than he had realized before.[27] This new technology seemed less important to the young boy than the arrival of the Henderson County Public Library bookmobile at the Green River Baptist Church parking lot on the first Monday of each month, beginning in 1956 or 1957. Morgan had never been to the library in town and assumed that it was for rich townspeople. But his father read to the children nightly from *National Geographic*, the Bible, or schoolbooks. By age twelve, Morgan was ready to delve into whole books waiting on those traveling shelves. Laura Ingalls Wilder's stories of prairie life, Jack London's Klondike books, and James Oliver Curwood's novels set in Canada's Northwest Territories transported him to worlds beyond his own.[28] He read in spare moments between shelling corn for chickens and milking cows, thrilled with these faraway worlds that made his own life seem easy.

About the same time, young Morgan began thinking of what he might do with the money he was saving. Following his sister, he joined the 4-H Club and honed his husbandry skills by raising a Red Devon calf named Ginger that he sold for seventy-five dollars.[29] To that money accruing interest in his post office savings account, he added pay that his father gave him for helping with pole beans, thinking he could "someday power [his] escape to somewhere faraway, maybe to college,"[30] a place teachers helped him to envision. When he did leave for advanced education, his country-lad entrepreneurial skills helped fund his transition to a new phase of life.

School experiences, especially in 1956 and 1957, moved Morgan another step toward the "foot in two worlds" position that has fueled his writing, one a rural world of physical labor and the other a cerebral world of literary art. As his sixth-grade teacher at Tuxedo Elementary School, he had Dean A. Ward, who was also the school principal. Born in 1904 on a nearby family farm on Bob's Creek, Ward was a distant relative, his grandfather being the brother of Morgan's great-grandmother Louise Ward Morgan, who married her first husband John's brother Lemuel after John died as a prisoner at Camp Douglas. Morgan's first male teacher, Ward not only looked European—a bit like James Joyce—but also played piano during assemblies, composed the school anthem, and loved literature and language. In fine tweed suits, he regaled students with stories of his own graduate studies in English and education at the University of North Carolina at Chapel Hill, and more importantly, he used lively storytelling skills to recount the *Iliad*, the *Odyssey*, and *Silas Marner*. Diagramming sentences with Mr. Ward showed Morgan that they are "firm, physical things," and this role model's love of grammar and clear enunciation made young

Morgan conscious of his own speech. He dropped vernacular pronunciations such as "ort to" and "yourn" and met Mr. Ward's expectation that he would do a good job making announcements on the school intercom.[31]

Most significantly, it was in Dean Ward's sixth grade class that Robert Morgan wrote his first story. On the spring day that students took a field trip to Biltmore House, George Vanderbilt's chateau near Asheville that Morgan's paternal grandfather helped build, Morgan stayed at school because he did not have the three dollars required for the outing. Mr. Ward told him not to sit idly but to write a story like those he enjoyed reading, sometimes with a novel hidden inside his spelling book during class. Mr. Ward gave his young charge a plot: a man is lost in the Canadian Rockies, with no gun or knife; get him back to civilization. By day's end, Morgan had created his first story, drawing on his own experiences in the woods as well as his reading of London and Curwood, and he soon learned that "only the act of writing made writing possible."[32] In the poem "Purple Hands," Morgan celebrates his kinship with this honored teacher, the pronoun "we" bringing him and all farm children into the story his father told about young Dean Ward appearing with stained hands at Green River School each year after his own Bob's Creek School ended its session: "If someone came to school with purple hands, / we knew they had been dropping taters." The speaker's admission that working-class children tried to hide that colorful evidence of labor turns into a nod to Ward's impact as the sliced potato starch becomes the "ink of yet another hopeful planting," a metaphor for Morgan's later planting of words in stories or poems.[33] Ward no doubt recognized in Morgan an intelligence leading to the boredom and dreaminess he sometimes exhibited in class or on hurriedly completed homework assignments. Morgan seems unsure whether Ward played any role in his skipping seventh grade, however, saying only that his move to eighth grade was likely his mother's idea.

After eighth grade, when Ms. Frances Satterfield enhanced Morgan's attraction to meter and rhyme by requiring him to memorize Poe's "The Raven" and Wordsworth's "I Wandered Lonely as a Cloud," Morgan attended Flat Rock High School, where he joined the debating team and again studied with influential teachers. His freshman English teacher, Ms. Julia Lappin, talked of Faulkner, Poe, and reading on the grass at Duke University. She required students to present oral book reports and to write short papers every few weeks, literary analyses or essays about personal experiences. She even told Morgan, when he complained that he had nothing to write about except his Green River farm, that his farm and native mountains would be important to his writing one day. Ms. Lappin's perception of Morgan's ability led her to give him a second chance when he submitted an untidy poetry booklet, his selected poems copied and illustrated messily. She allowed him to turn in an extra-credit book report to salvage his term grade, assigning an A-plus to his paper on *Quo Vadis*. The next year, his tenth-grade world history teacher, Ms. Sara Nickell, thrilled him with stories of the Russian Revolution, and his second male teacher, Mr. Leslie Fisher, taught him in biology that complex concepts can be understood by breaking them into parts. Fisher sent Morgan to Cullowhee for the regional biology competition. Morgan placed third on those exams and received the school medal in biology at year's end.

The most significant teacher of his secondary school career hailed originally from the Finger Lakes region of New York, just outside Ithaca, where Morgan later lived. Mrs. Elizabeth Rogers had moved to Chapel Hill, North Carolina, for a job at the end of World War II. There, she met her husband, and together, they moved to the western part of the state when he got a job as the Flat Rock High School basketball coach. In her Latin class at Flat Rock High, Morgan noticed and began to emulate her clear enunciation, building on the speech awareness Dean Ward had earlier inspired. Unlike many local residents, Mrs. Rogers did not slur syllables but gave each its proper articulation. Morgan began speaking more slowly to achieve the same effect, becoming more fascinated with the beauty and power of language. When East Hendersonville High School opened, consolidating smaller county schools, Morgan found himself in Mrs. Rogers's American history class. There, he honed his writing skills, answering questions in twice-weekly reports, and he became more enamored of history through her passion for it. In *Lions of the West: Heroes and Villains of the Westward Expansion*, which he dedicated to Mrs. Elizabeth Rogers, as well as in *Boone*, we see the influence of her focus on cultural contexts, leaders' personalities, and the importance of place in history's narrative. Morgan worked to get Mrs. Rogers as well as Mr. Ward and Ms. Lappin inducted into the Henderson County Education Hall of Fame, and he honored six of his teachers at a Flat Rock High School reunion in October 2013. Those teachers and his later achievements belie the stereotype of an impoverished Appalachian educational system.

Morgan also benefitted from teachers who instructed him in music, an early passion. He writes in his unpublished memoir that as far back as he can remember, he made up music in his head as "a correlation to the world around [him] but also a kind of grammar for [his] feelings, for the story of [his] life."[34] His melodies derived from whip-poor-wills, mockingbirds, gurgling creeks, raindrops, hymns, church bells resonating across the valleys, groans of wood settling in the house, or country-western or classical music playing on Grandpa Hamp's radio. Everywhere he turned, he heard music, because he listened for the world's cadence, from the hum of electric wires to the magical blending of voices when the church congregation sang. He eagerly began studying piano around age ten, practicing on the secondhand upright that his mother bought when his sister started lessons in Asheville, where she later studied organ, too. Morgan's first teacher was Mrs. Walker, a retired lady from Iowa who charged children one dollar per lesson on Tuxedo Elementary School's baby grand piano. Students had to wash their hands before touching the keys. When she later moved lessons to her house in Tuxedo, Morgan got off the school bus there. Mrs. Walker loaned students biographies of composers and required they read about Mozart, Brahms, Beethoven, and Haydn. Morgan also took a few lessons from a Hendersonville composer of musicals, Ray Taylor, and at age thirteen began to study piano with his most influential music instructor, Evelyn Thorne. Ms. Thorne had retired to Hendersonville from New York City and told the story of one day coming home to her studio to find Leonard Bernstein, whom Morgan later saw on a neighbor's television, practicing on her Mason and Hamlin piano, courtesy of a friend with a key to her apartment. She loaned Morgan issues of *Musical America*, and through her lively conversations, she became a mentor, modeling not just classical piano skills but also eloquent language and intellectual interests.

Music was just one of Morgan's wide-ranging interests that made his teenage years confusing as he began to consider careers. Thinking that he wanted to be a composer, he bought scores, such as those of Rachmaninoff, at the music store in Hendersonville. He did compose some musical scores during his teens, a time when he also enjoyed concerts at Brevard Music Center, about twenty-five miles west of Zirconia. It was there that he heard Byron Janis perform his first Brahms concerto. But Morgan's interest in history was also increasing, no doubt influenced by his father's zeal for it. From the library, he checked out biographies of Dwight D. Eisenhower and Otto von Bismarck. He studied Gerd von Rundstedt, seeing the Battle of the Bulge from the German point of view. He contemplated a career in the military, wanting at one time to attend West Point. At the same time, philosophy became a special interest. His high school teachers introduced him to English moral and political philosopher Thomas Hobbes, and on his own, he discovered Jean-Paul Sartre in the Hendersonville Library, reading *Being and Nothingness* and absorbing the tenets of existentialism. He read Colin Wilson's *The Outsider*, published in 1956 and espousing what Wilson called an optimistic existentialism. The book looks at social alienation in works by figures such as Albert Camus, Ernest Hemingway, Fyodor Dostoyevsky, Soren Kierkegaard, and Friedrich Nietzsche. These creators of modern thought hit a nerve with Morgan's own burgeoning sense that he did not fit comfortably in his community. Also, Nietzsche's emphasis on embracing the world we live in rather than the world beyond clashed with the Baptist and Pentecostal church tenets Morgan had learned since birth. Complexities and possibilities occupied Morgan's mind as he did farm chores, contemplating philosophers' comments on individuals' creative powers.

Morgan's reading of fiction continued, of course, with the bookmobile continuing to play a role in fulfilling his appetite for books. In 1960, he found on the bookmobile shelves perhaps the most important novel he read as a teenager: *Look Homeward, Angel*. He had seen a picture of local legend Thomas Wolfe in the Hendersonville newspaper, along with a photograph of the stone angel that had inspired the famous book's title. Wolfe's stonecutter father had sold that angel to a Johnson family, who placed it in the family plot in Hendersonville's Oakdale Cemetery. Morgan's response to Wolfe's novel was transforming: "I felt this was the book I'd always been looking for. It was a novel about me. . . . It was a revelation about how ambitious and thrilled and scared I was, and about how 'lost' I felt. . . . Eugene Gant's parents seemed like my own parents, and his anxieties and frustrations and sense of destiny were my own. . . . I became intoxicated with the elevated, poetic prose."[35] Gant's parents, of course, reflect Wolfe's parents, William Oliver (W. O.) and Julia Westall Wolfe, a pair biographer David Herbert Donald describes as "different in temperament" and antagonistic.[36] Like Clyde Morgan, W. O. Wolfe had little interest in money and property. Like Fannie Morgan, Julia Wolfe had ambition and a head for business, buying real estate and running the Asheville boarding house she called Dixieland. While Wolfe's parents' relationship seemed more melodramatic than that of Morgan's parents, with W. O.'s alcoholism leading to fierce arguments with his wife, it was their obvious opposition that most struck a chord. Morgan tells fellow Appalachian poet Jeff Daniel Marion that his parents' influence on him was "always contradictory." His father—an extrovert who "dominated conversations," talked of history, and spoke in tongues at public services—countered his mother's more tranquil, reserved "delight in the small and ordinary."[37] Wolfe helped Morgan to see that family differences provide two worlds that a writer can reconcile in art. When Morgan discovered that he and Wolfe shared a birthday, October 3, he felt even more thrilled, more connected to the man who had grown up not thirty miles away, in Asheville, and had become a famous writer. That Wolfe's book named places Morgan knew also helped him to recognize literary possibilities for the coves and mountains he had known since birth.

While Morgan points to Wolfe as the author whose work first made him entertain the idea that he too could be a writer, he mentions his youthful awareness of another local writer in his commemoration of Wolfe's one-hundredth birthday, published in the *Thomas Wolfe Review* in 2000. Carl Sandburg lived the last twenty-one years of his life in nearby Flat Rock, in the old Memminger house that he called Connemara, moving there with his wife and children in 1946. In Morgan's ninth-grade poetry notebook, he included Sandburg's poem "Harvest Moon," its imagery and rhythms stirring his nascent sense of language's possibilities. Although he never saw Sandburg, the proximity of a second famous writer heightened young Morgan's aspirations. Both Sandburg and Wolfe taught him, as he later studied their work, that "the best writing is poetic and for the larger audience of ordinary readers." [38] Remembering that nonacademics in his North Carolina home knew and cared about these writers, he later made it his own goal that his poetry and prose be accessible to everyone.

Morgan's sister, who was three years older than he, helped to open a literary world to him as well. Evangeline, or Sister, as Morgan called her, went to Bob Jones University in South Carolina for her first year of college in 1959. When she brought her anthology of American literature home in the spring of 1960, Morgan delved into it, thrilling to Wallace Stevens's forceful images and discovering Walt Whitman and the possibilities of free verse, which he saw as "a new kind of verbal music." [39] In his induction speech for the North Carolina Literary Hall of Fame, Morgan cited his early reading of Stevens's "Domination of Black" as his first encounter with the terror of the sublime, another moment that inspired him to understand the "geography of language" no matter how long it took. Morgan also attended concerts at Bob Jones University, once seeing a performance of Puccini's *Tosca*, compliments of family friends in Hendersonville who helped to nurture his love of music. When Evangeline transferred to Western Carolina University, Morgan drove her to Cullowhee in the family's pickup truck, no doubt dreaming of his own future college days. In 1960, he spent his own money to buy *Dr. Zhivago*, feeding his hunger for serious literature with this novel written by a poet, its rich language leaving a lasting impression.

In June 1961, Morgan made his first significant trip away from home, spending a week at a Civitan Club camp at Wildacres Retreat in Little Switzerland, North Carolina. His family drove him to the camp in their Studebaker pickup truck, marking the teenager's first trip that far east of Asheville. He remembers feeling released from the mountains as the truck made its way east on Highway 70 before turning north back into the mountains. With students from Pfeiffer University acting as counselors, and with instructors giving classes in history, philosophy, music, dance, folklore, and race relations, the camp stressed civil rights and liberal political ideas, an ironic theme given the origin of the charming center sitting atop Pompey's Knob. Thomas Dixon, author of the racist novel *The Clansman*, on which the film *The Birth of a Nation* is based, built the cultural center in the 1920s with royalties

from the movie. Dixon lost Wildacres in the Great Depression, but a couple
from Charlotte, the Blumenthals, bought the place and dedicated it to improving human relations. That summer, students discussed Anglo-Irish playwright
Dion Boucicault's *The Octoroon; or, Life in Louisiana*, an antislavery drama pro-
duced in New York in 1859, and they heard a Charlotte rabbi's address. When
Pfeiffer music professor Dr. Brewer lectured on Baroque, classical, Romantic,
Impressionist, and modern music, young Morgan found that he knew more
about musical styles and composition than other attendees who were more
affluent and, he assumed, more knowledgeable and culturally sophisticated.

A Chicago couple on the Wildacres faculty significantly influenced Morgan
and built his confidence. Mr. James Dodman Nobel, a 1925 Cornell University
graduate, had published a book of free verse poetry, and his wife was a modern
dancer. Morgan, in his letter introducing himself to faculty, had written that he
served as superintendent of Sunday school at Green River Baptist Church and
also that he wrote music as well as short stories, so the Nobels asked him to
pray before the first camp meal and then to improvise on the piano while Mrs.
Nobel danced and her husband read his poetry. When the couple left Wildacres
to attend their son's Cornell graduation, Mr. Nobel gave Morgan a copy of his
book of poems, *Modern Trilogy*. The inspired young man wrote words for a song
that campers sang the last evening.[40] Asked to describe his camp experiences to
Civitan Club members in the Skyland Hotel, where F. Scott Fitzgerald had written "The Crack-Up," he found the speaking easy. His strong voice and smooth
delivery surprised him. One impressed Civitan member told him that he would
make a fine lawyer. This Wildacres experience taught Morgan to move beyond
the embarrassment he felt when an instructor assumed that his daddy, coming
to get him in a pickup truck, must be looking for work. He saw that he could
compete intellectually and socially in the world opening up for his exploration.

Thus, while Morgan's experiences away from his small Green River community had been limited, he did have a significant intellectual perspective when
he ended his high school education with the eleventh grade. He skipped his
senior year, as already planned before his Wildacres adventure. A family friend,
Fred Toms Jr., had recommended that Morgan apply for early admission to
Emory College at Oxford, Georgia, the old campus of Emory University. With
Scholastic Aptitude Test scores as the only criterion for acceptance, Morgan
earned a spot. He sold the Guernsey cow that had earned a red ribbon at the
county fair years earlier for $150, adding that money to the profits from beans
he planted on the acreage his father allotted him to cover tuition and board
fees remaining after his scholarship was applied. He went off to Georgia at age
sixteen. "I wanted to get away from home, to more opportunities, more books.
I was tired of staying on the farm," he shares in an interview.[41] Perhaps Fred

Toms emboldened the teenager when he said, "it's guys like you who become successful."[42] Working-class upstarts full of ambition, Toms meant, those greedily wanting to get ahead and working for everything they get. Morgan proved Toms correct as his education and career unfolded.

Off to College(s)

At Emory's Oxford College, Morgan discovered new worlds during his one-year stay. He studied Plato and Aristotle, more than holding his own in the mostly Socratic classes, even among older, wealthy students from preparatory schools, who sometimes asked for his help with philosophy papers. He occasionally went home with friends for weekends, further expanding his perspective. In Dalton, Georgia, he picked up a *Saturday Review* at Bill Slate's house, reading about James Agee for the first time and seeing a review of *A Long and Happy Life*, the first book by North Carolina writer Reynolds Price, who was pictured on the magazine cover. With a friend who was a theologian's son, he went to Catholic and Episcopal churches, just as he was reading T. S. Eliot in his Emory poetry class. He found that he understood logic, including that of Wittgenstein, and the philosophy of mathematics, algebra, and calculus. When he earned top scores in math classes, as he never had in high school, he started toward a career in math and engineering, with his parents' enthusiastic approval. The United States at that time had begun its "beat the Russians" space program, and Morgan joined many young Americans in having his mind on rocket science. He dreamed of going to the California Institute of Technology but never applied, thinking that money would be a problem. So he focused on other institutions where he could study dynamics. The Georgia Institute of Technology, better known as Georgia Tech, awarded him a work-study position to defray costs for studying mechanical engineering, but he decided instead to return to his home state for the strong aerospace program offered there. In the summer of 1962, he visited the Northeast for the first time, driving to New Hampshire with a friend, expanding his horizons a bit more before beginning his second year of college in the fall.

When seventeen-year-old Morgan transferred as a sophomore to North Carolina State University (NCSU) in Raleigh to study aerospace engineering and applied mathematics, he felt excited but still confused about his career path. He received scholarship money for tuition, thanks to his mother's letter to Governor Terry Sanford asking for financial assistance. His scholarship came from escheated land funds, amassed by the state government's taking of unclaimed property. This funding covered his tuition at the University of North Carolina at Chapel Hill for the next two years as well.[43] In Raleigh, he worked part-time and also used money from his summer job to pay for room and board, living in room sixty-eight in the basement of Owen Hall. His mother, then working at the Hendersonville General Electric plant as an assembler, sent him what money she could spare. He again did well in mathematics and science classes, earning straight As as he studied physics, vector analysis, and differential equations.[44] In fact, Morgan completed his assignments in minimal time. Having no friends, and describing the NCSU year as extremely lonely, Morgan filled his free time with long walks all over the city, visiting museums and bookstores while thinking about what he wanted to do with his life. Making up for not being allowed to see movies as he grew up, he took in foreign films and every free movie he could find. Fellini's *La Dolce Vita* was the first film he saw. He walked to theaters, including the Rialto on Glenwood Avenue, over two-and-a-half miles from campus, where he saw *Lolita*, his "first encounter with Nabokov."[45] An NCSU student identification card also brought free admission to concerts held in Raleigh, so he nurtured his passion for music. Among many performances, he heard the Moscow Philharmonic at the Museum of Art. He read poetry books at Sembower's Bookstore. Rapidly growing beyond the country boy he had been and feeling increasingly alienated from his fellow engineering students, Morgan began to contemplate a turn to the humanities.

Taking advantage of his first chance to meet an established writer face-to-face, Morgan acted on his growing attraction to the arts. After a brief tenure at the University of North Carolina at Chapel Hill, actor and playwright Romulus Linney had landed in Raleigh. Morgan describes this artist's impact on his education:

> Romulus Linney was the first published writer I ever met. As the artist-in-residence at NC State in 1962–63 he conducted a writing workshop every Monday evening in the student union. Few attended, but I would sometimes bring a poem or short story and Linney would read it and discuss it. One evening he brought Reynolds Price, who was newly famous for *A Long and Happy Life*. Reynolds entertained us with stories of Oxford, and famous writers such as William Styron and Truman Capote. For a farm boy from the Blue Ridge Mountains, in the engineering school, it was a heady experience to be in the company of these distinguished writers. Later in the year Linney brought Edward Albee to the workshop, at the time *Who's Afraid of Virginia Woolf* was running on Broadway.
>
> It was many years later, when I saw Romulus Linney in New York, that I realized I had gotten from him at an early age ideas about how to conduct oneself as a writer. He was alert, courteous, but kind of

"neutral," like an actor not playing a part. He was very supportive of younger writers. Without quite knowing it at the time, I aspired to model myself on someone with such confidence and modesty.[46]

Morgan did develop the persona he admired in Linney, and understanding later that writing is very close to acting helped him to step aside and let his fictional narrators tell their stories. Poet Howard Nemerov also came for a reading in the fall of 1962, marking Morgan's first encounter with contemporary poetry, and Donald Hall read in the spring. Linney's presence at NCSU, his inviting writers to campus and modeling generosity as well as wide-ranging interests, was part of the fortune Morgan experienced that year.

Signing up for his classes for the spring of 1963, Morgan found his lack of a high school diploma stopping his academic progress for the first time, a stumbling block that soon proved fortuitous. His advisor would not let him advance to a course in partial differential equations because he had a deficiency in solid geometry, a course he would have taken his senior year in high school. So Morgan enrolled in a creative writing class taught by Guy Owen, the editor of *Southern Poetry Review* whose novel, *The Ballad of the Flim-Flam Man*, came out in 1965. Students wrote both prose and poetry, but Owen particularly encouraged Morgan's fiction. When he read to the class Morgan's story about his great-grandmother seeing corpses on porches during the Civil War, he told students it had made him weep. Morgan was hooked. No professor had wept over his mathematical calculations. While maintaining good grades in science and math courses, he found his mind more and more on the "power of words."[47]

Owen's enthusiasm for his stories led Morgan to transfer again for the fall 1963 semester, this time to the University of North Carolina at Chapel Hill, known for its humanities and writing programs. Thomas Wolfe had matriculated there at age sixteen, the same age Morgan had been when he began his college studies. Rooming in Chapel Hill with his Hendersonville friend Scott Ward, the son of the influential teacher Dean Ward, Morgan continued to work part-time jobs to cover living expenses. He ate most meals at the Pine Room, underneath Lenoir Hall, where a hot dog with chili cost ten cents, and a full meal, thirty-five cents. He delved into literature classes, one in particular making a lasting impression. In November of 1963, he sat in Dr. Joseph Flora's American literature class, discussing Hemingway's *A Farewell to Arms* when news of President John F. Kennedy's assassination arrived. He recalls that day in his poem "11/22/13," reflecting that the murder broke his youthful illusion that the "world had certainly improved" since the First World War that Hemingway described so poignantly.[48] In later years, Hemingway's spare, understated descriptions became a model for Morgan's own prose style. Professor

Flora also planted the seed of Morgan's interest in literature of the West. Two decades later, Morgan saw that Western writers gave him a sense of liberation as he returned to fiction and to writing in voices other than his own. John Steinbeck, Wallace Stegner, and Willa Cather gave him insight into writing about his own North Carolina frontier.[49]

Intending to earn a degree in mathematics as well as comparative literature at UNC-Chapel Hill, Morgan finished math requirements before abandoning that discipline once he met Jessie Rehder, and he never applied for the math degree. His most influential teacher at UNC, Rehder was devoted to her students and published their work every year in *The Young Writer at Chapel Hill*. Doris Betts and Jonathan Yardley were among many protégées whose work she nurtured. Morgan had asked Guy Owen, who had suggested the idea of using family history and Morgan's home landscape in his writing, to recommend him to Rehder. He wrote both poetry and fiction in the creative writing honors seminar she allowed him to join. One day, as he walked to Wilson Library, Rehder stopped her car in the parking lot, rolled down her window, and said, simply, "'You're the most talented writer I've ever taught.'" As Rehder drove away, Morgan finished his trek "about three feet off the ground."[50]

Fellow students also energized Morgan's expanding world. He fondly remembers the joy of meeting others as interested in the written word as he:

> Two important things happened to me that fall of 1964. I fell in with a group of students, all from the Northeast, who had gone to the finest prep schools in New England and been kicked out for various reasons. They had come to Chapel Hill to be beatniks and poets. They knew far more about poetry than I did. They could talk about metaphor and line breaks, French poetry, and William Butler Yeats. Every day we met and talked about poetry, read poetry aloud, lived and breathed poetry. I read Robert Lowell and Robert Bly, James Wright and Gary Snyder. Because my friends were so much more sophisticated than me, I was reluctant to show them the poems I was trying to write. But the best poet among them, Dudley Carroll, insisted that I show him some of my stuff. One day I gave him a sheaf of the things I'd done, with little confidence in their reception. That night around 2:00 am there was a knock on my door. Dudley and his friend Tim Perkins stood there holding my poems. Dudley said my work was so good, so exciting, he had to come tell me. I don't think any review, any award, any honor I've ever received since has been more thrilling than that. Dudley's praise gave me a new confidence—an energy—that reinforced the momentum already building

in me. I wrote a few more short stories, but my real concentration from then on was on poetry.[51]

Morgan's confidence continued to build as fellow students facilitated his entry into the world of print. His very first publication appeared in the student religious association's *New Wine*. When his second-year roommate, Wade Marlett, asked Morgan to write something for the publication, Morgan chose to review *A Death in the Family*, James Agee's Pulitzer Prize–winning novel. Morgan had read it after seeing the film it inspired, *All the Way Home*, and reading Agee's letters to Father Flynn, his teacher at an Episcopal boarding school. *Carolina Quarterly* gave Morgan his first story publication in 1964. "A Fading Light" has not been collected but was reprinted in the magazine's forty-fifth anniversary issue in 1993.[52] Soon, Morgan became the fiction editor of *Carolina Quarterly*, immersing himself in contemporary writing as he read manuscripts.

Although his prose publications delighted Morgan, they did not sway his vision. He saw himself as a poet. He had written his first poem in the summer of 1964 while working at the Hendersonville General Electric plant. On the loading dock after a thunderstorm, he saw a rainbow as "timbers bracing the sky" and jotted down a haiku. Back at UNC-Chapel Hill, he started writing poetry about the farm, the Cherokees, and his family, feeling that these subjects chose him to tell their story.[53] When he first met Shannon Ravenel, his future fiction editor at Algonquin, in the fall of 1964, he told her that he was moving away from fiction into poetry, thus declining a potential association with a major publisher. Ravenel had just landed a job at Houghton Mifflin as the first southerner on staff, and the house sent her south to pick up some southern writers. Her former Hollins College professor Louis D. Rubin Jr., who was teaching then at UNC-Chapel Hill, referred her to Jessie Rehder, who gave her Morgan's name. Ravenel met Morgan for breakfast at the Carolina Inn. She describes the twenty-year-old Morgan as nervous during that meeting, as was she, being only a little older than he was and just starting out.[54] Houghton Mifflin, of course, did not publish poetry, so the two left that meeting not expecting future connections. They could not predict that years later, after moving to Algonquin Books of Chapel Hill, Ravenel would ask Morgan for permission to reprint "Poinsett's Bridge" in *New Stories from the South: The Year's Best, 1991*. He subsequently asked if she might be interested in a longer work, and Ravenel fostered his first novel, *The Hinterlands*.[55] But before he associated with Algonquin as his fiction publisher, his career as a poet took off, from its launching in the respected journal his NCSU professor Guy Owen edited. Morgan "broke into print as a poet" in the spring of 1965 when *Southern*

Poetry Review published "The Swan of Tuonela," his composition after Finnish composer Jean Sibelius's tone poem of the same name.[56] *Carolina Quarterly* continued to publish his poems.

With his commitment to poetry intensifying, Morgan graduated from UNC-Chapel Hill in May 1965 with a bachelor of arts in English. The same year, he married Nancy Bullock, whose father, Richard Bullock, had moved his family from the Northeast to work as personnel manager, and later night manager, of the General Electric plant in Hendersonville. Morgan had gotten to know Nancy during visits with her brother, one of his good friends. With his new wife, he returned to Chapel Hill in the fall of 1965 to pursue a master of arts degree. But he dropped out after one year, and in the fall of 1966, he tried to join the Air Force. He was rejected for weak eyes. Back in Zirconia, he painted houses with his father to earn money. However, he continued to write and to study poetry, including Baudelaire's *Fleurs du Mal*, which he bought in paperback. He began graduate studies at UNC-Greensboro in the spring of 1967, drawn there by the legacy of poet Randall Jarrell, who had died in October 1965. With graduate courses transferred from UNC-Chapel Hill, he completed requirements for the master of fine arts in two semesters at Greensboro and received his degree in the spring of 1968.

Morgan's choosing of the University of North Carolina at Greensboro for his master of fine arts luckily connected him to Fred Chappell, who joined the English faculty in 1964, just as the university was adding its graduate writing program. A native of Canton in western North Carolina, Chappell knew the "cultural dissonances Morgan was undergoing" as he embraced the intellectual world of universities and French poetry, a world very different from the working-class mountain culture of his youth.[57] Chappell worked with Morgan when Morgan's necessary employment interfered with class attendance. The Morgans' first child arrived in July 1967, and he worked two part-time jobs to support his family, including being a teaching assistant in the English department. When work intersected with class meetings, Morgan submitted poems to Chappell and met him at the off-campus café Pickwick to discuss them. Morgan credits Chappell with inspiring and instructing him at this critical time in his development: "Fred brought a wide erudition and critical rigor to his discussions of poetry. He was much more connected to modern Southern poets than I was at that time, poets such as Jarrell and Warren and Tate. That encounter gave me a new sense of identity as a Southern writer." Other Greensboro instructors were valuable readers, including James Applewhite, who served on Morgan's MFA committee, and Robert Watson. But Morgan deems Chappell's influence crucial: "Every poet must have a reader. . . . That's why poets and writers often come in pairs, Wordsworth and Coleridge, Byron and Shelley, Thoreau and Emerson, Marianne Moore and Elizabeth Bishop, Sherwood Anderson and Faulkner. Young writers go looking for their true reader, their authentic reader. They go to Paris, London, Greenwich Village, San Francisco, MFA programs. I was very lucky: I found my true reader in Fred Chappell." [58]

Morgan's time at UNC-Greensboro also intersected with fortunate connections still emanating from UNC-Chapel Hill. Shortly before her death in 1967, Jessie Rehder took some of his poems to William Matthews, who was in Chapel Hill for his graduate degree, and Russell Banks. The two of them eventually started the magazine *Lillabulero* with Newton Smith. Morgan hitchhiked from Greensboro to Chapel Hill to meet with these ambitious young men. "Morgan would spend hours in the offices, talking about Mallarmé, Rimbaud, Baudelaire, and the concepts of correspondences and surrealism, reflecting the heavy influence of Fred Chappell, who also had felt the power of these writers," Smith remembers. He adds that "the most passionate discussions centered on the more recent poets, Robert Bly, James Wright, W. S. Merwin, Gary Snyder, and Robert Creeley, and whether the directions they were taking were the ones poetry should follow out of its entanglement with the halls of ivy." [59] These Chapel Hill friends published Morgan's poems in virtually every issue of *Lillabulero* from 1967 to 1971. Publication built the young writer's confidence and quickly extended his connections. "That magazine caught on and soon I got many invitations from other magazines to send poems," Morgan recalls. One little-known magazine that solicited Morgan's poems was *Choice*, John Logan's magazine that published Robert Bly, Robert Creeley, and other famous poets of the era. Morgan gladly joined this first-rate list. He also had poems published in *Midwest Quarterly*, *Southern Poetry Review*, and *Greensboro Review*. [60]

A Challenging but Valuable Interlude

The years immediately following his university education found Morgan determined to follow his compulsion to write. With his graduate degree, he began teaching at Salem College, a women's school in Winston-Salem, North Carolina, in the fall of 1968. But preparing to teach Dryden, Milton, and Pope, and reading creative writing students' submissions, left little time for his own work. [61] When he won a $1,000 National Endowment for the Arts Fellowship, he left Salem College after one year, planning to live on savings and grant money while working on poetry and a novel. [62] With his wife and son Ben, he spent much of the summer of 1969 with Nancy's mother in upstate New York, enjoying his proximity to William Matthews, who was now in the Northeast. Matthews and Russell Banks had moved *Lillabulero* from Chapel Hill to New Hampshire and then transitioned from magazine to book publishing. Lillabullero Press published Morgan's first book, *Zirconia Poems*, collecting work composed in the summer and fall of 1967. On July 20, 1969, Matthews hosted a publication party at his house, where the friends watched Neil Armstrong take his first steps on the moon.[63] Guy Owen's positive review of the collection appeared in the *News and Observer*, published in Raleigh, North Carolina.

Exhilarated by the NEA Fellowship and his first book, Morgan drove his family across the country in August and September of 1969. For the first time, he saw the wide expanses and inspiring landscapes of the West. Camping when the weather wasn't too cold, he fished in Idaho's Sawtooth Mountains, drove down the California coast to San Francisco, and stayed mostly with Nancy's aunt in Paradise, California. They visited Yellowstone, Glacier, Yosemite, and Sequoia National Parks. Back on the East Coast, they rented a house near Trumansburg, New York, in close proximity to William Matthews. After three months, they returned to Hendersonville, in December 1969, spending the holidays with Morgan's parents. In January 1970, he rented from a distant cousin, Leo Levi, a one-story, late nineteenth-century farmhouse just off Brevard Road for seventy-five dollars a month. Still planning to write while living on the NEA grant funds and his savings, he believed that he could find a full-time job whenever he needed it, for colleges were exploding in the 1960s as baby boomers reached college age. Many colleges were turning into state universities, and English teachers were in high demand. Saving time for his writing, Morgan spent one week a month working with his dad, painting or doing carpentry.

But when Morgan's wife, Nancy, became ill with severe asthma in the summer of 1970 and then spent a week in the hospital after her appendix burst, his expectations were turned upside down. They had no insurance, so Morgan used the grant money to make partial payments on hospital bills. Unemployed and suddenly in serious debt, he continued painting houses part-time, used up his savings, and relied on vegetables from his and his parents' gardens to keep food on the table. Criticism from those who thought he should just get a job—including his parents—made Morgan more determined to keep writing, suggesting a degree of negative capability, Keats's term for the ability to live in uncertainty. But soon, this experience changed Morgan into a realist. Before, he had thought that he could live like Thoreau, surviving through frugality while following his artistic calling. But when hospital bills piled up, he saw that the modern world requires money, and he realized that he had to use his skills to make money to match that need. His house-painting and farming skills went only so far. He had to borrow $187 from his mother to get his wife out of the hospital, and his mother-in-law lectured him about responsibility when she flew from Syracuse to take care of Nancy and Ben while he took more painting jobs.[64] His forced epiphany about money molded his stance toward the academic career that began to unfold within a couple of years.

Morgan sees the year and seven months that he spent as a self-employed house painter and farmer in Hendersonville as tremendously important—as significant as his year at NCSU. It was during this time that he began working seriously on the craft of writing, on cadence and sound. William Matthews, his only real correspondent during this isolated time, mailed books to him, and they exchanged their poems for critique, a practice they continued for decades. Taking long walks in the woods next to the farmhouse, he found a return to intimacy with the physical world reawakening his sense of nature's language, its smells, textures, sounds, and marking of time. He bought and borrowed botany books from the Henderson County Public Library. He read Thoreau's essays and Whitman's Specimen Days, starting his own notebook of weeds, flowers, trees, insects, and birds he encountered in the Blue Ridge. In silence he listened, observed, imagined, and wrote, looking forward to Matthew's letters and responses from little magazines accepting or rejecting his poems. An uncollected short story titled "Mailbox" captures the anticipation with which he walked down the lane each day, craving connection with the literary world. Matthews asked Richard Howard, the editor of New American Review, to solicit poems from Morgan. Howard published "House Burning," a poem later collected in Red Owl.

Matthews corresponded with Morgan during this time from Cornell University, whose faculty he had joined in 1969 after completing his graduate degree at UNC-Chapel Hill. In November 1970, Matthews invited Morgan to give a poetry reading at the Ivy League school. Morgan drove his family to New York, where they stayed with his mother-in-law near Syracuse, an easy drive from the Cornell campus in Ithaca. After the reading, he met English faculty, including Faulkner scholar Walter Slatoff, and Baxter Hathaway, who developed Cornell's creative writing program and started Epoch magazine. Energized by the kindness of these scholars, Morgan returned to Hendersonville, continuing his house painting, writing, and job seeking. He sent letters of interest to nearby Brevard College as well as to community colleges, seeking a teaching job in the area. Unexpectedly, just when he was talking to the Brevard College faculty about a position, a letter from the chair of Cornell's English Department, Barry Adams, arrived in May, asking him to take a one-year visiting lecturer position while A. R. Ammons, a poet hailing from eastern North Carolina, was on sabbatical. Morgan borrowed $475 from his mother-in-law to fund the move to Ithaca to begin classes in the fall of 1971. He left North Carolina with no outstanding hospital debt and paid his mother-in-law back within a year.

The family was glad to settle down, having lived in twenty different houses between 1965 and 1971. Morgan reflects on the Hendersonville farmhouse interim, finding positives in that worrying time:

> There was a lot of stress, doctor bills, low cash flow. But it was also a time of rapid growth and maturing. When I left for Cornell I was a much more mature person than the one who had taught at Salem in 1968–69. The reading, the walks in the woods, the study of local flora, and the writing of draft after draft of poems, helped me get through. I remember the day I walked to the mailbox and found a post card from Richard Howard asking me to send poems to *The New American Review*. I was very isolated, but heard often from Bill Matthews. And then one rainy day I got a letter from Cornell, inviting me to come teach for a year.[65]

Matthews died unexpectedly in 1997 at age fifty-five, and Morgan opens the collection *Terroir* with the elegy "In Memory of William Matthews." "Of our generation you were the most / generous behind the mask of irony," Morgan writes, paying tribute to his friend's role in jumpstarting his teaching and writing career.

Settling in at Cornell University

That first year at Cornell surprised Morgan as much as the offer of the visiting lectureship itself. His initial nervousness soon gave way to feeling at home, both in Ithaca and in the university setting. The northern Appalachian landscape felt familiar to the southern Appalachian native, the waterfalls, gorges, and rugged hills mirroring those he knew in childhood. Lying in a river valley south of Cayuga Lake, one of the Finger Lakes providing the area's regional name, Ithaca evidenced geological as well as human history that resonated with Morgan's earlier experiences. The Cayuga Indians' history echoed Morgan's sense that Cherokees haunted his North Carolina homeland. The Cornell atmosphere, reflecting that university's status as a land-grant institution and partner of the state university system, seemed down-to-earth and unassuming. Cornell's balance of science and humanities fit perfectly with Morgan's training in both worlds, and in his first semester, he met the well-known astronomer and astrophysicist Carl Sagan, who was then teaching in the astronomy department. Generous English faculty welcomed his perspectives. Gentle humanitarians such as Slatoff, who had suggested that Morgan be invited to teach, valued his working-class experiences and recognized his intellect. Morgan worked hard to fit in with his colleagues, reading their books while drawing on his knowledge of history as well as Russian and French literature to join them in intellectual discussions. His teaching of Ammons's poetry workshop went well, and when science fiction writer Joanna Russ left Cornell as the academic year came to an end, the administration offered him another one-year appointment.

Once he completed his second year, Morgan accepted an offer to join the Cornell faculty on the tenure track. His second chapbook, *Voice in the Crosshairs*, had been published by David Sykes, a student of William Matthews, in 1971, the completion of a printing project with Angelfish Press that had been arranged while Morgan was still in North Carolina. Another book soon followed. Almost as soon as he arrived at Cornell, someone recommended his work to John Benedict, the poetry editor at W. W. Norton. When Benedict asked to see a book manuscript, Morgan sent the poems he had composed during the uncertain house-painting period in Hendersonville. "Six months later he called me to say he was publishing *Red Owl* in the fall of 1972," Morgan remembers. "One of the many lucky breaks I've had over the years." [66] Certainly, Morgan's work ethic and acumen complemented his luck. Because he continued to write when he felt down and isolated in Hendersonville, he had a manuscript to send to Norton. Once on Cornell's tenure track, he suspected that diversifying might make him more integral to the department, so he asked to teach some literature classes along with his creative writing workshops. He particularly enjoyed the American Romantics and developed courses on Emerson, Dickinson, and Whitman to parallel other faculty's fiction classes. Teaching literature deepened his understanding of poetry and prose in ways that contributed to his own writing, and branching out did help to ensure his place on the Cornell English faculty.

Morgan continued publishing poetry as he settled into a tenured position. *Land Diving* appeared from Louisiana State University Press in 1976 and *Groundwork*, dedicated to William Matthews, appeared from Gnomon Press in 1979. These poems reflect his delving into his western North Carolina past soon after he got his feet on the ground teaching. Unexpectedly, his longing for home took him often to Cornell's Olin Library for books on the geography, geology, settlement, and Indians of his Southern Appalachian Mountains. He was doing this reading about the same time that Wilma Dykeman's *The French Broad* inspired him to think about the mountains and history in new ways, just as he was also probing Emerson's theory that language and nature mirror each other as well as the human soul. He began to see his Henderson County farm as the world of Emerson. Language, then, grew in importance as a home that connected him to North Carolina family and landscape. As he often says, without moving away from home, he might never have written as much about it.

His homesickness, but also his Cornell family, invigorated Morgan's deepening commitment to his art. One special faculty colleague validated Morgan's goals for his own writing. James McConkey (1921–2019), a World War II journalist whose essays often appeared in the *New Yorker*, completed fifteen volumes, including his memoir *The Court of Memory* (1986). Morgan attests in a 2010 Cornell Writers Series presentation, "James McConkey and the Quest for the Sacred," and again in a eulogy for his colleague that McConkey's ability to find the sacred in the ordinary, his search for human connection, and his honest portrayal of the poor and working class inspired him. McConkey's plain, authentic voice as well as his discovery that autobiography is a sort of fiction, with a narrative arc requiring the selection and shaping of material, also intersects with Morgan's decisions about prose. As his storytelling relatives continued to haunt his imagination after his first decade of writing poetry, Morgan's reading of McConkey showed a way to shape history and real lives into poignant fiction.[67] At the same time, Morgan's return to fellow Appalachian writer Thomas Wolfe, known for turning autobiography into fiction, helped him to find the new narrative voice that made his fiction writing career take off. He kept writing poetry as well, applying the work ethic instilled in his childhood to achieve in both genres and to add nonfiction and, later, a bit of drama. Even when he chaired the Cornell English Department in 1986, 1987, and again for part of 1988, he wrote each morning, continuing to rise early as his father did, before turning himself over to administrative duties. The Kappa Alpha Professor of English at Cornell since 1992, he comments on the work that sustains him in an interview with Robert West: "The sense of a job well done is one of the most important and lasting satisfactions we know."[68]

The interviewer who asked Morgan how he could possibly have gotten from his modest beginnings in Green River to Cornell University assumed that growing up poor in southern Appalachia limits possibilities. Intellectualism and creativity, however, can grow anywhere. As a child, Morgan attended the Baptist church three or four times a week. There, hymns, soaring metaphors, and the rhythm of the King James scriptures instilled an exciting sense of language in him. And listening to talk of a heavenly spirit while working the Green River soil gave him an early sense of the human complexity complementing the scientific intricacy of the universe that he touched, smelled, and heard every day. In New York, he eventually bought a farmhouse outside Ithaca, with ten or eleven acres of field that he cuts every summer on his John Deere tractor, after the birds have hatched in the grasses. With his face in the wind and deer watching his path, he connects to the natural world that provides imagery and inspiration for his writing. As he captures beautifully in his poem titled "Double Springs," the dichotomy of his southernness and his northern-ness enriches his vision, "separate currents merging" to form the intellectual, farm-boy-turned-successful-writer who still loves dirt, takes long walks in the countryside, and sees no contradiction in plowing a garden before relaxing to Haydn, revising a poem, or shaping accounts of human folly and persistence over time.

Sixteenth‑ through Nineteenth‑ Century History: Fictionalizing Pioneers and Conflicts

As the place that Morgan knew as a boy held his imagination after he moved to New York in 1971, he fed his hunger for home by creating fiction and poetry tied to family, regional lore, and historical events set in the Blue Ridge. Publishing eight poetry collections in the two decades preceding the appearance of his first story collection in 1989, Morgan found reading about his Mountain South's geography and past during those years was inspiring him to tell stories that would bring the area to a national audience. Particularly in three novels that take readers from 1770s pioneer life to the American Revolution to 1850s slavery, he explores southern Appalachian settlement and conflict central to the country's identity. Numerous short stories complement these novels' historicizing, as Morgan clarifies that everyday people experience history as deeply as powerful leaders whose decisions drive storylines about the past.

The success of these works lies partially in Morgan's discovery of a new narrative voice. He again read Thomas Wolfe in the early 1980s, this time realizing that what inspired him most was not his fellow Appalachian's poetic language but his mountain people's stories. Reflecting on this epiphany, Morgan articulates his newfound fictional goal: "I wanted to let those people [who were also his people] tell their stories in their own idiom. The lost language I wanted to recover was the living language of a culture almost vanished when I was a child."[1] In his first short story collection, *The Blue Valleys* (1989), he uses some dialect, for instance "you was" or a nonstandard irregular verb such as "brung," that helps to establish the southern Appalachian setting. These stories, told mostly in a male's third-person limited omniscient point of view, are beautifully crafted, but their voices do not seem definitively tied to mountain storytelling.

Morgan's reading of a Wolfe novella, even more than his reading of Lee

Smith's *Oral History*, prompted him to try a new path into his mountain people's oral tradition. He recognized *The Web of Earth* as "different from almost anything else [Wolfe] wrote, for it is without a third person narrator or editorial comment."[2] Wolfe wrote *The Web of Earth* soon after his mother visited him in Brooklyn in January 1932. Her incessant talking inspired Wolfe to write a story "about an old woman, who sits down to tell a little story, but then her octopal memory weaves back and forth across the whole fabric of her life until everything has gone into it," as he describes the story in an April 1932 letter to Julian Meade, an author working on an article on Wolfe.[3] *Scribner's Magazine* published the piece in July that year. Called Delia Hawke in this version, the garrulous mother becomes Eliza Gant in the novella's 1935 reprint in *From Death to Morning*. Morgan says that reading this piece "helped steer [him] toward writing in the voice of a woman character, toward letting the character tell her own story": "One of the special things I learned from 'The Web of Earth' was that it is the unpredictableness of a narrator that makes the voice most alive. The speaker keeps surprising us, but the sentences seem inevitable once we hear them. I also saw the advantages of a woman narrator. Women are usually closer observers of detail, and they are more willing to talk about their feelings, their relationships, than men are. The novella was a revelation of intimacy, paradox of close characterization, and toughness."[4] The "toughness" that Morgan recognized in Eliza Gant parallels the strength he observed in his mother. He transferred this feminine resilience to memorable women storytellers in his fiction.

Morgan published for the first time in a woman's voice in *The Mountains Won't Remember Us and Other Stories* (1992). Five of the eleven stories feature female first-person narrators, from Martha Sue describing her marriage to a Confederate prisoner of war, to 1970s women working in dime stores. In the title story, which at seventy-three pages is a novella like *The Web of Earth*, Morgan uses Wolfe's model of an older woman narrator. In a nursing home to recuperate from a leg amputation, Sharon shares forty-five years of memories, analyzing her life after her first love's death in World War II. This story derives from Morgan's Uncle Robert's death in a 1943 plane crash in England. He talked several times with his uncle's fiancée over the years, although when he wrote the novella in the spring of 1989, he had not seen her in almost forty years.[5] Like Eliza in *The Web of Earth*, Sharon moves back and forth through time, playing narrator and all the characters' parts in vignettes that transport readers into moments fixed in her memory. Morgan saw this novella as "the best thing [he'd] ever written,"[6] and he sticks with this older female storyteller strategy to open his first novel, a chronicle of early Appalachian settlement.

Frontier Settlers in *The Hinterlands* and Stories

Published two years after *The Mountains Won't Remember Us*, *The Hinterlands: A Mountain Tale in Three Parts* (1994) presents a pioneer woman who claims the adventurous spirit of frontier male explorers as the narrator of the first and longest of its interlocking tales. Introducing the 1772 story of settling in the Appalachian backwoods, Petal Jarvis Richardson explains in the first paragraph of "The Trace" that "every young girl dreamed of running off to the West." Her statement recalls Eliza Gant exclaiming to her son when she hears a ship whistle in New York Harbor, "Say, boy! I tell you what—it makes me want to pick right up and light out with it! Why, yes, I'm not so old! I could start out now . . . and just see everything . . . England, where all our folks came from, and France, Germany, Italy—say! I've always wanted to see Switzerland."[7] Like Eliza, Petal subverts the plea to "Go West, Young Man" that Horace Greeley popularized in the mid-nineteenth century, declaring, "I've heard it said men like to up and move on and women want to nest and stay. But I've never noticed it was so. I've seen just as many women as men with a hanker to move on, to light out and try a new place. Couldn't have been so many people settled here if the women didn't want to come too."[8] Through Petal, Morgan honors women's role in America's settlement.

Petal's stalwart disposition mirrors that of Wolfe's tale-teller. According to Douglas Johnson, in "Eliza Gant's Web: Her Role as Earth Mother and Moral Hub in *The Web of Earth*," "Wolfe . . . found . . . [in Eliza] . . . an unshakable psychic stability. She could always wait things out, size things up, strike when the iron was hot, tie loose ends together." Eliza draws her strength from the earth, seeing it as she sees herself—"powerful [and] self-sufficient."[9] She exclaims, "didn't we learn to do everything ourselves and to grow everything we ate and to take the wool and dye it, yes, to go out in the woods and get the sumac and the walnut bark and all the walnut hulls and elderberries for the dyes."[10] When a neighbor, distraught over losing his money in the 1920s real estate bust, cries to Eliza that both of them, past seventy, are too old to start again, she shows her ability "to keep her focus on the . . . whole of life rather than the frustrations and setbacks of the moment":[11] "'I'm going to pitch right in and work hard till I'm eighty and then . . . I'm going to cut loose and *just raise hell*.'"[12] While eschewing Eliza's chattiness, Morgan instills her can-do spirit and practical resolve into Petal and the other women who tell their stories through his pen.

Following Wolfe's fictionalization of family, Morgan bases one scene showing Petal's strength on a true story his maternal grandfather, Robert Hampton

Levi, told about his own grandmother Beddingfield, who was left alone during the Civil War:

> One night a panther climbed up on the house and screamed and tried to jump down the stick-and-clay chimney. She built up the fire to keep the cat away but realized she didn't have enough wood to feed the blaze all night. As she looked around the cabin in terror she saw there was nothing to burn but her furniture. The panther had killed her cur dog just outside the door and clawed on the door itself before jumping on the roof. All through the night she broke up chairs and fed the pieces to the flames. She even had to burn up the breadboard carved from a wide piece of yellow poplar, and the ladder leading up to the loft.[13]

Morgan translates his great-great-grandmother's tale into a wrenching child-birth scene. Alone and in labor with her first baby, Petal stays up all night burning her few pieces of furniture, cradle included, to keep a panther from coming down her chimney. Her account of labor and childbirth rivals Ivy Rowe's lyrical description of birthing Joli in Lee Smith's *Fair and Tender Ladies*. Morgan allows Petal eleven pages to tell her birthing story, from the time her water breaks until she cleans up the dirty sheets and falls asleep. Like Wolfe's Eliza, she shows that women embody the Emersonian ideal of self-reliance as well as men.

Another trait that Petal shares with Wolfe's Eliza is the ability to size up a situation, a particularly useful trait for a pioneer woman. Giving birth while her husband Realus supposedly rides fifty miles to find a midwife, Petal does not know that he led her in circles when they eloped to make her think their homestead is out West. She discovers his lie eight years into the marriage when, disobeying his orders to stay close to home, she follows the riverbank to pick foxgrapes with her children and hears the bell from her daddy's cow. Realizing that she has lived those years just over the mountain from her parents, she contemplates leaving "such a lying polecat" (118). But hearing her parents' stories of the American Revolution raging around her—neighbors dead, families driven out of the community for being Tories—she returns home to confront her husband. Unable to find Realus at their house, which marauding Indians have ransacked, Petal discovers a rotting corpse tied to a scarecrow frame and sees that "they wasn't nothing to do" but cut the body from the frame and bury it (139). She gets the corpse on a sheet and drags it to the burial ground by hooking a sled's trace chains over her shoulders and pulling the sled like a draft animal. Realus later returns but hides by the barn, knowing that Petal has discovered his ruse. She erupts: "It riled me anew that he was afeared to face me" (144). But as she evaluates her situation, her anger gives way to reason. If she leaves Realus, she will raise her children alone. "Realus could go off to the west," she knows, "and start a new place and a new family. A man could just vanish into the wilderness and clear him up a new place and find another wife." Conceding that she "was going to have to forgive Realus" (145), she leads him to the house, extending human connection and showing that, like Eliza Gant in Wolfe's fiction, and like Morgan's own mother, she is emotionally stronger and more responsible than the man she married. Martha Green Eads analyzes Petal's response to Realus's deception in light of Kathyrn Norlock's *Forgiveness from a Feminist Perspective* (2009), a text that explains women's pardoning of wrongdoers who are undeserving of their mercy. Tracing Petal's stages of forgiveness, and arguing that her bathing of Realus is sacramental, Eads elucidates Morgan's secular spirituality as well as his ability, surely enhanced by observing his mother, to understand the way women negotiate their reality, often extending "irrationally generous acts of grace."[14]

Petal's reflections on her woman's place complement other historical realities in "The Trace." Blacksmith shops, a reference to "long hunters" who hunted the Holston River Valley for six months or more at a time, and Realus's description of the West as Edenic, with plentiful deer, buffalo, and turkeys, give lessons in late eighteenth-century life and the mythology that kept settlers traveling west to fulfill their vision of America's manifest destiny. Realus and Petal encounter a rough band of gold diggers, and they girdle trees to clear their land for crops. Through Petal, Morgan offers lessons in planting corn as well as in its many uses as a staple of pioneer survival. He alludes to the American Revolution when the gold-digging preacher shows up having lost a leg fighting with John Sevier, called Nolochucky Jack, against the British major Patrick Ferguson at King's Mountain in 1780. Morgan's historically accurate details reflect his insistence that fiction writers get the facts right when describing bygone days.

Morgan's intention to chronicle a history of his southern Appalachian territory led him to write two stories predating Petal and Realus's settling in the hinterlands. Fictionalizing the sixteenth-century incursion of Spanish explorers into the area, Morgan invokes an Indian girl's pragmatic voice to tell the tale. "The Tracks of Chief de Soto," published in *The Balm of Gilead Tree*, explores the colonial exploitation that began when Hernando de Soto led Spaniards northward from Florida around 1539. In the story, they arrive in the Blue Ridge when the Native men are away, leaving the women to be pressed into service as sexual partners and gold diggers who are forced to turn the branch and its banks into a muddy defilement. Since de Soto named the Appalachian Mountains for the Apalachee Indians of Florida, Morgan has the chief bring roped Apalachee slaves with him into the area, along with black-robed Christian missionaries describing the great father in the sky and a bound Creek princess translating de Soto's Spanish into "human language" the Indian villagers can understand.[15] Horrific violence toward the Apalachees, especially after their refusal to dig in a cave housing rattlesnakes, clarifies the Spaniards' cruelty and disregard for the Natives' beliefs. Not romanticized as purely victims, the Indian women show practical good sense by willingly engaging in sex with the invaders, avoiding their fury or abuse. The young narrator worries that she cannot plant corn on the half-moon's schedule while occupied with these men, and her insight that humans depend upon nature's cycles contrasts de Soto's desire for quick and easy wealth. When leaving, the "hair faces," as the narrator calls the white men, steal the Indians' food after also taking, by engaging the women in a drunken orgy, their ability to meet the sacred duty of keeping the council fire burning. Obligated to start a new community, the women "'scrape away the tracks of the old village'" and the hair faces as they wait for their men to return to start a new fire, a hallowed responsibility reserved for males (23). The speaker does not yet grasp that the "red spots [running] like tracks down [her] arm" signal smallpox, another track of European exploitation (25). In "The Tracks of Chief de Soto," we see the sacredness of nature losing to the worship of mammon and power, as well as the beginning of Native devastation.

Morgan fills the time gap between "The Tracks of Chief de Soto" and *The Hinterlands* with another story featuring beautifully crafted descriptions of Blue Ridge Mountain vistas:

> the valley draped from ridges for miles ahead. . . . And beyond the valley another ridge rises like a great ocean wave about to spill over, and above that ridge another, blue not green, and beyond that another, hazy with distance, as if fog or smoke were lifting out of the valley between the ridges. And beyond that mountain still others rise higher and higher like steps, wave on wave breaking in haze so high they seem to float among the clouds, the hunting ranges of the Cherokees, the gateway to the west, to the wilderness of the interior, to the edge of the world, lost finally in mist at the edge of infinity.[16]

This vision comes in "The Distant Blue Hills," published in *As Rain Turns to Snow and Other Stories*. It is a third-person limited omniscient tale that follows a blue-eyed boy for several hours in 1752. He hoes corn some distance from the home he alludes to, where he imagines his mother cooking the deer that he has shot with a long rifle. The slow-moving sentences convey how the observant boy carefully notices his surroundings and hides from passing Cherokees, one sporting a blond scalp tied around his midsection. The scenes show the boy's skill as well as survival customs we seldom witness in historical fiction of the time: he drinks milk straight from the deer's udder and bites into the heart of the panther he slays as it tries to eat the deer corpse he cached in a tree. "The Distant Blue Hills" presents the collision of peoples and the morally fraught consumption of nature that we see in other works detailing the history of settlement. Notably, the boy wades through lush, fragrant wild peavines that smother a clearing with pink and white blooms. As Morgan's poem "Wild Peavines" bemoans, by the late twentieth century, one "must look through several valleys / to find a sprig . . . / like some word from a lost language / once flourishing on every tongue."[17] In the story, the paradox of settlement complicates our response. We applaud the boy's resourcefulness and bravery, as well as the natural world's cycles, as a wolf, drawn to the smell of blood, heads toward the panther's carcass as the story ends. But the scalp the Cherokee carries and the slaughter of living creatures create an uneasiness about white men's encroachment into this mountain terrain.

The masculine perspective in "The Distant Blue Hills" appears in *The Hinterlands* as Morgan shifts, after Petal, to male narrators to extend the saga of America's settlement of the eastern frontier. Nodding to frontier humor, "The Road" weaves the folk tradition that a pig will take the shortest route possible to its feeding trough into the true story of trailblazer Solomon Jones, the husband of Morgan's maternal great-great-grandmother's sister.[18] Morgan changes the last name, having Petal's grandson Solomon Richards tell his grandson a rollicking tale about his 1816 adventure of dashing through the woods, holding the tail of his sow named Sue, to chart a course for a road through Douthat's Gap. Solomon's son David tells the last story, recounting to his adult granddaughter in "The Turnpike" the 1845 rebuilding of Solomon's road. Morgan explains that the road Solomon surveyed went through Jones Gap in what became Jones Gap State Park but that no highway followed that route in later times.[19]

Because Solomon and David tell their stories to family, they use natural mountain language like Petal does, rich in double negatives and irregular verbs. But Solomon Richards also ushers in a more literate mountain culture than his grandmother described in "The Trace." While Solomon has had no more than a few weeks of formal schooling, he reads every night, trying to win the daughter of a local college teacher, one of Morgan's ancestors:

When I wrote "The Road" I was thinking of Solomon Jones, who married Mary Hamilton, daughter of Robert Hamilton, my great-great-great-grandfather, who founded a school, first in Asheville, then Hendersonville. The schools were referred to as "colleges," but were probably more like high schools or even middle schools. Robert Hamilton's other daughter Elizabeth married John Jones, my great-great-grandfather, who died in the Union army in 1864. Robert Hamilton was from a distinguished family in Ulster, but as a younger son he could not inherit, and immigrated to North Carolina to found a school. He was known as "Professor Hamilton." [20]

Courting Mary MacPherson, Solomon tries to speak as townspeople do, although he exhibits traits of eighteenth- and nineteenth-century Appalachian dialect. Both Solomon and Petal regularize irregular verbs, for instance, using -ed past tense forms like "knowed" (88, 161) and "catched" (106), a characteristic of early Appalachian English documented in Walt Wolfram and Donna Christian's *Appalachian Speech*. Both rely on other nonstandard verb forms such as "I seen" and "had took" (181), "run" for the past tense "ran" (176), "had give" (81), "come" for the past tense "came" (56), and "eat" for the past tense "ate" (62). They modify the unstressed -ow at the ends of words to -er, as in "feller" (153) and "foller" (168). Both use "hisself" and "theirselves," as well as "painters" for "panthers," terms of rural working-class Appalachian vernacular. But signaling a slight shift, Solomon avoids an early Appalachian English form that Petal's narrative offers: the regularization of the irregular adverb or adjective superlative form in "favoritist" (28, 97), "awfullest" (73), and "wonderfullest" (89). Having spent his adult life with his educated wife Mary at the time he tells his story, Solomon has also adopted some regular forms, such as "half-grown" (154) rather than "half-growed," showing an evolution that reflects the novel's time frame, similar to Lee Smith's matching language to time in *Oral History*.

Like Wolfe's *The Web of Earth*, all three narratives in *The Hinterlands* achieve the effect of dialogue as speakers repeat a listener's question or incorporate it into a response, an oral storytelling strategy that Morgan had applied in the opening tales of *The Mountains Won't Remember Us and Other Stories*, set in the late eighteenth or early nineteenth century, when orality dominated Appalachian culture. The narrator of "Poinsett's Bridge" tells a younger family member, addressed three times as "Son," about helping to build a bridge as part of the turnpike that opened up a route between South Carolina and North Carolina close to Morgan's childhood home. Built in 1820 with locally quarried stone, this bridge with a fourteen-foot Gothic arch stretches over Little

Gap Creek, the North Fork of the Saluda River. Perhaps the oldest bridge in the southeastern United States, it bears the name of Joel Roberts Poinsett, a member of the South Carolina House of Representatives and the first United States minister to Mexico, who is also credited with bringing the poinsettia, which is named for him, to America. The narrator, who offers the local pronunciation of "Pineset," introduces the class consciousness that Morgan observed as a child, locals' resentment of wealthy low-country South Carolinians finding leisure in the cooler temperatures of Flat Rock near Morgan's home. When the narrator begins the first paragraph by mentioning "the most money [he'd] ever had, one ten-dollar gold piece and twenty-three silver dollars,"[21] he invites his young listener to notice wealth inequality, capitalism, and class conflict, all recurring themes in Morgan's Appalachian stories.

Class discord, of course, relates closely to America's legacy of discrimination, a reality appearing in "Poinsett's Bridge" in the presence of slaves as well as in an outsider's dismissal of Appalachians as ignorant. An enslaved water boy plays harmonica as his fellow slave dances, entertaining white workers and reinforcing stereotypes of Black people's natural rhythm. Barnes, the English master mason, denigrates locals, calling them superstitious for worrying about natural hazards such as landslides or panthers. He belittles their understated talk when the flash flood that the narrator predicts ravages the landscape: "'You folk never know how to say what you mean'" (16). When local boys rob the narrator, his wife reflects working locals' resentment of wealthy intruders, saying that his pay for months of work was seeing "the rich folks going up to Flat Rock for their banquet" after the bridge ceremony (19). While the slaves subtly note that "'Massa Barnes sho like to have his say,'" the narrator openly acknowledges his anger, noting that his grandfather fought the revolution "to get rid of such strutting peacocks" (17). Poverty and indignation are as important for this story as the history of Poinsett's Bridge and the droves of cattle, sheep, hogs, and turkeys that the narrator encounters as settlers drive animals from Tennessee and Kentucky to markets in Atlanta or Augusta, Georgia, on trails that buffalo and Indians first scored.

The second story in *The Mountains Won't Remember Us* intersects with a scene from *The Hinterlands*, both of them describing eighteenth-century settlers' clashes with Indians. While Petal Richardson's family escapes harm from the Indians who ravage their homestead in "The Trace," the older male narrator of "Watershed," who also narrates the third tale in *The Hinterlands*, confesses to his grandson that he murdered a Cherokee girl in his youth, helping adult men attack "the heathen" in the Cherokees' huts.[22] Describing scenes that are among Morgan's most violent, David recounts white men's pouring onto Indian hunting grounds after the American Revolution, with the government

selling land it did not own. David reflects on the long-lasting impact of his pulling the trigger in terms of the watershed, where adjacent drops choose to flow
to the Atlantic Ocean or the Gulf of Mexico. In this "place a decision is made
close up in just a matter of a fraction of an inch yet it has such a long-range
consequence," he muses (28). The watershed represents David's regret that he
followed the adults' killing. It is also Morgan's commentary, in this and other
works, on Americans' shameful treatment of Indians.

Morgan balances such carnage with comedy that few critics have noticed
in his work. In *The Hinterlands*, "The Road" entertains with its episodic series
of obstacles that Solomon and his hog Sue encounter as they survey a path
through Douthat's Gap to Cedar Mountain after Solomon signs up sharehold-
ers willing to back his plan to build a toll road. Holding a darting pig's tail while
trying to hack notches in trees to mark the trail, Solomon overcomes hurdle
after hurdle, much like Phoenix Jackson in Eudora Welty's "A Worn Path,"
though he faces encounters more amusing than Welty's protagonist does. After
fighting off a pack of beagles, Sue leads Solomon into a moonshine blockaders'
camp. Some of Morgan's relatives spent time in a penitentiary in the 1940s
and 1950s for making moonshine in Chestnut Springs, South Carolina, "in the
Dark Corner,"[23] and he uses this history in "The Road," naming "Morgans" as
one of the Dark Corner families who are "always fussing and feuding" (182).
Solomon paints a hilarious scene of Sue getting drunk by gorging herself on
the mash that keeps the blockaders' hogs "drunk half the time, grunting happy
and fat" (183). After they escape this riotous skirmish (with Sue bringing the
blockaders' tent down around her while they point their guns but decide they
cannot shoot a crazy man with a drunk pig), Sue runs straightaway toward
a waterfall, prompting Solomon to think, "The sow seemed bent on suicide"
(189). His narrative voice throughout the tale maintains this droll humor, reflecting a take-what-comes attitude. Even Sue's frequently breaking wind in his
face does not divert Solomon from his goal.

"The Road" in fact seems to be almost a tall tale, especially in its hero's
constant escapes from danger. Solomon confronts a Cherokee, a group of
bathing Melungeon girls whose old woman supervisor runs a needle though
his lip, a preacher who tries to talk him out of building the road, a bear who
scares Sue into releasing her bowels as Solomon runs behind her, a raggedy
family that tries to kill Sue for their supper, a "frog rain" storm that drops
toad frogs among hailstones, a black spider, a rabid panther, and lead miners
who threaten to shoot him and Sue. As he meanders from his memories of
these action-filled scenes that intimate outlandish southwest humor to his
present-day responses to his grandson's implied questions, Solomon imparts
wise advice: humans must respect animals, such as the pig Sue, the bear, and

even the rabid panther; people everywhere have the same basic needs as well as both good and bad traits and should try to see others' points of view; humans do not always control events; and "Everybody's life is hard" and "The only thing that can get you through so much messiness and grief is a plan" (257). The plan he espouses entails work and determination: "We have to believe we can do great things even to accomplish little things," he tells his grandson (276). His definition of work resonates with Morgan's many comments on the value of staying busy: "that's what work really is, something difficult, something to fill up the time. Every day is a long day if you don't have work to do. Every hour is long unless you have something that has to be done" (230). Like Petal, Solomon shows himself to be a philosopher-storyteller, intending not just to entertain but also to instruct.

Also like his grandmother, Solomon faces a choice near his story's end, and the decision he makes shows her influence as well as that of Tracker Thomas, a mysterious fellow who supposedly came into the Carolina and Tennessee mountains when Daniel Boone was scouting those hills. Solomon's encounter with Thomas opens the road builder's eyes to the world's beauty, to the apple orchard he has not noticed, and to the vastness of time that humans can hardly understand. Tracker Thomas relishes the way his perspective enlightens Solomon about people who might have lived in the mountains before Cherokees. He also predicts road-building's ultimate destruction of the wilderness: "And next thing we'll have is wagons and dust, peddlers, new ground cleared and gullies washing every holler. The game will be gone, like the Indians is gone" (250). Tracker Thomas extends a token of connection, a gold piece. Solomon pays that favor forward when he assists a snakebitten boy, cutting the boy's flesh with his hatchet, risking his own safety by sucking poison from the boy's hand, and finally carrying the boy home. "I thought about my road and my plans and I seen they wouldn't be worth nothing if I couldn't stop and help somebody bit by a rattler. They wasn't no road that important" (278), he reflects. Ironically, Solomon achieves success anyway, for Sue continues "heading lickety for Cedar Mountain" (286). The last lines of "The Road" signify that Solomon's destination is not a physical space but an understanding of his place in the world. Watching his gold nugget sparkle in the moonlight, Solomon remembers the millions of butterflies that periodically fly through Douthat's Gap. His reverie evokes his grandmother's belief in the kinship of humans and of humans with other creatures.

Petal establishes early in *The Hinterlands* that storytelling builds these desired bonds. She tells her grandchildren that her direct ancestral knowledge is limited to her grandparents, with family members from previous generations being "lost in the fog and dust," reduced to "a name here, a fact there, a rumor." She offers a vivid metaphor for humans' place in time: "We are isolated in the little clearing of now, and all the rest is tangled woods and thickets nobody much remembers. I always said it's how you enjoy that little opening in the wilderness that counts. That's all you have a chance to do. That's why I'm telling you this story" (14). To prepare her grandchildren for their little opening of lifetime, Petal explains to them all she's learned, including human weaknesses and the naturalness of sexual feelings. Over and over, this book's storytellers emphasize the connection that humans need. When Petal tells her grandchildren that she and Realus will be with them as they grow up and begin their own families—even though Realus is dead as she makes that statement—she adds, "Don't worry if you don't understand. I don't think the young is meant to. . . . But I wanted to tell you anyway, so's you'll remember it after I'm long gone" (149). Her great-grandson David brings this notion of story full circle in the book's last section, as he recounts hearing about his "Great-grandma Petal Richards staying up all night to keep a painter from coming down the chimney" the night his Grandpa Wallace is born (299). Passing this tale to his granddaughter, he illustrates Petal's explanation that story connects us with people that we will never know, providing a sense of our place in the universal scheme.

Yet David's short tale also interrogates this comforting sense of place by forwarding an ecological consciousness reflecting Tracker Thomas's prediction of reckless ruin. Describing the 1845 rebuilding of the road that Solomon eventually builds based on his survey with Sue, "The Turnpike" depicts not so much David's sense of accomplishment as it does his anguish when he sees his work's effects. David's theory of roadbuilding paints him as a nineteenth-century environmentalist: "you have to work with the soil and rock and slope you find," trying to "make your idea fit the place you're working on" (311). But his supervisor does not adhere to this philosophy, instead letting cost and speed guide his orders. David expresses palpable despair at the raping of the land: "After they got through clearing the right-of-way, it looked like a storm had hit the mountain and broke off all the trees. . . . And the ground looked ugly as the mange where it was exposed" (317). He tries to stop workers from dumping dirt down the mountainside, killing bushes and trees, but to no avail. When a long summer rain comes, the bank above the road caves in, sending two slides of ruptured dirt to cover all the progress made on the road. David laments the disaster: "It seemed impossible this was the beautiful gap where we had started working a few months before. The whole mountain was filth and waste, like a wound festering and running its corruption down the slope. It made me mad all over again just to look at what we had done" (326). Telling his granddaughter this story, he passes on a plea for people to be good stewards of the land.

David's distress over the spoiled topography mirrors his response to the inhumane behavior he witnesses toward Black and white convicts who are working on the turnpike and replacing the road that Solomon charted and that enslaved men built years earlier. He feels sickened by the warden whipping a convict until his back is raw and bloody. David, in a supervisory position, digs with the convicts despite his co-supervisor's admonition that he should not do so. These incidents show David's deep sense of human community, a value he learned from his father, Solomon, who learned it from his mother, Petal. We see the same humanity triggering his regret for his youthful killing of the Cherokee girl in "Watershed." David's integrity and work ethic color everything he does in "The Turnpike": showing convicts how to dig straight so they will take pride in their work, declining money from Mr. Lance because he is guilty of usury, taking on the job of building the turnpike when his father falls too sick from a stroke to do it. David's actions reinforce the fact that voices in *The Hinterlands* convey a cooperative generosity of spirit.

Morgan also portrays community by repeating tales that bind generations. In "The Turnpike," David's "painter" story mimics the yarn that Solomon tells in "The Road" about a panther stalking a betrothed girl traveling home with fresh meat from a hog-killing. She drops all the meat and then pieces of her clothing to distract him, finally dashing into her house stark naked. David experiences practically the same fate. After the turnpike's opening ceremony, he returns to his boarding house, run by his betrothed Miss Lewis's family, and sheds his clothing piece by piece to divert Old Tryfoot, who is attracted to the barbecue smell on his hands. David explains the evolution of story into myth as he introduces the legend of the three-footed panther: "You know how stories like that will start on their own and grow" (300). Like the young girl in Solomon's story, David bursts into his beloved's parlor wearing only his drawers and one wrist cuff, ending a hilarious journey marked by the throwing of galluses and trousers. Panther tales create a vivid sense of place and community through time in these narratives.

"The Turnpike" shows family connections becoming more intimate, pointing the way toward the close kinships that form a core of Morgan's fictional world. Calling his adult granddaughter "sweetheart" and "my child," David consoles her for having a baby out of wedlock: "They will be another boy come to love you, and your baby. You've got to see this through" (306). "I know how you feel," he commiserates. "That's why I'm telling you this. When your heart is about broke, ain't nothing helps but knowing other people have their troubles too. That, and getting on with your work" (307). Recounting his happy arrival at his beloved's home, where Miss Lewis laughs at his near nakedness, he shares the human kindness that Petal illustrates in the story of Realus's gift of late-blooming witch hazel at the end of "The Trace." The building of relationships in this first novel parallels the building of homesteads and roads, with each tale portraying the beginning or making of a marriage. The three generations of storytellers also introduce Morgan's commitment to creating a multibook depiction of family and place. In response to an interviewer's 2004 question of whether he intended "to create a mythology for Appalachia analogous to Faulkner," Morgan responded, "All the novels are, yes. That is, the Richards family in . . . *The Hinterlands* is still there a hundred and fifty years, almost two hundred years later."[24] In his more tightly family-focused novels, *Gap Creek*, *The Truest Pleasure*, *This Rock*, and *The Road from Gap Creek*, future generations of the Richards family continue working the land that Solomon and David Richards traverse.

That Morgan had a vision of interconnected work early on is evident in a minor detail that Solomon Richards mentions in his section of *The Hinterlands*. On his way to see Mary MacPherson in "The Road," he stops for food at Kuykendall's store, the inn and tavern run by Morgan's ancestor Abraham Kuykendall in the late eighteenth century. Kuykendall, born in New York in 1719, migrated south and fought with a North Carolina militia in the American Revolution. For his service, he received a land grant of more than six hundred acres along Mud Creek, the area known as Flat Rock. He built his tavern on Old State Road, the route that drovers used to drive herds from Tennessee and Kentucky into South Carolina or Georgia, and he built pens to hold the animals while drovers ate, slept, or drank his whiskey. Morgan captures the lore of this famous settler in "Kuykendall's Gold," published in *The Balm of Gilead Tree: New and Selected Stories*. Narrated by the man's second or third wife, this story preserves the legend that locals long tried to find gold that Kuykendall buried,[25] and it also shows Morgan's sympathetic view of pioneering women. Young Falba realizes, when her father accepts fifty dollars to leave her with a married man, that sexuality is her only power. Escaping to follow her father and brothers, she then seduces the wealthy, eighty-year-old Kuykendall, seeing marriage to him as her only option. He gives her father one hundred dollars to leave without her, again emphasizing the status of women in this backwoods culture. But Morgan gives Falba the upper hand by ending the story with her plan to secretly dig up the hidden gold that frail Kuykendall dies trying to locate. Her prediction that people will call the pine woods haunted reflects history, as Morgan heard it growing up in the vicinity of Kuykendall's inn, the same history his fellow Appalachian writer and Kuykendall descendent, Jeremy Jones, notes in the prologue to his memoir *Bearwallow* (2014), set near Morgan's Green River landscape.

The American Revolution in *Brave Enemies* and Stories

Morgan continues his focus on America's founding in a book of historical fiction set around the time of "Kuykendall's Gold," a novel that again conveys a woman's perspective on our national story. *Brave Enemies: A Novel of the American Revolution* depicts the Battle of Cowpens, a clash referenced in "Poinsett's Bridge" when the narrator mentions that his grandfather helped fight in it. Morgan's author's note in *Brave Enemies* addresses his writing in a woman's voice. After citing Defoe's *Moll Flanders* to prove that men commonly write in a female voice, he points to William Butler Yeats's antimask, or opposite identity, to explain that writing through the voice of Josie Summers, whose experiences are so foreign to his own, triggered his creativity and discipline. But noting his memory of sitting in the corner as a boy, listening to female relatives talk while peeling peaches or stringing beans, he clarifies that Eliza's particular mountain voice in Thomas Wolfe's *The Web of Earth* most enabled him to revise a ten-year-old draft of this novel describing the South's role in the American Revolution. Once he imagined Josie's fighting in the war, he shifted from the third person to two first-person narrators, following his belief that "novels are about people. They're not just about historical events . . . or about warfare," despite his desire to tell the story of the battle.[26]

Morgan's research into the American Revolution in the South revealed it as a civil war as well as a fight against the British Crown. In *Brave Enemies*, neighbors fight neighbors as each person has to choose to be Tory or Patriot, with whole families hanged, beaten, or burned out for perceived misplaced loyalties. After a beginning-at-the-ending prologue that establishes Josie's battle injuries, the first chapter moves back in time to show ubiquitous violence. When local men whip her stepfather for sympathizing with redcoats, the sixteen-year-old Josie tends his wounds until he heals enough to follow her into the woods and rape her. She splits his skull with an ax and runs away, cutting her hair and stealing her rapist's clothing because "if [she] could look like a man or boy [she] might be able to survive while traveling in the hills."[27] Her unstable mother blames Josie for Mr. Griffin's depravity, reflecting assumptions about female sexuality and emphasizing the cruelty of the times, which is soon evident again when Josie helps to cut down and bury a family lynched by white men dressed as Indians. Their disguise points to European settlers' abuse of those inhabiting the land they want, and it also symbolizes the liminality of this period of upheaval. Shifting power structures trigger hostility and create a world of uncertainty that Morgan's gender-disguised protagonist represents: "Josie's identity is in constant flux—no longer a girl and not yet an adult, she is neither the Josie she has always known or the Joseph she pretends to be. In this sense, Josie's life is a metaphor for the country itself, as it grows away from its past but has not yet determined its future."[28] Even the landscape seems unsettled, as represented by a massive forest fire that burns Josie's co-narrator.

John Trethman, a Methodist circuit preacher bringing God's word to the hinterlands, narrates four interludes interspersed among Josie's fourteen chapters, his romanticism and ability to remain apolitical balancing the story's violence to give a fuller picture of the Revolutionary South. A nature lover who plays flute and sings to woods creatures, John wishes to bring peace and joy to the world. He fears that his conviction that the natural world, indifferent to humans, follows its own laws that need no "divine explanation" (125) might border on pantheism. But he understands that humans need the community that religion helps them form. His study of Thomas Cranmer, the archbishop of Canterbury and author of *The Book of Common Prayer* who was eventually burned at the stake for upholding his faith, inspires John's efforts to overcome his human frailties, his quick temper, and his selfish concern for his reputation. That Cranmer secretly marries relates to John's falling in love with the homeless Josie, who introduces herself as Joseph when she stumbles into a church service and accepts John's invitation to stay at his cabin. John feels sinful after their night of intimacy and so performs a nuptial ceremony, but he keeps the marriage secret so that congregants will not know that he lived with a woman before marriage. Throughout the story, John and Josie think that their miseries might be punishment for their wrongdoings and quarrels, a sensibility reflecting Morgan's upbringing in a fundamentalist church. As usual, Morgan treats religion respectfully, presenting objectively the biblical teachings that John struggles to follow. Falsely accused of being loyal to the Crown because he is literate and speaks proper English, John is drafted into service as chaplain to Banastre Tarleton's British soldiers to inspire them in the "justice of their cause" (180), evidence of the military's use of religion for political purposes. While John sees the futility of war, he genuinely desires to comfort young men who are longing for home or suffering from battle injuries. His vanity about his linguistic and vocal talents, as well as his thinking that God sends Josie to be his helpmate, reveals an arrogance, yet John's basic decency validates the Christianity that creates a degree of community and stability in this chaotic world.

Morgan makes Josie Summers the protagonist in this war novel, and like women in his earlier and later fiction, she possesses remarkable strength and practical intelligence. Recognizing her limited options after the British kidnap John, Josie does not hesitate to continue to cross-dress or to join the militia, knowing that "a boy might have a chance to live in this world gone crazy. A girl unprotected would be shamed and killed, or beaten and cast away" (171). Less petulant than John, Josie understands people's motivations and knows how to survive. She never reveals her rape, she hides an attempt by a fellow soldier, Gudger, to rape her when he discovers her gender, and she shoots some of Tarleton's Green Dragoons during the Cowpens fighting. As the battle ends, Josie feels proud that she has kept up with the men. If John represents Morgan's view of war's absurdity, Josie articulates his strategy for meeting challenges: tell yourself the worst will soon be over and go a little further; "break the hardest jobs into little pieces and finish them one piece at a time" (229). Like John, Josie finds strength in thinking that she suffers to pay for misdeeds, a religious notion making misery seem just and survivable. Morgan rewards Josie for her stamina and humanity, illustrated in deeds such as bringing water to, and then burying, an Indian woman dying alone in a cave. Pregnant and delirious from the laudanum that eases pain in her badly shot foot, at the novel's end, Josie sees her husband approaching her wagon bed that soldiers guided across a swollen Broad River. All the trauma points toward this reunion.

Continentals won the Battle of Cowpens, and Morgan works diligently to give the historical facts of this January 17, 1781, turning point in the American Revolution. Nathanael Greene, commanding the Continental Southern Campaign, sent General Daniel Morgan to impede the British back-country operation, centered at Fort Ninety-Six in South Carolina. British General Cornwallis directed Lieutenant Colonel Banastre Tarleton to block him. As Tarleton pursued General Morgan's men along the Pacolet River, Morgan turned north toward the Broad River, then in flood. When the swollen Broad River hemmed him in, General Morgan decided to make a stand against Tarleton at Cowpens, a well-known pasturing ground near present-day Spartanburg, South Carolina. Andrew Pickens's militia met Morgan there, along with Continental units from Maryland and Delaware, former Continental Virginia militia, men from Georgia and other states, and Colonel William Washington's cavalry. True to this history and to Daniel Morgan's and Tarleton's strategies, *Brave Enemies* shares how General Morgan ordered men in the first and second lines to fire two rounds at officers and fall back to the next line, though they panicked in the second line and fled but later regrouped. "'Shoot epaulets and stripes, boys. Two shots and you pull back,'" Josie hears from the Old Wagoner (246), the nickname Daniel Morgan earned when hauling supplies for the British Army and for George Washington years before the revolution began. Josie's battle experiences cover approximately eighty pages, her voice recounting the historical detail of troops' movements as well as the fiercely intense battle chaos, with sabers, gunfire, and rolling heads forcing readers to see the awful realities of war. In an interview, Morgan explains his narrative strategy of having Josie, lost from her troop, "run back from the second battle line with the South Carolina militia" so that she can describe the battlefield from several angles.[29] Having found that many people in the Northeast knew little of the South's role in the revolution, he wanted to educate readers on this encounter that followed the better-known Patriot victory at Kings Mountain by three months. He wished to credit the Southern backwoodsmen whom the highly trained British army assumed were unprepared to match their skill and to highlight Daniel Morgan's giving Tarleton his first defeat. And having three of his own ancestors fight in the battle, besides Daniel Morgan, to whom he is distantly related through Llewellyn ap Morgan of Bala in North Wales,[30] he also wrote this book of historical fiction to honor them as well as his father's stories of the revolution in the South.

A story published in *As Rain Turns to Snow and Other Stories* follows a Virginia militia soldier whose travels after the Battle of Cowpens portray settlers' interactions with Indians and their effect on the natural world's transformation. In "The Jaguar," after helping General Daniel Morgan rout Tarleton at Cowpens and fighting at Guilford Courthouse and Fort Ninety-Six, Nathaniel heads home when Cornwallis surrenders at Yorktown, dreaming of the girl he hopes to marry. But when a Coosa woman called Sarah joins him at the story's end, he accedes to life's mysterious unfolding. After the death of the Tory sympathizer who bought her "'for a musket and a jug of applejack,'"[31] Sarah acts to secure her future in this chaotic world, attaching herself to the man who appears and treats her respectfully. Not romanticizing Indians, Morgan includes the fact that Cherokees captured this woman and sold her to McIver after burning her village. Another point of this story of eighteenth-century backwoods survival is to reveal that jaguars once lived in the Southern Appalachians. Sarah, whose Coosa tribe lived in the regions that became Georgia and Alabama, recognizes the spotted skin of the big tiger cat that Nathaniel kills as it attacks his mare as that of a jaguar, a cat he did not know lived in these hills. Morgan's poem "Jaguar" clarifies that historical habitation, noting that "such speed and power and prowess once / patrolled these forests . . . / where fastest killer's now the car."[32] Nathaniel's sense of the mystery of decision making—Sarah, or maybe the flood that sent him back to McIver's trading post, decided that he would be with her rather than with his Virginia sweetheart—makes us ponder humans' decisions. The collective decision that the jaguar and Sarah are commodities, a decision based upon the assumption of ownership and superiority, warrants collective examination, Morgan implies.

The Civil War Era in Stories and *Chasing the North Star*

Moving from the American Revolution to the nineteenth-century, Morgan again draws upon family connections to create Civil War fiction. He begins his first story collection, *The Blue Valleys*, with "A Brightness New and Welcoming," a tale based on his paternal great-grandfather, John Morgan, who died in 1863 at Camp Douglas, a Federal Civil War prison camp near Lake Michigan. The story never identifies the camp by name but places the dying captive in a low-lying area with a boat bringing water from Chicago for officers and guards. Orderlies call the prisoner "Reb," for Southern Rebel, but as the third-person narrative consciousness moves to thoughts of home, we learn the real first names of Morgan's paternal great-grandparents, John and Louise. He gives them the surname Powell, the name used for their descendants in later novels: Tom Powell of *The Truest Pleasure*, whose wife and sons tell their story in *This Rock*, is modeled on the son of John Morgan, who is called John Powell in the fiction.

Water becomes a motif in "A Brightness New and Welcoming," the muddy camp drink triggering John's memory of three springs that intersect near his home in North Carolina's Blue Ridge, his recollection of that cold water related in beautiful, synesthetic imagery. John remembers his desertion from the Confederacy, when he hid in the loft from the Home Guard before turning himself in after harvesting crops. Morgan renders John's pain through a mind groggy with morphine, mingling prison-camp time with John's past mountain-home time to lead to the surprise of the last line, where the "he" walking north from the Greenville, South Carolina, train station is revealed to be his friend Woodruff, coming from Camp Douglas to deliver John's watch to his wife. The entire penultimate paragraph describes Woodruff's slow imbibing of the life-giving mountain spring water, its purity countering human carnage and disease. Morgan reflects that his mountain community was preoccupied with good spring water and that the Celtic "tradition of springs as sacred places" might inspire their frequent appearance in his work, given his Welsh heritage.[33] The spring water in this evocative narrative counters its portrayal of the horrendous emotional and physical burdens that war brings to soldiers and civilians alike. In this story, Morgan does not include the fact that John's wife, Louise, married his brother and added more children to the Morgan line.

Another great-grandfather imprisoned during the Civil War made it back home to become a tremendous influence on Morgan's imagination. *The*

Mountains Won't Remember Us and Other Stories includes "Martha Sue," a story based upon Morgan's great-grandmother Mary Ann Jones's marriage to John Benjamin Franklin Pace (Frank), who survived New York's Elmira prison camp. This story incorporates mountain people's divided allegiances. Pro-Union sentiment ran strong in North Carolina Appalachia, where few held slaves since land was not amenable for growing the cotton or rice that enslaved laborers cultivated in the Deep South. Mary Ann's father, called Johns rather than Jones in the story, went to Tennessee to join Union forces and died at Cumberland Gap, whereas Frank Pace, named Ben Peace in the story, joined the Confederacy on the promise of serving one year, a government lie also mentioned in "A Brightness New and Welcoming." Pace's experience inspired Morgan's poem "Confederate Graves at Elmira," published in *Terroir*. In these lines, Morgan captures the starving, the typhus, and the carting of survivors south on cattle cars at war's end, as Pace traveled to Greenville, South Carolina. The poem "The Road from Elmira," which appears in *Sigodlin*, also recounts this journey, this time balancing Frank Pace's civilian traversing of the road through Saluda Gap with his walking north on it as he returns from war a "ghostlike," ragged man. Learning that a Black custodian spent twenty years identifying men buried at the New York prison camp and having their names etched on stones, Morgan ends "Confederate Graves at Elmira" by honoring that man's work for the "decent thing." Here again, Morgan's investigation of his ancestors' lives connects us to facts and ironies of the American story.

Frank Pace's Elmira religious experiences form a significant thread in "Martha Sue," narrated by the title character. The religious rifts appearing here as in *The Truest Pleasure* and *This Rock* stem from the late eighteenth- and early nineteenth-century religious revival termed America's Second Great Awakening. During the Civil War, traveling preachers held camp meetings for soldiers, particularly Confederate units or prisoners. Emotional worship and singing helped Elmira detainees survive starvation and gruesome living conditions. Pace returned to Green River experienced in the charismatic worship that led to Pentecostalism in the twentieth century's first decade, a movement emphasizing baptism with the Holy Spirit, evidenced in speaking in tongues or dancing. Through Martha Sue, this story recounts Mary Ann Jones's discomfort with such goings-on and the fact that after two tent meetings, she refused to attend another. Morgan's Hard-Shell Baptist great-grandmother disapproved so fervently of Pentecostal emotionalism that she would not be buried in the Pace cemetery. She is interred at Refuge Baptist Church, where the fictional Martha Sue directs her children to put her body, "in the Baptist ground out near Upward where [her] folks is." [34]

Martha Sue depicts the war on the home front as she tells of putting in crops with her mother and of outliers stealing their horse and ruining their corn, and she introduces characters who are important to later work by Morgan. She also shares the true tale of Morgan's maternal great-grandfather's run-in with outliers as a child. As a boy, Fidelie Capps, surnamed Cape in the story, was home with his sister after his father's conscription when outliers ransacked their place, as Morgan tells in his play *Homemade Yankees*. The play includes the sexual violation of his sister that Martha Sue does not mention. Moving beyond the war years, Martha Sue describes her children with the exact traits they have in *The Truest Pleasure*, from Florrie's flirting to Joe's stuttering to Ginny's reading to Locke's attraction to medicine. Defining marriage as making-do, Martha Sue introduces the theme of surviving in the world we create and as it evolves. She notes that the railroad bringing a "new age of prosperity" up the mountain destroys the business of the drovers' market where she and Ben sold farm goods (69), showing that women understood the economy outside the home that nineteenth-century society considered their place.

Frank Pace figures in another Civil War era story important for Morgan's career, a story appearing in *The Balm of Gilead Tree: New and Selected Stories* and one that again recounts events true to his ancestors' lives. "Little Willie" tells of escaping slaves leaving a boy with his great-great-grandparents Daniel and Sarah Pace and their son Frank in the 1850s. The Paces share their supper with the three adults and child, who are probably from Georgia or South Carolina, before the grown-ups dart away when fugitive hunters arrive. The enslaved woman says that Little Willie, about five years old, cannot run any more. Sarah, named Celia in the story, hides the boy in the attic while authorities search the house. Since the 1850 Fugitive Slave Act required that anyone caught harboring a runaway be subject to fines and jail time, the family hid him from neighbors for a time before pretending that they bought him in Greenville, South Carolina, as Morgan explains in an essay titled "Little Willie and the Blue Jacket," published in *The Algonquin Reader* in 2015. While helping the Pace men cut timber, Willie dashes to grab the blue jacket that Sarah made for him and is killed by a falling oak tree. As the narrator, Celia, mentions at the end of "Little Willie," the family buries the boy at the edge of the woods in the Pace family cemetery. Morgan grew up seeing remnants of the undressed stone marker, and in July 2017, he spoke at a ceremony marking the erection of a stone that he and family members purchased to memorialize the child.

In *The Algonquin Reader* essay, Morgan explains that Little Willie's story helped to inspire his novel *Chasing the North Star*, a fictional neo-slave narrative that won the 2017 Southern Book Award for Historical Fiction. At Cornell University's October 2019 MorganFest: A Celebration of Robert Morgan, he also shared that he wrote the book to address the scarcity of Black characters in Appalachian literature. In this book, Jonah Williams begins his trek north when he turns eighteen, leaving his home in upper South Carolina, close to where Little Willie supposedly joined the Pace family as a purchased slave. Jonah runs for five months, ending up in Ithaca, New York, Morgan's home since 1971. There, Jonah finds welcoming human beings, a job, and a loving relationship with the enslaved woman Angel, who joins him on his journey. Telling Jonah's story, Morgan adapts the strategies of antebellum narratives, creating an episodic plot structure while including subthemes of literacy, identity, and sexual exploitation.

Chasing the North Star begins like most slave narratives, establishing birth and thus highlighting the reality that most enslaved persons had no written certificate marking their entry into the world. *Narrative of the Life of Frederick Douglass, an American Slave,* starts on this bitter note: "I was born in Tuckahoe . . . in Talbot county, Maryland. I have no accurate knowledge of my age. . . . By far the larger part of the slaves know as little of their age as horses know of theirs. . . . They seldom come nearer to [their birth date] than planting-time, harvest-time, cherry-time, spring-time, or fall-time." [35] Morgan's novel follows this model, announcing in its first line, "He was called Jonah because he was born during a terrible storm and his mama said soon as she let go of him and put him ashore in this world of folly and time the thunder quieted and the wind laid." [36] Jonah enters a violent landscape, both physically and psychologically. "The granny woman that delivered him said he would always be darting away . . . [being] no more dependable than Jonah in the Holy Book" (2), an analogy introducing the biblical allusions that also form a motif in traditional slave narratives.

As the first line shows, Morgan writes Jonah's chapters from a third-person limited omniscient perspective, although he shifts to the first person when the enslaved woman Angel shares her interpretations of events. In both voices, the plain prose style that Morgan uses for his fiction perfectly reflects the forthright sentences indicative of the prose of traditional slave narratives. Morgan does create an interiority surpassing that of most antebellum narratives. Readers live inside the minds of the escapees, who evidence little consciousness of audience, unlike Douglass and the North Carolina writer Harriet Jacobs, who both crafted autobiographies to sway American readers to press for slavery's end. Jacobs apologizes for her writing skills in the preface to *Incidents in the Life of a Slave Girl, Written by Herself:* "I wish I were more competent to the task I have undertaken. . . . I remained in a Slave State twenty-seven years. Since I have been at the North, it has been necessary for me to work diligently for my own support, and the education of my children.

This has not left me much leisure to make up for the loss of early opportunities to improve myself." [37] Morgan's narrators, less aware of the larger world, readily let readers into their emotional lives, sharing fears and doubts as they work their way through dangers. They focus on daily experiences, not showing anger or judging the whole institution of slavery as explicitly as Douglass and Jacobs do. In line with this change in voice, Morgan does not begin with a white character's prefatory comments attesting to the narrators' authenticity and reliability. Less polemical than Douglass or Jacobs, Morgan couches his book's argument for freedom in its narrators' simple strivings for dignity.

Striving for dignity includes craving literacy in *Chasing the North Star*, just as it does in the best-known slave narratives. Jonah's education corresponds to the famous learning-to-read scene in *Narrative of the Life of Frederick Douglass*, when the twelve-year-old Douglass, then Frederick Bailey, listens to a group of white boys reciting passages from Caleb Bingham's *The Columbian Orator*. A house boy, Jonah observes the white children's lessons and learns to read, write, and count along with them. Soon, the young mistress catches him taking *Robinson Crusoe* from the family library to read during free moments. Not highly literate herself, as most women were not, she promises to keep his secret if he reads to her from the good book. She gives him his own little Bible, saying that it will teach him "not to steal and deceive" (5). She also gives him newspapers, instructing him to tell his mama they're to start fires with—after he reads every word. Ms. Williams evidently considers her own deception just fine, and Jonah does not betray her when Mr. Williams catches him reading *David Copperfield* and whips him "for [his] own good" (10). Whites correctly assumed that learning to read would foster resentment toward bondage. Having read of the Underground Railroad and the Fugitive Slave Act and having studied maps with the white children, Jonah can imagine a new life and cannot stay where he has been shamed. He leaves the night of his beating, stealing his mama's few saved coins and one kitchen knife.

Jonah's owners and most other white people in the novel illustrate the hypocrisy and moral miasma that slave narratives typically expose. "'I'm a fair man,'" Mr. Williams says just before lashing Jonah, adding that he "wanted everyone on the Williams Place to live in Christian harmony," claiming, "'We are a family here'" (9). In Virginia, the white whorehouse madam who employs Jonah for a while marches her girls to the Presbyterian church every Sunday, each carrying a Bible. But with no compunction, Miss Linda calls her partner, Mr. Wells, to physically torture the girl Prissy with a dreadful ice-insertion punishment for stealing from a customer. Linda illustrates white women's complicity in the sexual violence that marked this era of servitude, as Stephanie Jones-Rogers documents in an essay in *Sexuality and Slavery:*

Reclaiming Intimate Histories in the Americas. Notably, Prissy's "honey-colored skin" marks her as "Indian, or part Indian" (126), a person of color who is especially liable to whites' cruelty. Shortly thereafter, Wells abusively punishes Jonah for having sex with Prissy, alternately pouring scalding and freezing water on Jonah's body until he begs for mercy. Jonah notes that Wells "didn't seem at all angry or upset" (135), suggesting that he is diabolical, emotionally detached from his brutality. Wells clarifies that he leaves no bruise or scar on Jonah, as he does not on Prissy, thus not lessening their monetary value and maintaining his public persona of moral rectitude. Early in his flight, while hiding outside the church that Ms. Williams and her children are attending, Jonah thinks that the "love and mercy" Jesus preached "must be only . . . for white people. If Jesus loved everybody the same way, why had he made some masters and some Negroes?" Jonah does not rage against injustice as he ponders that puzzle. He once asks Ms. Williams that very question, eliciting the standard reply that the Lord's ways are "a mystery beyond human understanding" so that people simply must have faith "to accept the world as it was . . . [and] to live their lives in harmony with God's plan" (47). Obviously, Jonah needs more faith than whites, who must find it easy to accept their world of power over other human beings.

Morgan's second runaway also interrogates the slave-owning society's assumptions. Jonah meets Angel in the North Carolina mountains, at a gathering Morgan calls Jubilee. He says in a *NC Bookwatch* interview that he made up Jubilee but got the idea for it from his grandfather's story about a Blue Ridge community of freed slaves, Kingdom of the Happy Land, that is also referenced in *The Truest Pleasure.* In *Chasing the North Star,* enslaved people sneak out at night to play music, to hear preaching, to drink—alcohol and chicken's blood—and to dance naked and engage in sex. When Jonah asks who let them have a party, Angel answers, "'Nobody but ourselves'" (72). Feminist historian Stephanie M. H. Camp argues that bondpeople organized these outlaw gatherings in woods or swamps to enjoy their own bodies that whites saw only as property. Camp's account of enslaved people's three bodies—the body acted upon by owners, the body subjectively experiencing that domination, and the reclaimed, empowered body acting outside that domination at the revelries[38]— illuminates our reading of this and other scenes in Morgan's text as Angel, especially, reflects on her experiences. As an adolescent, Angel becomes her master's concubine. Mrs. Thomas may or may not be aware of her husband's purpose for bringing Angel into the house but, despite being infirm, she does find the strength to hit the girl with a stick for poor sewing. One theory of white women's compliance with their slave-owning husbands' infidelity is that they saw so much violence enacted upon enslaved people that they perhaps "saw sexual exploitation as part of that continuum," or perhaps they thought their husbands' power included the right to sexually violate enslaved females.[39] But rather than feeling victimized, Angel relishes the increased food allowance that makes her fleshy, as Master Thomas demands, and she quickly learns to use what she possesses: "my power and my value were in the softness of my skin and the shape of my shoulders and new breasts and the roundness of my butt," she realizes during her first night with Thomas. "For the first time in my life," she thinks, "I saw I was not helpless, for I had something that people wanted" (82). Using her body as a site of "transcendence,"[40] Angel resists feeling the inferiority her society tries to impose. At Jubilee, she leads Jonah through his first sexual experience and then secretly follows him, assuming that he is a runaway and her only chance to get to the North. Her sense of agency serves her well.

Angel's practicality about her limited options resonates with and challenges Harriet Jacobs's plea to Northern readers in *Incidents in the Life of a Slave Girl*: "I feel that the slave woman ought not to be judged by the same standard as others."[41] Unlike Jacobs, Angel accepts no stigma for the sexuality that she, like Jacobs when she chooses a relationship with the white lawyer Sawyer to thwart Dr. Norcom's advances, wields as a survival tool. When Angel finds Jonah working at the house of prostitution, she becomes one of Miss Linda's girls, taking money for sex, as she does later at a hotel in Ithaca, New York. However, when Angel shares with Jonah that she follows him because she "'didn't want to be the play toy of white men the rest of [her] life'" (252), she reflects Jacobs's sentiment that sexual exploitation did indeed trap enslaved women. Angel's willingness to do what she has to do—at another point, she lifts her skirts for jailers when she sees that they intend to use her sexually—shows her common sense, her manipulation of the subordinate place her first body, in Camp's terms, holds in American society. Her disposition to use the empowered body that whites refuse to see enables her eventual arrival at a place where her body becomes her own.

Angel also provides needed levity during this tense journey through a dangerous United States, often delivering truthful but hilarious put-downs of her co-traveler's posturing. When Jonah covers himself in clay, hoping that people seeing him float in a stolen boat on the French Broad River will think him a white man, Angel thinks, "a colored boy covered with clay didn't look like anything but a colored boy covered with clay" (112). Her six chapters of first-person narration and witty comebacks provide a counterpoint to the serious-minded Jonah's accounts of their travails, adventures they sometimes experience separately because Jonah leaves Angel three times, sure that he can travel more quickly and safely alone. Their getaway-and-pursuit escapades temper the dangers they face and slowly evolve into a love story as well, another part of *Chasing the North Star* that counters nineteenth-century thought about Black people. Whites during slavery supposed that Blacks did not love but only lusted, an assumption fitting their categorization of Black people as beasts. Critics argue that neo-slave narratives help to complete the picture of enslaved people's humanity by granting them romantic desires and loving relationships.[42] Romance, as well as Angel's ability to see ironic humor in potentially tragic situations, contributes to the novel's interrogation of nineteenth-century stereotypes of enslaved people's emotional and intellectual lives.

Morgan keeps this narrative moving as his fugitives find their way, putting them into one difficult situation after another. In fact, *Chasing the North Star* has something of an episodic, picaresque plot, as do other slave narratives. Mostly walking north, but also steering a stolen boat and later riding a train, the runaways confront all sorts of people and dangers. Jonah's first adventure involves carrying jugs of liquor for two mountain bootleggers. When the drunks decide not to bother with him any longer, they tie Jonah's feet to a persimmon tree and set leaves on fire under him. He stomps out the flames and escapes. Soon, he climbs a tree to evade men on horseback and breaks into a general store at night, hiding in an empty coffin when the storekeeper comes in to get laudanum for a neighbor's wife. He rides a shack down the raging Shenandoah River during a flood, gazing at skulls grinning from open coffins that have been pushed out of the ground. With Angel's help, he digs himself out of jail after dodging bullets a drunk white man shoots at him from a nearby cell while yelling that he won't lie down beside a "nigger" (201). This scene, both horrific and somewhat comic due to the drunk man's giggling nonsense, recalls Douglass's jailing as well as the prison metaphors in his *Narrative*. When Jonah and Angel hop a train after running from the jail in Winchester, Virginia, he kicks another fugitive slave who threatens him out of the boxcar. Then Jonah cries, thinking he might have killed or hurt the man. In Harrisburg, Pennsylvania, he descends into a white man's well to clean out a rotting raccoon and other debris, sinking "below grave level" (230) yet seeing stars in midday—a scene of both hell and hope. When a mad dog bites him, Jonah's integrity requires him to kill the animal so that it will not hurt others. He and Angel pick up fallen apples in an orchard, thinking of the Garden of Eden as they rest on a sunny hillside, but Jonah soon finds himself locked in a basement until the orchard owner makes her son set him free. The plot keeps readers on edge as Jonah and Angel spin between brutality and the good fortune of leaving cruelty behind.

Chasing the North Star also features the trickster motifs that traditional slave narratives—or perhaps "freedom narratives" is a better term—employ. Readers have a chance to identity with the guile that fugitives use to seize opportunities and escape varied dangers. Both Morgan's protagonists deceive with aplomb. Angel, for instance, during a period when Jonah has left her, travels with the Goat Man, a tinker who mends pots and sharpens knives as he journeys on a wagon pulled by his beloved goats. When he suffers a stroke, Angel cares for him and pretends to be a gypsy tinker, learning the trade by doing the work. She once steals a fine piece of cloth from a lady's house to make herself a dress befitting her new gypsy identity, demonstrating Camp's point that "when [enslaved] women adorned themselves in fancy dress of their own creation, they distanced themselves from what it felt like to wear slaves' low-status clothing." [43] Jonah tricks people by slipping into Black English dialect when responding to their questions—for instance, saying "I be hungry" (196) if he's trying to beg some food—although Morgan has him think and talk to Angel in Standard English. Jonah also deceives by writing his own passes to show to whites who might stop him along the way, following Douglass's example of writing in an owner's hand a permission for him to be on the road to a certain destination.

Name changes are part of the trickster motif, and Morgan ties the slave narrative tradition of making biblical allusions to the trick of changing identity. With a few exceptions (Julius and Jeter Jenkins), Jonah chooses biblical names as he tries to keep sheriffs from reporting that they've found Jonah Williams, his true name he sees on a fugitive flier that he tears from a post office wall. At Miss Linda's whorehouse, he presents himself as Ezra, a Hebrew name meaning "help." When he escapes Miss Linda's, Jonah claims to be Isaac on a note giving permission for his travel to Tennessee to help his master's mother. Abraham's plans to sacrifice the biblical Isaac parallel what many slaves must have felt—that their heavenly father was sacrificing them to the white man's whims. Jonah selects Joshua Driver as his final name, written on a fake note of purchase printed by an abolitionist preacher who befriends him in Ithaca: Joshua for the prophet who made it to the Promised Land, and Driver, perhaps, for its sound of potency. Joshua celebrates his strength in Ithaca by moving a heavy rock on which he carves his new initials before placing it at the base of a noble oak tree, a witness to his freedom journey. Angel selects Sarepta as her new name, one she earlier claimed at Miss Linda's house in Virginia. That name appears not only in Morgan's genealogy in the person of the nineteenth-century Nancy Sarepta Morgan but also in the biblical books of Luke (4:26) and 1 Kings (17), where God sends Elijah to the town of Sarepta (also known as Zarephath) to care for—and be sustained by—a widow and her son during a famine. Angel's new name thus represents the mutually helpful relationship that brings her and Jonah to a new life as free Americans.

As historical fiction, *Chasing the North Star* asks readers to face the hardships and terror that people escaping slavery endured, while also appreciating their spunk and ability to read whites' intentions. Morgan offers similar opportunities to deepen our view of the past in all his writing. His novel following fugitive slaves picks up essentially where his nonfiction *Lions of the West* ends, with the death of John Quincy Adams in 1846. In that nonfiction series of biographical sketches subtitled *Heroes and Villains of the Westward Expansion*, Morgan interprets national figures who were important to expansion west of Appalachia, leaders and adventurers such as Thomas Jefferson, Andrew Jackson, Sam Houston, David Crockett, Nicholas Trist, and John Chapman, who was known as Johnny Appleseed. In the prologue, Morgan says that while this book considers the famous "lions" of the period, it was really "the unnoticed thousands on foot and on horseback, in wagons and ox carts, who . . . wrote history with their hands and feet, their need and greed, their sweat, and often their blood." [44] It is these unseen people to whom he gives voice in his fiction. Like his historical fiction, the vignettes in *Lions of the West* embrace the missteps and moral flaws central to our history, especially the brutal displacement of Native Americans. Morgan notably draws upon Mexican historians' perspectives, as well as those of Americans, in his discussion of the Mexican-American War, another way that he refuses to romanticize the meaning of westward expansion. In his biography *Boone*, he notes the frontiersman's realization that opening Kentucky up for settlement would bring floods of people to destroy the wilderness he loved in the same way the Indians loved it, one of the ironies of the United States' settlement story. In this examination of the man behind the myth of Boone, Morgan also highlights Rebecca Boone's resourcefulness, her role in settlement paralleling that of Petal, Josie, Angel, and other fictional females who help to set straight the historical record of America's early years. Uncovering silenced voices while exploring complex collisions of peoples and cultures in the Appalachian South seems to be one of Morgan's special contributions to the literature of this place.

Chapter 4

The Family Novels: Two Generations of Paternal and Maternal Ancestors

I n a 2001 *North Carolina Literary Review* interview, Morgan professes a passion that his historical fiction reveals: "one of the motivations to write fiction is to make the past come alive—to try to understand it, to get into it, to see it in the kind of intimate detail and complexity with which we see contemporary life. We know who we are by knowing something about the past." He explores his own past in family-focused novels that capture the complexity of seemingly simple lives in the rural Blue Ridge of the late nineteenth and early twentieth centuries, a time when western North Carolina was "on the brink of . . . industrialization." The transformation captured his imagination: "I think that cultures become particularly available for fiction writing just as they're disappearing." Family gave him firsthand knowledge of this changing world: "I'm fascinated with the generation just before my parents' and knew some people in that generation—people who had lived through Reconstruction who could remember the post-Civil War mountains and who spoke the old dialect. . . . I had a great-grandmother who could remember the Civil War. . . . It was like a contact with the past, the living past."[1] Morgan transmits this living past in four novels based directly upon his relatives. His paternal line offers the characters and plot for *The Truest Pleasure* and its sequel, *This Rock*, while the narrators of *Gap Creek* and its sequel, *The Road from Gap Creek*, are fictional representations of his maternal grandmother, Julia Capps Levi, and his mother, Fannie Levi Morgan. But these books go beyond honoring Morgan's family members. Their characters' lives reflect a larger American story as well as conflicts of the human heart that mark successful fiction of any place and time.

The Truest Pleasure

The first of these books Morgan published is *The Truest Pleasure*, a work signaling his intent to chronicle a family saga covering multiple generations.

Narrated by Ginny, who is modeled on his paternal grandmother, Sarah Pace Morgan, the book recounts her marriage to Tom Powell, who has grown up from being the baby propped on Louise's hip at the end of "A Brightness New and Welcoming" when she opens the door to hear of her husband's death. When Tom, now in his late thirties in the 1890s era of straw boater hats, tells Ginny that his father died in an Illinois prison camp, he evokes the story of Morgan's great-grandfather John Morgan's 1863 death at Camp Douglas in Chicago. Unlike Tom's father, Ginny's Pa returned from the Civil War, just as Morgan's great-grandfather John Benjamin Franklin Pace came home when he was released from New York's Elmira prison camp. The story "Martha Sue" recounts his return—he's Ben Peace in that story—and introduces his children Ginny, Locke, Joe, and Florrie, who are all crucial to *The Truest Pleasure*. The novel connects to earlier generations as well, all the way back to the Morgans' Welsh origins.[2] Locke shares that their great-great-great-grandma, Petal Jarvis, was "wound" through the mountains by her husband Realus so that she would think they were traveling to Tennessee to settle (39), as Petal tells in *The Hinterlands*, and Ginny mentions their great-great-grandpa who helped build Poinsett's Bridge, as Morgan recounts in his story of that name. Ben shares that his great-great-grandpa fought in the American Revolution at Kings Mountain and Cowpens (124), reminding readers of Morgan's *Brave Enemies*. Ginny writes to Locke that she "feel[s] close to Great-grandpa Peace who cleared the place up long ago and set out arborvitaes and hemlocks, magnolias and junipers" (247), referring to Morgan's great-great-grandfather Daniel Pace, who in 1838 bought the square mile of land that established Morgan's Blue Ridge home. Creating a family lineage leads marriage itself to form a theme of intimacy, especially in the first-generation novels, and the work involved in making a marriage echoes descriptions of the physical work that defines these people's lives in their historical setting.

Morgan tightly interweaves the main thematic subjects of marriage and religion in *The Truest Pleasure*. At the first chapter's brush arbor meeting, Ginny reflects on the Baptists' condemnation of such services before she speaks in tongues for the first time, mesmerized by the charismatic preacher's eye contact, which Morgan understands to be a common trigger for glossolalia. Tom visits Ginny's Baptist church in chapter two, and they marry in chapter six. Tom's resistance to Ginny's Pentecostalism soon appears, driving the rhythm of their relationship until Tom dies at the book's end, a reversal of the historical fact that Morgan's grandmother Sarah Matilda Pace Morgan died when her children were young. Ginny, like her model Sarah, follows her father's attraction to the emotional worship he learned in services led by a fellow captive at the Elmira Civil War prison camp. The novel reviews the history of Frank

Pace's wife so despising speaking in tongues and dancing in services that she left orders to be buried at her childhood Baptist church rather than with him in the Pace cemetery, as recounted in "Martha Sue." Morgan explains the religious argument's effect on subsequent generations, starting with Frank Pace's daughter accompanying him to Pentecostal Holiness brush arbor meetings led by traveling preachers:

> My grandmother, Sarah Matilda, spoke in tongues and performed holy dances at the services. Her sister and several of her cousins bitterly disapproved. The argument over doctrine and manner of worship, baptism of fire versus the traditional baptism of water, was passed down to Daddy's generation. Though his mother [Sarah] died in 1912, when he was seven, he followed her example to the Holiness services when they were held, even though he remained a member of the Baptist church.
>
> My grandfather [John Mitchell] Morgan was violently opposed to the Holiness meetings and furious when his wife kept attending after she was married. One evening he was so angry that she had gone to a prayer meeting at her brother's house that he got out his shotgun and fired repeatedly across the pasture. Not only did she attend the services, she gave money to the visiting evangelists. My grandfather Morgan was an especially frugal man, raised during the hard years of Reconstruction, and resented her openhandedness most of all.[3]

Morgan saw the impact of this quarrel in his father, whose grief over his mother's untimely death from measles perhaps compelled him to endorse her Holiness worship. As Morgan explains in his essay "Work and Poetry, the Father Tongue," he was "always aware of the tension revolving around the conflict in the family and community," and he came to believe that his father's connection to Pentecostalism, and many family members' ridiculing him for it, contributed to the inner conflicts that kept him from moving ahead in life.[4] The ironies in this dispute gave Morgan plenty to explore, including the fact that John Mitchell Morgan's quiet demeanor, the model for Tom Powell's temperament, erupts in such ferocity. Morgan transfers his grandparents' disagreements about worship and money to the novel, gunfire included.

Morgan does not judge Pentecostalism, but he does tie Ginny's need for the excitement of brush arbor worship to her place as a woman. At her first service, she feels "a great burden . . . falling away," including her worry about her lack of beauty (8). In her cyclical "need" for brush arbor fellowship, she often expresses "boredom" (235). Ginny craves learning in a world where her sister

Florrie accuses her of reading too many books, adding that "'a woman wasn't meant to think so much'" (63). Several times, Ginny repeats Petal Jarvis's sentiment in *The Hinterlands* that women, like men, "dream of wandering away" (317). She writes to her brother Locke, "I envy you men, able to go where you want . . . and find an occupation" (246). When Tom is dying of typhoid, Ginny feels energized as she takes control of his care, thinking, "I was completely in charge" (310). Earlier, in a land dispute, Ginny takes a leadership role by insisting that she and Pa visit a lawyer, but she has to abide the lawyer's bypassing her to talk to Pa. The Pentecostal services and speaking in tongues give Ginny a voice beyond her place of domesticity. As Nicole Drewitt-Crockett notes, Ginny refuses to "forego her own religious needs and desires to maintain" marital accord,[5] certainly a manifestation of her independence and determination to empower herself in a patriarchal world.

Tom, unlike Ginny, seems uncomfortable with speech, both in church and at home. "'People get in trouble talking,'" he tells her. "'It's the tongue that destroys you'" (98). Tom interacts with the world through bodily movement. Ginny admires Tom's strong muscles and attributes his success as a lover to his confidence in his physical being. This preference for concrete physicality gives Tom a mostly literal vision of the world, as shown in his confusion when Ginny says that the Romans saw a hearth as home to the gods: "'A hearth is in plain sight and you can see no god lives on it,'" he retorts (78), a sentiment relating to his rejection of baptism by fire. Tom approaches life pragmatically, knowing that plants put into soil turn into food that can bring in money if they're sold. His physical competence translates to his improving the farm and turning a profit from it, as Morgan's grandfather John Mitchell Morgan did.

While Tom focuses on the soil's potential yields, seeing it as a commodity, Ginny's musings on spirituality include metaphors of nature as well as sexuality. Once, when she and Tom fight about the revivals, Ginny finds solace in the woods, loving the shoals where "it was like the water was talking, quoting scripture or muttering a poem" (125). She finds that walking in dirt "cleanse[s]" and "heal[s]" (170) as brush arbor meetings do. Ginny's extensive use of earth, air, fire, and water imagery, a pattern evident also in *Gap Creek*, suggests a pre-Socratic, classical sense of the four elements as the foundation of all matter, a view growing from intimacy with the physical world. Ginny's description of a ripe apple captures the elements' creative powers, evoking the concept of "terroir," the French term for the unique combination of soil and climate that produces grapes for distinctive wines, as Morgan explores in his poem "Terroir." Ginny says that the apple's "flesh . . . smells like the essence of earth. The sap is an extract of all the sun and wind and rain of the summer" (90). Morgan often intertwines these primordial elements into a unified image in *The Truest*

Pleasure with delightful synesthesia, such as the brush arbor's "drown[ing] in flames" (13) when it catches fire during Ginny's first service. Her later description of sexual ecstasy blends all four primordial elements: "There was rivers of sparks in the soil and they swirled through the dark and spread in wind to the end of the earth" (177). After speaking in tongues during this orgasm, Ginny reflects that she fails to understand "how the pleasure of the flesh could be so similar to the pleasure of the Spirit" (245), repeating her earlier thought that "the thrill of loving was almost the same as communion with the Spirit and the thrill of solitude by the river" (130). Her sense that religious and sexual passions are the same places her in the tradition of Lee Smith's Appalachian women who seek the wholeness of the sacred sexual female—for instance, Red Emmy of *Oral History* and Ivy Rowe of *Fair and Tender Ladies*. Realizing that reaching to nature or to another human—a horizontal connection to the things of this world—complements a vertical reaching heavenward, Ginny sees a unified universal order.

Ginny's brother Locke enables her final epiphany when he responds to her letter—written over thirteen days as domestic chores take her away from the pen—asking if he remembers why their mother hated Holiness worship. Composed as she struggles to understand Tom's resentment of her Pentecostalism, the letter reviews the denominational history central to Morgan's family. Ginny and Locke's mother, who represents Mary Ann Jones Pace, was a Hard-Shell, Old Regular Baptist. They were a group also known as dryhides, who believed in predestination and thus saw trying to convert people as useless. Hard-Shells also thought it sinful to play musical instruments in church and felt one baptism by water was sufficient.[6] Used to sober services, these Baptists found dancing or speaking in tongues heathenish, as Florrie and Tom do, opposing the emotional "baptism by fire" worship of Pa, Ginny, her brother Joe, and his wife Lily. Locke leads Ginny to consider Tom's anger not in theological but in human terms. Seeing loved ones "lose their willpower and dignity" makes others fear that they too could lose control, Locke says, adding that "no one wants a spouse to escape to a place of their own" (305). His guidance helps Ginny accept Tom's full worth during and after her frantic, futile efforts to keep him alive after he fights a fire that burns much of their land. When he dies from what turns out to be typhoid, she heeds Locke's suggestion that she find and receive Tom's "truest pleasure," the strengths and talents that he gave (306). In a final epiphany, after hinting that religious fervor or eroticism or the thrill of creation in nature might be the truest pleasure in life, Ginny realizes, when a voice in her own head repeats, "'Service is also praise,'" that giving of oneself to others is sufficient tribute to a higher being and, in fact, the truest pleasure. "'The tabernacle is with men,'" the voice quotes from

Revelation, and "'Human things are all we know'" (323). Ginny accepts that Tom's truest pleasure was work, a gift she appreciates as she finds his cigar box full of money, his corpse still on the bed.

Morgan's play with the notion of "word" enriches this novel's exploration of religion. Ginny recites many biblical verses, the scriptural Word. But ironically, reticent Tom's final words, muttered in delirium shortly before his death, enhance her epiphany as they remind her that childhood poverty motivated his frugality: "'Mama, we got fifteen cents and a gallon of cornmeal. . . . I know where they's a rabbit,'" he babbles (300). Ginny also now accepts that she does not need the speech of (male) charismatic preachers, for "silence is the language of God. . . . He prefers to speak to us that way, and through our own voices" (334), an insight shared by Florida Grace Shepherd as God speaks to her through her own woman's voice at the end of Lee Smith's *Saving Grace*. Ginny's thoughts about her own voice resonate with her lifelong love of language. As a child, she made lists of her favorite words from the dictionary, and when she makes notes "to put the mouth of the branch and the sand and trees into sentences" while walking their land's boundaries with Pa and Tom (267), her verbal expression echoes the Word in its biblical sense of articulating creation. We see Morgan's explicit verbal play with religious language when Tom calls his final illness, triggered by fighting an immense conflagration threatening to destroy the farm, his "baptism by fire" (299), evidence that he sees the irony of a literal fire consuming what he worked so hard for while disparaging Pa and Ginny's spiritual zeal.

The Truest Pleasure follows the material world housing this family's spiritual deliberations, of course. Tom's fervent work to expand the farm's productivity intensifies when a cotton mill opens nearby in 1904, industrializing Green River. Tom becomes an entrepreneur, peddling vegetables, molasses, wood, and hogs to mill hands. By 1905, the mill whistle orders their lives, blowing at seven in the morning, noon, and midevening, an artificial marking of time encroaching into the natural world's signals of the hours' progression. Mill houses have the first electricity in the area, but Ginny expresses no jealousy of mechanized progress. On her way to the train that takes her and Pa to town to press charges against their neighbor Johnson, an outlier during the Civil War, for cutting wood on their land, Ginny sees mill hands "slumped in the morning cold," arriving for work or leaving the night shift. She thinks that they "looked like prisoners lined up to go through the bars" (257), on their shoulders the lint that gave textile mill workers the name "lintheads," as immortalized in songs such as "Lint Head Stomp." On the train, Ginny notices that the fields by Mud Creek look "sooty" (259), a mark of the changing landscape modernity brings, as are the pits that she later encounters while walking the boundary line. Her brothers Joe and Locke had dug holes in a futile search for zirconium silicate, inspired by their uncle, Dr. Johns, selling tons of zircons from his mine to Thomas Edison for early experiments in incandescent bulb filaments (272). Another man claimed mineral rights on that land, and before he and Johns settled the dispute, electric companies found that carbon and tungsten worked more effectively than zirconium silicate. Morgan notes his great-uncles' digging in the poem "Zircon," explaining how the zircon "keeps / the fingerprints of isotopes from clouds / of the original primordial dust," reminding readers that the industrial age is but a spot in time's whirling progression.[7]

Tom's labor to sell products in the mill village stands alongside work of all sorts in *The Truest Pleasure*. Through Ginny and Tom, Morgan describes processes that enable people to maintain a homestead: peeling and canning peaches, making apple cider and molasses, pulling fodder, building spring-houses, fishing, washing clothes outside in a snowstorm, moving manure to expedite its decay into fertilizer, building gates, and widening dirt roads. Both enjoy the order their efforts bring to the land: "There is a thrill to cleaning a row, getting rid of ragweeds and bull nettles," Ginny says (171), her sentiment mirroring Morgan's zeal for clearing away weeds that he honed as he started hoeing corn at age five, and reminding us of the metaphor he offers in his unpublished memoir as well as in his poetry. Weeding is editing the soil, ordering nature and ordering words being comparable art forms in his agrarian/literary world.

Locke, too, though no longer on the farm, values work, a complement to his role in bringing a firsthand account of the larger world into this Appalachian narrative. Locke joins the army during the Spanish-American War of 1898 when "recruits were give bonuses to go to Cuba" (40). Home on furlough, he shares stories of seeing a demoniac healed in a Manila prison and of treating soldiers suffering from tropical diseases after San Juan Hill. The screaming, diarrhea, retching, and death he confronts on a hospital ship in Havana almost convince Locke that he is not cut out for nursing despite having the caregiver bent of his granddaddy Johns. But Locke sees that helping the sick men lifts him as well as his patients: "'I got hold of myself through hard work. . . . I was more than myself, and better than myself. It seemed I become the work, and was no longer me at all'" (42). Riding a train to California, Locke travels through snow sheds constructed by "Chinese coolies" (33) helping build America's railroads, and he writes to Ginny about experiencing the 1906 San Francisco earthquake. He reads Christian Scientist publications and considers psychology's impact on health, pushing his family to think beyond their religious teaching and limited schooling. Ginny and his Pa also read newspapers. Their sometimes oblique references to history, such as Teddy Roosevelt's Rough Riders fighting in the Spanish-American War, President McKinley's assassination in 1901, or the

Japanese bombing of the Russian port Vladivostok in the Russo-Japanese War of 1904 and 1905, ground the novel in its time period and recall how Morgan's great-grandfather and father read widely in history.

Illnesses in *The Truest Pleasure* also reflect its early twentieth-century setting. Morgan says that the prominence of sickness in the novel grew as he imagined Ginny's world and remembered family stories of deaths from pneumonia, typhoid, and lockjaw and realized the vulnerability of people facing ailments without modern antibiotics or sanitation. He knew that his great-great-uncle, Dr. Levi Jones, whose medical training was as a Union army corpsman, began his examinations by saying, "'What this case needs is a little whiskey,'" and he knew the hollowed-out Medicine Rock on family land where Dr. Jones "washed those bloody from gunshots, knife wounds, and amputations."[8] When Ginny gets pneumonia in 1905, the family triggers her recovery by putting a fried-onion poultice on her chest to make her throw up mucus since Dr. Johns, who is modeled on Dr. Jones, has no remedy—just as he does not for the typhoid that Tom contracts a few years later. "There wasn't anybody to help," Ginny laments (319), reflecting the isolation of rural Americans as well as the lack of medical treatment. As she tries to keep Tom warm by putting heated rocks under the bed and feeding him hot sassafras with whiskey, she says the secret name that Dr. Match, a Cherokee, gave her decades earlier, along with a concoction that helped her to start her menstrual period. These details reflect Frank Pace's taking his daughter to a Cherokee doctor when she needed medical help, a trip that Morgan sees as possible validation that his great-grandfather carried Cherokee blood, although the family claimed that his dark coloring stemmed from Italian ancestry. Ginny clearly finds strength in the name that is unknown to her family, repeating it right before Tom's death as she finds that her prayers and "feelings from . . . the brush arbors" seem disconnected from his suffering (320). Her occasional return to the pigeon imagery that Dr. Match suggested, such as when hard labor with her third child ends in the baby's death, also pays tribute to American Indians' insight into the psychology of healing. Morgan thus places the Pentecostal versus Baptist conflict into the spiritualism of an older Green River world.

Ginny's final hours with her dying husband end *The Truest Pleasure*, as she reflects on "the story of a marriage" that could be this book's subtitle, as it is *Gap Creek*'s. Ginny comments explicitly on marriage's ups and downs throughout the book. She learns to read quiet Tom's body language to tell when he is "sulling" and observes that "the sweetest thing about little quarrels is the making up," when all wrongs seem "forgivable" as "the charge of anger . . . becomes pleasure" (112). Their hostility erupts every time Ginny attends Pentecostal meetings, and its intensity is exacerbated when her sister

Florrie, who disapproves of those services as much as her brother-in-law, flirts with him. Tom then sleeps in the attic, as he does when Ginny's birthing time nears. Often revealing intimate details of their lovemaking, Ginny also reflects that "when a man and woman ain't sleeping together they don't feel the same toward each other. . . . I reckon the sex thing is a lot of the glue that holds people together" (184). Ginny advises her unmarried brother Locke to realize that marriage is "mostly a matter of . . . steady work" (241). She and Tom do that work to withstand troubles until pleasure's interlude returns.

This Rock

Ginny continues as a widow in *This Rock*, carrying Morgan's paternal story forward as she raises the children alone. Ginny's prologue and epilogue frame three dated sections—1921, 1922, and 1923—whose narrative voices shift between hers and that of Muir, her second son. Ginny and Tom's firstborn, Jewel, born in 1899, has died during the 1918 flu pandemic. Moody, born in 1902 and based loosely on Morgan's uncle John Dwight Morgan, who was involved in moonshining as a young man, and Muir, born in 1905, the year of Morgan's father's birth, enact a Cain and Abel conflict. Fay, who is based upon Morgan's Aunt Mae, was born in 1908 and is thirteen as the novel begins, and she reacts to her brothers' clashes mostly from the background. Characterizations set in *The Truest Pleasure* guide *This Rock*, with ironic twists that are true to characters' real-life models. Ginny names her first son after the nineteenth-century evangelist Dwight L. Moody, the founder of Moody Bible Institute and Moody Publishers, which sold across the country inexpensive religious books and tracts, including *Moody Monthly*, which Ben Peace, and his real-life model Frank Pace, read. But Moody Powell in no way follows the evangelist. From the outset, he is an aggressive child, knocking his sister's snowman down in *The Truest Pleasure* and, as Ginny remembers in the prologue to *This Rock*, setting fire to the little cabin that his younger brother builds at age ten. Muir, whom Tom names after the Scottish boss he worked for before marrying Ginny, a nod to Clyde Morgan's claim of Scottish heritage although he was Anglo-Norman, is the son who feels called to preach. Morgan also explains that Muir's name pays homage to Scottish poet Edwin Muir and the naturalist John Muir.[9] Muir represents Morgan's father, exemplifying Clyde's frustrations, his obsession with religion, and his aborted attempts to escape Green River as a young man. Muir's articulation of his angst—"I didn't know what I wanted to be, and I didn't know what I could be"[10]—ties his and Morgan's father's anxiety to the kinds of sentiments most adolescents feel as they seek their own identity.

Narrating more chapters than his mother, Muir claims *This Rock* as his initiation story, reflecting Morgan's father's long years of settling into adulthood. When Ginny urges Muir not to waste time on tasks that make no money, she echoes Clyde Morgan's family's frustrations with his penchant for doing work around the farm that earned no profit. In fact, Muir's dreaminess and quick rages in the face of criticism, his inability to work with other people, his preference for being alone, and his love of working in the rain and of trapping, a skill that ties him to the nineteenth century, are all traits of Morgan's father. Like Muir, Clyde Morgan stopped going to school at age twelve and dreamed of building a castle; in fact, he commissioned his portrait with his dog Prince that features a castle in the meadow background. Muir's several attempts to leave the mountains come straight from the biography of Morgan's father. Clyde once bought a train ticket to Minnesota to trap for fur but decided not to go. In 1927, heading to Canada to trap, he drove his Model T as far as Toledo, Ohio. He picked up a man claiming his Packard had broken down near Lima, Ohio, which in the 1920s was a Chicago gangster hangout. When Muir reenacts this scene in the novel, the stranger leaves after discovering that the North Carolina boy is not hauling moonshine as he assumed. Like Clyde, Muir heads back home after this scary encounter, glad to get away from the city's stench and noise. In 1928, Clyde tried again to leave the mountains, taking a train to eastern North Carolina to trap on the Tar River between Rocky Mount and Greenville, as Muir does immediately after his Ohio adventure.[11] Morgan collapses the time frames of his father's trips, fitting them into 1922 and 1923. In the fiction, these trips revealing Muir's inner conflicts occur as interludes among his fights with Moody who, as Muir admits, is one reason he needs to leave home.

Morgan centers Muir's frustrations mostly on religion, feeling that much of his own father's exasperation stemmed from quarrels within the Baptist church and from his draw to Pentecostalism in a family and church community that disapproved of Holiness worship. In the novel, Muir does not feel this pull but remembers the fear and shame he felt as a child when he witnessed his mother dancing and speaking in tongues during the brush arbor scene described in *The Truest Pleasure*. Muir's discomfort is resonant of Morgan's response to his father's speaking in tongues, a painful memory that he recounts in "The Gift of Tongues," a poem that opened up his feelings about Pentecostalism at age forty and enabled him to write *The Truest Pleasure*.[12] In *This Rock*, Muir delivers his first sermon in the Baptist church as a teen, stirring Ginny's dream of having a son preach. But Moody, jealous of his mother's favoring Muir as "marked for something special" because his tied-down tongue had to be clipped (11), disrupts the sermon by breaking wind, loudly, from the back pew. Muir stays away from church for nearly a year, engaging in violent physical fights with his brother in cycles of rancor and guilt, discord and reconciliation. An early scene introducing the metaphor of the biblical Cain and Abel story occurs when Moody's volatile temper erupts in violence against the family's cow. Muir tries to intervene, resulting in the brothers fighting with a two-by-four and pitchforks. Religion then takes a back seat to secular affairs until Muir replaces his preaching ambitions with a passion to build a church, a vision that comes only after his journey into the wilds of bootlegging danger.

The mountains' moonshining legacy shapes this novel's brother-against-brother plot and that of one of Morgan's short stories as well. Moonshining developed out of corn's quick growth in southern Appalachian soil and the lack of decent roads for getting that corn to market. Condensed to whiskey, corn could easily be transported out of the hills for significant profit. Even before the beginning of Prohibition in 1919, mountain people made and sold liquor covertly at night—thus the idiom "moonshine"—to avoid paying taxes on their product. When Prohibition raised prices just as the mass production of automobiles made them affordable, the bootlegging business boomed. Morgan shares in an essay that some of his relatives spent time in an Atlanta prison in the 1940s and 1950s for selling liquor in Gap Creek and Chestnut Springs, the Dark Corner of South Carolina. The bank took one uncle's farm while he served time, and one "cousin was murdered on Gap Creek because he was caught cutting whiskey with too much spring water,"[13] an offense that gets Moody tied to a tree and whipped with a razor strop in chapter four of *This Rock*. In a chain gang narrative published in *The Balm of Gilead Tree*, Morgan portrays an even more revolting beating as a warden convinces the prisoner Mike, stripped naked and tied to a tree, to identify his cousin who hid liquor close to the prisoners' work site for them to drink. This "Sleepy Gap" inmate divulges the name only after he fouls himself. Unlike this short story's protagonist, Moody never admits that he is broken. Ginny and U. G., the son of her sister Florrie, find him hurt, along with a young girl from moonshiner Peg Early's house of prostitution. Moody cries in pain but lashes out at family for discovering his vulnerability. About his liquor-making relatives who inspired his portrayal of this part of history, Morgan speaks with largesse: "Making spirits and avoiding the taxes gave romance to their hard lives," he recognizes, as he describes their *making* as comparable to his writing, which is almost as "suspect, dangerous, maybe disgraceful" as moonshining in his Appalachian South.[14] He relishes that *making* as he transforms history into scenes of horror and delight, such as the car chase that follows Moody's thrashing.

Still recuperating, Moody drags his brother into a one-night bootlegging adventure, a riotous car chase through rugged backwoods terrain and creek beds that showcases Morgan's talent for infusing humor into serious scenes. Moody tempts Muir with money to buy traps and invokes the biblical principle that brothers should take care of each other, and he finally persuades Muir to drive him to Chestnut Springs to pick up liquor and transport it back over the state line to North Carolina. George Hovis argues that this scene, with Moody riding shotgun while Muir steers the Model T to evade pursing law officers, would transfer well to the big screen, one reason that *This Rock* would make a superb movie portraying early twentieth-century America.[15] This nighttime chase through the "wildest section of the mountains" (86) shows bootlegging in its glory days, when hauling huge cans of liquor in the backseats of early automobiles led to confrontations with rural sheriffs, who sometimes took bribes to ignore illegalities. In *This Rock*, the scene also reinforces Moody's willingness to misuse his brother. But by rolling out of the car to save himself while Muir endures a run-in with lawmen, Moody unwittingly helps the younger boy to mature while his own alcoholism and delinquency soon earn him a stint in a Greenville, South Carolina, jail for cutting a man. Moody's 1918 letter to his mother during his sarcastically termed "vacashun" (180) gives readers another chance to feel the grief he causes Ginny, who again asks for U. G.'s assistance to rescue her wayward son. Morgan does not glamorize moonshining, although he obviously enjoyed creating the comically exciting car chase that is a key in Muir's development, along with a later droll scene when he slips in pouring rain while doing moral duty as a pallbearer, dropping the casket whose lid he has not securely fastened. As the corpse rolls onto the muddy ground, readers enjoy the wry comic relief, a moment of southwestern humor that deepens Muir's frustration with himself.

Readers expect a subsequent scene to continue a lighthearted portrayal of Muir's adventures as he takes Annie to the circus, but his efforts to impress his sweetheart take a tragic turn that again contributes to his maturation. As he often does, Morgan uses a historical event, the true story of a circus elephant's killing of an unqualified trainer in Kingsport, Tennessee, in 1916. The next day, "Murderous Mary," as she came to be known, was hanged in nearby Erwin, a small town in eastern Tennessee roughly seventy miles from Morgan's home. In the novel, days after Muir, Annie, and Fay see the elephant stomp a roadster and its owner, they return to witness the execution, this time taking Annie's brother Troy, who is central to *The Road from Gap Creek*. Morgan moves the hanging to Tompkinsville, North Carolina, where an industrial-sized crane mounted on a train car hoists the elephant into the air and men shoot bullets into the strangling body, just as it happened in 1916.[16] Muir focuses on the elephant's eye during both scenes, sensitive to the animal's panicked weeping. Identifying with the unfortunate beast, Muir castigates himself as he wanders through the woods trying to relieve his shame at exposing Annie to the awful demonstration of inhumanity: "like the elephant you blunder around and hurt people. You are guilty and you are trapped, and nobody is able to help you" (205). But when Muir stumbles upon Moody's bootlegging money and liquor, he drinks some moonshine and gains courage, inspired by the sunlight's coloring of the thickets and the memory of seeing Chartres Cathedral in Henry Adams's book. Muir's vision of "the curve of the world" expands to "the curve of time stretching beyond that, far as the curve of thought" (207). The suffering elephant, the moonshine, and Adams's description of Chartres blend lowbrow affairs with high art to evoke Muir's epiphany: when a voice tells him to build a church, he knows he must build it of rock, "like the churches in Europe," a suggestion of Morgan's community across time and space as well as a nod to his father's building of the rock house that Morgan moved into as a child. Muir's decision to "preach with [his] hands" (208) emulates his father Tom's physical work as praise of a universal order. Once again, Morgan connects spiritual fulfillment to worldly objects and manual labor.

When Liner, a Baptist preacher, questions Muir's motivation for building a church atop Meeting House Mountain, Muir stands up to him, another important step in his maturation. Liner, whose theology assumes that everyone is a sinner, fears that Muir wants to start his own church. The preacher feels threatened by the young man whose relatives engaged in the Pentecostalism he claims to have stopped from splitting his congregation. Muir retorts that his Pa, Ben Peace, gave the land for the church that Liner leads. The historical parallel is Frank Pace's donation of land for Green River Baptist Church after the Civil War. Pace and his daughter Sarah, whom Ginny represents, ignored the congregation's "churching" them, or throwing them out, for attending Pentecostal meetings. Muir demonstrates the same resolve by defying Liner's directive to forget his dream. Obsessed with a "rage" to clear the mountaintop for a new place of worship (214), Muir channels the early settlers' urge to tame the wilderness and mark their presence in the world. As he plows a road up the mountain with the horse Old Fan, Muir wishes that he "'had a sow like old Solomon Richards did'" (224), referring to the trailblazing settler in *The Hinterlands*. Muir's growth is supported by Hank Richards, a neighbor and church board member, who teaches Muir as he helps him build, leading the young man who detests criticism to accept an experienced builder's suggestions. This relationship makes discernable the ties that bind Morgan's four family novels, for Hank, a *Gap Creek* protagonist, becomes Muir's father-in-law in its sequel, *The Road from Gap Creek*.

Secular and spiritual matters weave more tightly together as *This Rock* nears its climactic scenes. Morgan complicates the fraternal conflict when Muir assumes that Moody destroys his church's foundation, and the book's "Second Reading" section ends with Muir's ferocious retribution against his drunk and sleeping brother. As the 1923 "Third Reading" section opens, Muir again leaves home to work through his frustration and guilt. His climb to Black Balsam mirrors the times that Morgan's father Clyde camped alone in those high elevations, and Morgan blends this mythic journey of self-discovery with local geography and history. After Muir shares his food with a demented old man caring for a deserted community, he sees a red rag tied to a cabin post, a sign that typhoid wiped out the settlement. The vicinity this man roams encompasses the Pink Beds, a lovely area of spring blooms that drew families to camp there, bringing cows and chickens to sustain them. Muir lauds Looking Glass Rock as nature's cathedral, and then, consulting his map, he decides that a cliff in his line of vision is Devil's Courthouse, where, according to legend, the devil held court in a cave beneath the stone peak. The poem "Devil's Courthouse" in *Groundwork* suggests whites feared this place, and Morgan's unpublished story "Devil's Courthouse" suggests that Cherokees possibly left Spaniards to die in the cave when they went looking for gold. Cherokee lore says the slant-eyed Judaculla lives there. Muir also remembers—and teaches readers—that the balsams have been stranded in these Southern Appalachians since the last Ice Age, when massive ice sheets drove northern plants south. Muir's encounter with industrial age destruction triggers an unspoken epiphany that sends him back home. When a guard from the Sunburst Lumber Company threatens him, Muir considers shooting the man, a fictional event that Morgan bases on his father's telling him that when he camped in the Black Balsams in 1927, he saw where the Sunburst Logging Company had stripped balsams from the high peaks, and they had not grown back.[17] Muir's mood changes when he sees the danger this ranger is in as he tries to free a jammed log in the water chute that brings logs down the mountain to be loaded onto train cars. He considers warning the man that logs from above are rushing his way. But he stays silent, and when the man is thrown off the mountain, Muir heads home, ashamed that he failed to help a fellow human.

Muir's self-confrontation soon comes to a head, triggered by the brother whose role as his nemesis ends in death. Moody, it turns out, did not destroy the church foundation. The Willard brothers demolished Muir's work to punish Moody for cutting into their bootlegging business. Muir's earlier thinking that his brother's tearing up his work "was almost the same as if [he'd] done it [himself]" (237) emphasizes their emerging bond. Standing up for his brother, Moody kills Zach Willard. Muir sees his culpability for the deaths of the ranger and Zach and for Moody's crime, admitting that he has been "blinded by . . . anger and . . . vanity" (267). When church deacons rebuke his continuing efforts to build his church, adding to his angst, Muir sees "nothing to do but start over" (276). He begins with Moody, leaving food, socks, and money near a cave on Ann Mountain, where he thinks his brother might be hiding. Moody responds by sending his second letter in the novel, sharing his true feelings better in writing than in speaking. Ordering Muir not to search for him, Moody acknowledges his anger at being seen as the family black sheep but adds words of encouragement: *"You want to be a preacher you go ahead and be a goddamned preacher. . . . I heard you practicing out in the woods. . . . And you sounded good as a real preacher man to me"* (283). Ironically, reconciliation comes too late, for a deputy who plays a trick to find Moody's hideout kills the wayward brother.

The story suggests that Moody's purpose has been to propel his little brother into greater insight. Morgan's own comment that Moody's role in the novel grew during revisions as he kept wondering why Moody was so insolent[18] supports that purpose, as it also takes into account Moody's feeling that the family saw him as someone lesser than Muir. Liner, the weak preacher, refuses to hold Moody's funeral at the Baptist church, citing his criminal behavior and lack of church membership. He also declares that Moody's death is punishment for the family's defiance of Baptist doctrine. In the face of such an insult, Muir steps up to do the decent thing. As Ginny lays her son's body out on the kitchen table, Muir builds and lines his brother's coffin. He preaches at Moody's funeral himself, in the incomplete mountaintop church that community members fill. In his simple sermon, Muir testifies that Moody taught him that we can learn from our mistakes, and his sense that he has been preparing his whole life for preaching at Moody's funeral indeed gives meaning to the clashes that marked their time together. Articulating Morgan's respect for community across generations, Muir says that "'the dead never leave us . . . [but] give dignity and weight to our confused lives'" (311). Recognizing the role of the word in his own breakthrough, Muir finally understands Ginny's passion for speaking in tongues but sees his "stream of words" as more ordered, as "building a church of words a sentence at a time" (312), a metaphor related to the masculine, earthly building of edifices prominent in Morgan's work. In a landscape metaphor based upon seeing valley land, mountains, and heavens in one gaze from Mount Pisgah, Muir states that truly seeing is a twofold Pisgah vision: "'this world and the next, the natural vision and the spiritual vision'" (312). His lauding the "'gift of each other, and the gift of the trees and soil and sunlight to nourish us'" (313) reminds us that Morgan considers the material world part of our saving grace.

While Protestant denominations in southern Appalachia impose the otherworldly perspective that Morgan rejects, Jim Wayne Miller argues that the region's literature has always been as secular in outlook as it is otherworldly.[19]

This world and the next remain separate in Appalachian culture, he says, with traditional religion teaching that a better world awaits and that God won't help us much in this one. But true to Morgan's unifying vision, *This Rock* blurs this dichotomy. Particularly during his journeys of escape, Muir encounters people who deter his quest—gangsters in Ohio, locals running him off from Tar River, and the logging guard and the demented old man on his Balsam Mountain trip. They signal a spiritual power sending him home to his destiny of preaching. Morgan himself comments on the mad old man's unwittingly speaking directly to Muir's inner chaos by asking if he's a preacher, confirming that he sees a mythic element, a kind of spiritual intervention, in the literal journeys that direct Muir to the moment of delivering his brother's eulogy.[20]

Only Ginny's epilogue follows the funeral, relaying the fate of the never-completed rock church. Muir stops building when springtime calls him to plant a garden, and then he gets busy answering calls to preach at nearby churches. Abandoning yet another project—although starting this one has given him direction—he leaves the church's skeleton to ghostly lore. Like the closing frame of Lee Smith's *Oral History*, this story ends on a haunted mountaintop. Gathering herbs around the church, Ginny thinks she hears Moody laughing, just like Red Emmy's laughter haunts the Cantrell homeplace in Smith's Hoot Owl Holler. A neighbor reports seeing Moody's ghost. Then, the novel closes with a widely circulating tale that Morgan once thought was just his Grandpa Hamp's story, a tale forming the basis of his poem "Mountain Bride," published in *Groundwork*. In *This Rock*, young lovers awaken a den of slumbering snakes during a nighttime tryst in the woods. Tragedy ensues, with the girl succumbing to rattler bites.[21] Ginny accepts that "the haints or the snakes, or both" keep folks away: "people want to believe there is places in the world that is cursed. It reminds them there is things they can't see with their eyes wide open in broad daylight, and makes them feel other places may be blessed" (323). Her practical take on humanity shows again, as it does at the end of *The Truest Pleasure*, that her Pentecostalism never overcomes her grounding in secular reality.

Gap Creek

In truth, these mountains do sometimes seem cursed. The hardscrabble existence that people eke out of rocky soil explains why they hope for a better world in the next life. Morgan's characters face the fact that "human life didn't mean much," as Ginny says when her baby girl dies at birth in *The Truest Pleasure* (150), and this same realistic sentiment begins Morgan's best-known novel, *Gap Creek*, the first of two novels based on his maternal ancestry. When the narrator, Julie, sits on the frigid ground in the middle of the night after her little brother Masenier chokes to death on worms, realizing that "human life didn't mean a thing in this world . . . [that would be] going on about its business,"[22] she acknowledges the philosophical acceptance of life's trials that all the novels display. According to Morgan, Masenier's death is the only true scene in this book that is loosely based on his mother's parents' first year of marriage. It's absolutely true that his grandmother's younger brother died by choking on worms.[23] From this factual account, *Gap Creek* goes on to fictionalize natural disasters, near starvation, and the triumphs that hard work, sexual pleasure, nature's beauty, and human kindness can bring to a life of abject poverty lived in isolation near the turn of the twentieth century, just between the time settings of *The Truest Pleasure* and *This Rock*.

Morgan hit the jackpot with this third novel when Oprah Winfrey picked *Gap Creek: The Story of a Marriage* for Oprah's Book Club, a monthly book discussion segment of her television talk show. His publisher printed 600,000 hard copies in a week to prepare for Winfrey's public announcement. The book eventually sold two million copies worldwide and was a bestseller in Germany.[24] It also received the Southern Book Critics Circle Award and the Appalachian Book of the Year Award. The novel's success owes much to the plain, simple voice of its female narrator. Julie Harmon Richards represents Morgan's mother's mother, Julia Capps Levi, who often kept Morgan before she died in 1948, when Morgan was three years old. With a few direct memories of this grandmother, he challenges himself to convey through her words the inner life of a girl who sometimes was "ashamed that [she] couldn't think of what [she] wanted to say" (133). "My tongue was never loosened by my feelings," Julie thinks. "It was with my hands and with my back and shoulders that I could say how I felt. I had to talk with my arms and my strong hands" (122), similar to Tom Powell in *The Truest Pleasure*. Perhaps her serious work—plus "just a touch of dialect" that Morgan holds himself to, mostly with verbs such as "I knowed" or "I seen"—appealed to readers worldwide, many of whom wrote letters saying that he had captured their own grandmothers in Julie.[25] Indeed, her persistence in the face of one setback after another speaks to a human resilience that knows no boundaries of place or time.

Julie sees that work gives her the only control possible in life. When her father dies of consumption in chapter two, Julie is outside cutting firewood in the middle of the night, unable to watch his last minutes of labored breathing. Even after marrying, she does men's work as well as the scrubbing and cooking expected of women. While she expresses resentment about heavy work falling to her, her oft-repeated notion that "there was nothing for me to do" (82) but what has to be done reflects a stoicism born of necessity and deprivation.

When the eighteen-year-old Hank Richards from nearby Painter Mountain sees that Julie has cut corn tops and pulled fodder after her father's death, he says, "'You will make somebody a good wife'" (44), signaling the hard work required in rural Appalachia but also foreshadowing how Julie's stamina will get her through the trials that continue unabated when she marries him, at age seventeen, less than a month after they meet. "Like any bride," Julie muses, "I thought my husband was wise and on his way to riches" (51). She learns straightaway to temper her expectations, realizing the truth of her mother's verdict that marriage is simply work. As the novel progresses, Julie applies her work ethic to control the narrative of her marriage. On her second morning as a married woman, wishing she could go back home, Julie admits that the "shame of a failed marriage" was not worth the move from her new life of work back to the original, so she lets "the thought of the work . . . [clear her] head" (57) as it always does.

Hank Richards is modeled on Morgan's maternal grandfather, Hampton Levi, whose 1955 death gave the young Morgan time to hear his stories, many of them featuring panthers, bears, or rattlesnakes as well as family, such as his father, Lafayette, who fought in the Civil War. Hamp married Julia Capps on Mount Olivet and took her over the state line to South Carolina, where he worked at a new cotton mill in Cleveland, just south of Gap Creek. "One of his jobs was to tend the kiln where they baked the bricks," Morgan explains. "It was a very hot job, with 12 hour shifts. He did some carpentry also, but I don't think he worked inside the cotton mill." [26] In the novel, Hank arranges, without telling his bride, for Julie to cook and clean for the widower Mr. Pendergast in exchange for their rooming in his house, which is a considerable walking distance from Hank's brickmaking job site. Morgan creates a temperamental Hank Richards, a good-hearted but emotionally fragile young man whose moods Julie must learn to read. Despite praising and taking advantage of Julie's ability to work, Hank reflects his culture's assumption that women are inferior to men, and he uses that theory to cover his own weakness. Like his wife, Hank grows during their hard year on Gap Creek, progressing toward the man we see in *This Rock* and the *Gap Creek* sequel.

Women in this culture expect male dominance. When Hank's mother visits and overhears Julie directing her husband to make a coffin for the deceased Mr. Pendergast, she supports Hank's retort, "I'll decide what I do and when I do it,'" by telling him that he's "'got to show who's wearing the britches in this house'" (110, 111). This motherly push to make Hank a man follows Ma Richards's irritating criticism of Julie's cooking as well as her admission that Hank fails to "'finish what he starts'" and "'loses his temper too easy'" (90). That temper and the assumption of women's inferiority explode when the naive Julie falls prey to a shyster pretending to represent a bank holding a lien against Pendergast's property. Hearing that she gave the con man Pendergast's pension money, Hank slaps Julie after spitting hurtful words: "'You stupid heifer'" (129). Hank gets his comeuppance when he hands to swindlers—people pretending to be Pendergast's stepdaughter and her husband—his last five dollars, Julie's mother's necklace and brooch, and other valuables they take from the house as back rent. Seeing that "it was easier to let him blame me than to live with a man who was enraged at hisself" (168), Julie provokes a sugar-bowl throwing with her reasonable suggestion that they record what the swindlers took. Little by little, she learns to stay silent as Hank works through the anger that erupts when he thinks that he is not in charge. She quietly acts on her ingenuity—for instance, by going alone to the store that women seldom visit but men "slouch around . . . every day" (169) to trade ginseng she finds in Pendergast's attic for sugar and coffee. Julie's acceptance that she must play a subordinate role shows a kind of strength: she plows ahead, doing what she must to survive, reminiscent of Morgan's mother. In "*Gap Creek*'s Celebration of Women's Subjugation," Michelle Justus argues that Morgan portrays Julie as content with Hank's dominance, thus condoning patriarchal control and abuse. Julie does learn to placate him, to "keep [her] mouth shut" to avoid conflict (65). But Morgan's purpose seems to be to portray the realities of Appalachian rural life as the nineteenth century gave way to the twentieth, and among those realities is the fact of male privilege. If Julie sometimes uses silence to deal with Hank's immature volatility, she models a strategy common to generations of women without means to live outside their culture's mores.

Pendergast's death ends one of three calamities marking Hank and Julie's Gap Creek year. When Julie hits a canner of boiling grease with another pot while rendering lard after a grueling morning of hog butchering, fire erupts. Pendergast crawls through flames to retrieve his pension jar, and Julie nurses him as best she can until he dies of his burns. The next traumatic event highlights Hank's weakness, creating a bad memory that he shares with Muir in *This Rock* to make that young man feel better about his own failures. When days of sleet and rain make Gap Creek overflow its banks, Hank abandons Julie after they become separated while fighting raging waters to get to higher ground, escaping the flooding house at night. Julie finds him hiding in the hayloft, where he shoots his gun into the barn roof, threatening to kill himself and Julie as well. She manipulates Hank, telling him that he suffers no worse than others and challenging his resolve, saying that he "'won't do it'" but is "'just showing out'" with his threats. "'Get down from there and act like a man'" (221), she finally erupts. Their fortunes keep declining. The cow hangs herself trying to escape rising waters, just when Julie has discovered she is pregnant. Hank loses his job and the prospects for another by hitting a supervisor at work. Despite Hank's hunting turkeys, Julie's finding a little food such as horse apples on the farm, and neighbors' sharing jellies, the couple lives hungry. After Julie gives birth early, alone—reminiscent of Petal Jarvis Richards's birthing Wallace in *The Hinterlands*—she has no breast milk and almost dies along with the baby. Hank's mettle grows as he cares for the malnourished infant, who is named after Julie's mother (and Morgan's real great-grandmother), until her demise. The young couple survives these and other unrelenting tragedies, both of them turning to intense physical work to make sense of the "days . . . thick and cluttered with grief" (311) after baby Delia's death. Hank makes the decision to leave Gap Creek when a legitimate lawyer brings news that Pendergast's heirs will sell the house. As they climb toward North Carolina in the novel's last pages, leaving the lush rewards of their spring planting, Julie is again pregnant, marking a new beginning.

Throughout the novel, joys such as lovemaking, family, and nature do offset Hank and Julie's persistent troubles. Like Ginny in *The Truest Pleasure*, Julie describes sexual pleasure in vivid hues: "All the colors started running through my head in the dark. Purples and greens and yellows and blacks. They blended into each other. . . . The colors was melodies, like shaped note singing" (53). Or, "I felt my bones melting and my legs melting in the color that roared through me. But it was not a red flame or an orange flame. It was a blue flame that started at the back of my head and burned down my spine to my belly and out to the tips of my toes, as the blue turned to purple" (138). Both Julie and Hank enjoy the visit of her sister Lou, along with her new husband and her younger sister Carolyn, whose flirting with Hank causes Julie some distress. And despite the disasters of ice storm and flood, the natural world energizes Julie's positive outlook. When scouring Pendergast's place for food, she walks all the way to Gap Creek, "feel[ing] something [she] couldn't name" (148) as she takes in the rock cliff and ridges. Free of worries, she dashes through leaves and lies on the ground to gaze at the "*depth* in the sky" (151), pleasures that she keeps secret from Hank. As in all Morgan's work, the natural world strengthens characters who appreciate its gifts, and it was his mother and grandmother Julia that he observed relishing nature. He commends his mother's appreciation of the environment and of the wonders of food growing and bird nests, and he also applauds the way she modeled for him a "calm and lucid feeling for things in their objective fullness."[27] In his poem "Cowbedding," he describes Julia's seeing decaying leaves as "treasure." When the speaker twice says, "I want to go back" to help Grandma rake leaves for stalls, we feel a nostalgia that Morgan seldom lets his work reveal.[28] We also see why nature enthusiasts in his poetry and prose often appear as women.

Church continues as a mostly positive force in *Gap Creek*, but this novel emphasizes the community that religion affords, not the doctrine and conflict that *The Truest Pleasure* and *This Rock* portray as pivotal in Morgan's father's family. As Pendergast dies, he slips into a terrifying memory of Preacher Liner, who told him decades earlier that he was "'in danger of hellfire'" (107) for his sins, part of the same strict, fundamentalist doctrine that the older Preacher Liner hopes will persuade Muir Powell to bow to his wishes in *This Rock*. Pendergast and Ma Richards represent the pessimistic religion of doom that Morgan knew as a child: "'The good Lord made the world so we could earn our joy,'" Ma announces as she, Julie, and Pendergast relish the taste of fresh tenderloin. "'But it's no guarantee we'll ever be happy.'" "'There's no guarantee of anything except we're going to die,'" Pendergast replies (90). While these lines set a glum backdrop, religion plays relatively little role in *Gap Creek* until the last third of the novel, when Preacher Gibbs and his wife check on Julie and Hank after the flood. Gibbs's sermon for Pendergast's funeral in the Gap Creek Baptist Church had been of "'the wages of sin is death'" variety that Julie "hated" (115). Yet his and his wife's singing had lifted Julie. And when they visit on Christmas morning after the flood and again on New Year's, Gibbs concentrates on human community, bringing peppermint candy canes and encouragement and responding to the drunken Timmy Gosnell with practical humanity, not sermonizing. Gibbs invites the couple to services to meet their neighbors: "'the church is where we strengthen each other and support each other,'" he says (239). Both Julie and Hank join the church, and before Delia's birth, church ladies bring baby clothes and jellies, extending the bonds that Morgan feels are the best feature of religious congregations and giving Julie a needed community of women. And Hank's improving ability to handle the vagrant Timmy Gosnell owes something to the church and Preacher Gibbs's influence.

Showing up periodically to demand money he claims Pendergast still owes him and to insult women as whores, Timmy Gosnell is a tragicomic figure. Partly, his role is to show Julie's strength of character, as she runs the drunk man away with a stick the first time he visits, aghast that "Piieendergaasss," as Gosnell calls him, hides in the house. Hank's initial angry, masculinity-fueled responses to the inebriated man also give Julie early warning signs of her husband's temper. By the novel's end, Hank kindly tricks Gosnell into leaving by praying aloud for him, evoking Preacher Gibbs's earlier humane response to the sad fellow when he appeared after the flood covered in filthy mud, looking "like something that had been buried for weeks and rose from the dead" (233). Hank's lighthearted turning of religion against one resisting it shows his new self-confidence along with his down-to-earth understanding of faith as it later manifests in his attempt to help Muir build his church in *This Rock*.

These characters, major and minor, help Morgan to build the postage-stamp-of-southern-Appalachia world that his fiction and much of his poetry create. Through them, he exposes the profound poverty, as well as the know-how that got people through it, in the time that Julia and Hampton Levi lived. Ma Richards shares how poor she and Fate—who was based on Lafayette Levi, born in 1848 in Greenville County, South Carolina—were when they married after he returned from the Civil War. "'We didn't have a dollar between us,'" she remembers. She made coffee in the "water bucket" and "cooked soup in the washpan" (89). They lived in a bartering society, where no money exchanged hands but people traded work and goods, such as hen eggs for coffee or sugar. When Mr. Pendergast recalls the Confederate Army's having nothing but corn-meal to feed soldiers, he assures Ma Richards that the starving privates should not be called bushwhackers because they took a hog from a farmer's pen. The amount of the pension that Pendergast dies trying to retrieve also gives a stark reminder of the economic times: $47.86, which the shyster banker makes sure is not useless Confederate money before he steals it. As in his other historical and family novels, Morgan provides meticulous details about the work people did to survive: exacting descriptions of killing a hog, dressing a turkey, picking creasy greens, tending the sick, and laying out a corpse show how self-reliant his ancestors had to be.

People's difficult lives in *Gap Creek* fuel Papa's ghost's prediction about Julie's future when he appears during her near-death experience following baby Delia's birth. He comes to tell Julie that she "'will live and . . . will continue to work and to love,'" to which Julie responds, "'That sounds simple . . . and hard.' They was two words that fit . . . the life I had lived" (299). By twenty-first-century standards, Appalachian life in the family novels is simple, indeed, and certainly hard. But Julie appreciates the continuity that undergirds her modest life. When walking alone in the Gap Creek valley, Julie comes across the salt lick that Pendergast had put on a stick for his cow. A deer comes out of the woods to enjoy it. "'Mr. Pendergast is gone but his salt is still shining up here,'" she muses, not totally understanding what she means (149). This sense of continuity reappears near the novel's end, when Hank says that Delia, born in 1900, "'will live to see the end of time. For preachers say the world will come to an end at the end of the millennium.'" He continues, exclaim-ing, "'This little girl will . . . live to see Jesus bust out of the eastern sky in all his glory.'" Julie, however, questions Hank's literal understanding of the biblical prophecy from Revelation: "'Time can't end, for what would follow would be time, too'" (297). Her view of creation is bigger and more metaphoric than Hank's, as shown when grass makes her think of music or her bones feel "music coming from under the ground" during hallucinatory moments when she hears Papa's ghost. "Everything had a different voice, but the voices all harmonized like a congregation at church," she thinks (298). Earlier, she heard music in Hank's splitting wood, in clouds, and even in dust. Julie's instinctive grasp of universal harmony resonates with Morgan's poem "Time's Music," where "Insects in an August field seem / to register the background noise / of space" and grasshoppers and crickets make "crackling music" that "whisper[s] of / frost and stars overhead." [29] Julie's sense of universal unities heightens her role in Morgan's portrayal of Appalachian women as "compelling females who meet daunting circumstances with dignity, knowledge, and fortitude," as Nicole Drewitz-Crockett argues in an essay presenting Julie, Ginny Powell, and Petal Jarvis as "homestead heroes." [30] Continuing her life in the North Carolina mountains where she and Hank end their journey on the road from Gap Creek, Julie handles more hard physical labor as well as the severe emotional toil that decades of living bring, especially during economic depression and war.

The Road from Gap Creek

When Robert Morgan prepared to leave his mother's Green River home after helping producers film scenes in Gap Creek, South Carolina, for *The Oprah Winfrey Show*, he kept thinking that she had not said anything about *Gap Creek*. As he lingered on the porch, she stood in the doorway and asked, "When are you going to write about me?" [31] He recalled that question as he began to think seriously about a sequel to Julie and Hank's story that he initially thought Julie would narrate. His decision to let her daughter pick up the tale perhaps had as much to do with his mother's plea for attention as with his realization that a younger voice would more logically take his maternal family forward. Sadly, Fannie Levi Morgan died in July 2010. She never got to read *The Road from Gap Creek*, published three years later.

   Although *Gap Creek* ends with just Hank and pregnant Julie trekking up the mountain to establish a home near their folks, in reality, Morgan's mother, Fannie, walked that trail as a little girl with her parents and siblings. Fannie, born in 1912 and the second-youngest of six children, was five years old when her family took the road from Gap Creek to Green River, North Carolina, to move into the house that her father, Hampton Levi, had bought from Volney Pace, the model for Locke Peace in the family novels. As *The Road from Gap Creek* details, when Volney's wife died in childbirth, he gave his baby daughter to his sister Rose, the model for Florrie Peace, and returned to work as an army nurse. Fannie's brother Robert, the model for Troy in the novel and an inspiration for some of Morgan's short stories, was a baby during that trip, and Julia held him on her wagon seat. Fannie's sister, Wessie, and her older brothers, William Velmer, James, and Charlie, walked with Fannie so that the horse could pull the overloaded wagon up the steep hill. Morgan's mother remembered that they burned what they couldn't carry before leaving in the dark to start the four or five mile trip up the mountain to Green River, just as Julie and Hank head out before dawn at the end of *Gap Creek*. Morgan says that this walk from Gap Creek began his mother's lifelong obsession with transportation, aggravated later by her husband's refusal to buy a car or truck, a point of contention covered in some short stories, although not in *The Road from Gap Creek*.

In the novel, Fannie Levi becomes Annie, narrating the story as a married woman in the late 1940s. Her memories flow the way memories do, back and forth through time, from tragic days to lazy summer swims in the river, pulling us into an ordinary American family's experiences during the Great Depression and World War II. Characters enjoy a break from the constant calamity besetting Julie and Hank's early marriage. *The Road from Gap Creek* balances heartbreak with more cheerful scenes, many of them involving the German shepherd Old Pat, as the outside world infiltrates the Blue Ridge Mountains, bringing advances in technology along with national troubles that change the lives of the characters that we follow through Annie's intimate reflections.

The book opens with its greatest tragedy, as government officials deliver a telegram announcing Troy Richards's death in World War II. This scene immediately connects characters to the larger world, denoting a contrast between the modest Richards household and the complex military machine that leads to so much death and destruction across the globe. Morgan uses the factual details that cast a pall over the family he was born into. His mother's brother Robert Levi, after working on the Blue Ridge Parkway as a powder man with the Civilian Conservation Corps, joined the United States Air Corps when it seemed likely that America would be drawn into war. The promise of studying mechanics intrigued him. After training in Biloxi, Mississippi, and in Sarasota, Florida, he then went to a Massachusetts factory that made the type of airplane engines he would work on overseas. His deployment took him to Buckinghamshire, England, with the Eighth Air Force, as well as to Cambridge and Huntington.[32] As the telegram says of Troy, Robert Levi was "lost in the crash of a B-17 heavy bomber on Nov. 10, 1943, near the village of Eye in East Anglia."[33] Although not part of the fictional story, Morgan, born eleven months later, lived his youth under the shadow of this man:

I grew up with the legend of my uncle Robert Levi. . . . I was named after him, and many people compared me to their memories of him. . . . Women who had been in love with Robert would stop me in the church yard and say I "favored" him. He had been popular with everybody, a basketball player, tall, with red curly hair, handsome, a life guard, a powder man in the Civilian Conservation Corps. He was also an artist, and I grew up surrounded by his watercolors and oil paintings. He wrote poetry, too. One of his hobbies had been collecting arrowheads and other Indian artifacts, and I inherited some of those. He was an impossible ideal to measure up to. My poem "Uncle Robert" expresses some of my admiration and some of my frustration at always being compared to him, for after his death, he had become a martyr.[34]

A shrine to Robert Levi remains in the home Morgan grew up in and inherited. Pictures and awards in a den corner keep him in living memory, even after Morgan's mother's death in 2010.

His uncle's hold on his imagination led Morgan in 1986 to England, where he found the site of the crash and talked to a farmer who witnessed it. He kept researching military records, trying to discover why Uncle Robert, just a mechanic as far as the family knew, was in the B-17. Robert's buddy Frank O. Conwell finally contacted Morgan from Arizona in 2012, revealing that he and Robert also flew on missions: "It was their job to check all gauges, do repairs in flight, keep the wing fuel tanks balanced, and when under attack, man the guns in the overhead turret." Conwell also shared that Robert's plane had been to France to drop leaflets before heading north to bomb Ruhr Valley steelworks and that the mission involved experimenting with white phosphorous as an incendiary. Conwell, in another plane, "saw Robert's plane catch fire and crash and explode."[35] Though Morgan uses details of this research in his novella "The Mountains Won't Remember Us," he omits the explanation of Troy's presence in the plane from *The Road from Gap Creek*, sticking to the family's lack of knowledge about the mission.

Morgan's mother had a vision of her brother's death, an experience that Annie recounts in the book. Gazing out a window one evening, Annie sees Troy, looking worried and sad, seeming to want to speak to her right before a deafening roar and "whoosh of flame" erased his visage, leaving a sickening smell. In reality, and in the novel, that incident occurs two weeks before the family hears the dreadful news, thus around the time of Robert's death. The next morning, Annie's husband Muir dismisses her story as a dream, following his conviction that superstition shows a "lack of faith" (13). Muir "just laughed and shook his head, like he usually does when I get mad," Annie says, "acting like I'm not worth arguing with, just being an emotional woman" (14). Muir condescends, as men feel entitled to do in this place and time, ignoring his wife's anxiety. Late in the novel, Annie shares a plane crash memory somewhat foreshadowing her vision of Troy's fate. During his last Christmas visit home, a training plane from the Air Corps base near Greenville, South Carolina, crashes near the Richards home as Troy, his girlfriend, and Annie hunt for mistletoe on Meetinghouse Mountain. They see paratroopers parachuting out, and they try to pull the dead pilot out of the wrecked plane before soldiers training nearby warn them against meddling with a crash. "It seemed the war had been brought right to the ridge behind our house," Annie muses, "and there was no safe place anywhere" (261). When Troy dies, that feeling seems prescient.

Between chapter one and chapter nineteen, when Troy's body is shipped home for burial after the war ends, he appears often as Annie remembers family scenes. Like Uncle Robert, Troy paints—oils and watercolors—and collects Indian arrowheads. He gains self-confidence by taking responsibility for work on the small family farm, a noteworthy part of the cultural portrait. Like Robert, he plays high school basketball, practicing at home with a makeshift goal and an old ball the coach gives him, and he accepts a canoe from a man whose summer home he helps construct, the one Morgan sat in as a boy, "fearing to see / a body inside," as he notes in the poem "Uncle Robert."[36] Troy's charm attracts young ladies, and his engagement to Sharon relates tightly to the perspective on the relationship she narrates in "The Mountains Won't Remember Us." Troy, like Robert, chooses not to marry before departing for military service, though Sharon, mirroring the fiancée on whom she is based, wants very much to take wedding vows. Morgan visited Uncle Robert's fiancée in a Hendersonville nursing home at her request, learning that she never really got over Robert Levi. Through her conversations as well as his conversations with his family, Morgan gathered hints of frictions between her and his family that build dramatic tension in the narratives.

Annie brings Sharon Peace home for a weekend during the time both work at a dime store, introducing her to Troy and interpreting the changing dynamics of their interactions. Annie describes Sharon as "so dark skinned you might have thought she was an Indian" (180), reminding readers of Frank Pace's dark skin, and Muir in fact wonders if Sharon is a cousin in the Peace family who represents the Pace clan. Sharon's father owns an apple orchard close to nearby Saluda, six or seven miles from Zirconia. While Robert's fiancée wondered if the Levis felt she was not as good as they, in reality, both families were equally poor. Troy seems taken with Sharon, and Annie observes that falling in love "puts everything in a new brightness" (183). But immediately, Annie finds herself annoyed at Sharon's flirting. These two girls present different sides of womanhood: Sharon seems stereotypically feminine, more shallow and possessive, while Annie sticks to the practical work ethic Julie taught her and finds young men uninteresting. Sharon is angry that Troy joins the Air Corps without telling her and openly seeks to marry him: "'A soldier's wife gets special benefits. . . . But you have to be married to be eligible for them'" (250). Troy finally sends an engagement ring from Biloxi, but when he's home on leave in late 1941 and the next summer, he plans no wedding. When news of his death reaches Green River, Sharon shows up at the Richards home with a suitcase, intrusively hugging Julie, a woman who expresses little emotion even to family, and asks for some of Troy's paintings and arrowheads. Annie senses that Papa had "always liked Sharon better than me and Mama had. She had always kind of flirted with him. But then a man can never see through a woman the way another woman can," a judgment Annie applies also to her husband, Muir (124). But her conclusion that Troy "sensed that [Sharon] just wasn't right" for him (252), given his diverse interests and intellectual curiosity, implies she thought he was smarter than other men, this brother that people several times deem "'the best this family has seen'" (9). As Morgan indicates about Uncle Robert, grief inspires people to idealize Troy, an all too human response to loss.

Sharon reenters the narrative near the book's end, sharpening one of its main themes. Running into Annie in town, now-married Sharon shares that her husband gets angry at any mention of Troy. "'He threw away the boxes of arrowheads you give me,'" Sharon admits, adding that Albert claimed that "'he couldn't compete with a dead man'" (304), just as Robert Levi's fiancée, Sue, told Morgan that her husband threw away Robert's arrowhead collection and the pictures of her and Robert.[37] But Sharon takes a taxicab to Troy's funeral, and at the graveside service, with soldiers firing a three-volley salute, her veteran husband shows up with a pistol, calling his wife to leave with him, making Muir, who is preaching the funeral, cut his prayer short. Morgan complicates the notion of heroism in Albert's retort to Muir's plea for calmness: "'You think the only brave soldiers are them that died?' he said. 'Them that returns is just as brave as them that died.'" Sharon's sadness is discernible as she walks to the car "like somebody that has been give a long sentence" (310). Sharon recounts the same trouble with her husband in "The Mountains Won't Remember Us," his jealous anger erupting at any discovered memento of Troy. Annie's thoughts at the funeral capture Morgan's perception of war's effects: "I thought how the war wasn't really over. For us in Troy's family, for those that had loved him, and for former soldiers like Albert, the war was far from over. In fact it would never be over for any of us" (311). That statement is palpably true, particularly for the mother of this fallen soldier.

Julie's reserved strength continues from *Gap Creek*, and her inarticulateness is clearer in the story her daughter narrates. Annie marvels several times that Julie knows what to do in any emergency. For instance, she calmly takes over the laying out of Ginny Powell's body when Ginny dies of a stroke. Annie also notes that her mother increasingly keeps her emotional pain inside. Julie simply stares at the telegram reporting Troy's death, turning away from the officer as she does from family. As in her youth, she covers her anguish with work, completing chores as usual. Annie shares her mother's stoic demeanor, thinking that crying is for lesser pains, that "what had happened to Troy was too awful for crying" (118). Yet Annie also reflects that "over the years Papa had got stronger" while "Mama had got wore down . . . [and] less certain, like the wind had been knocked out of her," with a gendered analysis her own experiences support: "Maybe that's what happened to women. The world wasn't fair to women and always wore them down. It made me shiver to think that" (157–58). Over time, Annie begins to see Julie's refusal to talk about Troy, and her use of work as "a way of avoiding herself" (268), as problematic. When her mother's headaches and mental confusion finally prompt a visit to an Asheville doctor, he finds a brain tumor, the condition that killed Morgan's grandmother Julia Capps Levi at age sixty-four. Asked about Julie's keeping her sorrow inside, Morgan replies, "My grandmother would never talk about her grief and depression. She devoted her life to working for others. The death of her youngest son devastated her. She did die of a brain tumor, but in 1948, not 1945 as the character Julie does in the novel."[38] His comments on his grandmother tempt us to connect Julie's illness to the simmering melancholy that she never released, as Annie thinks moments before her mother dies: "She'd not let out her grief. And that grief had poisoned her" (291).

Annie's remarks about her mother's status as a woman reflect Morgan's sense that gender shaped his mother's difficult life to a considerable extent, as explained in chapter two, although in this novel, economics constrain as much as gender. Like Annie, Fannie Levi acted in high school plays and imagined becoming an actress, a dream her drama teacher encouraged. Similar to Troy when he makes the basketball team, Annie feels pleased to get a leading role since the town students "looked down on us kids from the country" (200), a truth that fit Morgan's next-generation experience as well. Evoking Morgan's two worlds of Blue Ridge rural poverty and physical labor and his relative affluence and intellectual work at Cornell University later on, Annie reflects that rehearsing after school and then going home to gather eggs and shell corn felt "like jumping between different worlds." But she knows that she will not pursue an acting career: "I didn't have enough money for new shoes for graduation, much less enough money to go to college" (82).

Although some in her community think theater sinful, Annie never lets religious censure overwhelm her view of acting: "I felt more like myself when I was playing a part than I ever did when I was just being me," Annie says. "I never was sure who myself was." But since she "didn't know how to play the part of somebody that is going off to study to be an actress," Annie accepts her destiny: "The only part I would play would be myself, and that wasn't wrote too good" (202). Hints of Annie's acquiescing come particularly in the story of her marriage, based upon Fannie Levi Morgan's life.

Annie's examination of the choices she makes concerning men shows Morgan's sensitivity to his mother's difficult life in a time when women faced limited possibilities. Boys who line up to walk her home from church seem tiresome, and the reality is that she "never did care nothing about" boys despite enjoying flirting with them (187). Her references to Muir Powell's longtime attention, noted in *This Rock*, summarize the plodding nature of their relationship. Annie is eight years old when she hears Muir preach his first sermon as a teenager, the one that Moody disrupts by breaking wind. She reflects on that day: "Now I wonder how much feeling sorry for somebody has to do with loving them. You might think that pity and sympathy are different from love. But I think they must be close together, especially for a woman" (40), perhaps a comment on the expectation that women be good nurturers. Annie explains several times that she views marriage as limiting: "I wanted something more than just settling down to raise babies and keep house and go to church on Sundays" (206). She also notes that she felt her mother's influence: Julie "had had such a hard time herself . . . that she didn't want to see [her daughter] tied to a husband" (188). Annie claims that she felt confused, afraid that she did like Muir when she "didn't want to be in the power of no man or boy" (192). Clearly, Annie feels an unnamed feminism, a desire for independence in a culture where she cannot see a way to make a life outside marriage. When Muir declares his third proposal as his last, she immediately thinks of her aspirations, which are ironically resonant with Muir's multiple attempts to leave Green River in *This Rock*: "I thought of all my dreams of going away and doing something with myself" (207–208). Annie consents, rationalizing that never leaving to make her way in the world signals her latent desire to marry Muir. She also worries that if she does not accept, she will "be an old maid" (208), and another conjecture reflects a judgment that Morgan finally made about his parents' union: Muir "had no head for business at all. I'd thought I wanted to marry a businessman, but I didn't. I was the one who was good at business" (209). Morgan suspects that his mother thought Clyde was so feckless that she could control the purse strings, a prediction that turned out to be true, though it had frustrating ramifications in Fannie's world, where only men could make business decisions and where Clyde left the moneymaking up to her when public jobs became necessary, as chapter two details. Annie's references to Muir's love of classy clothes, herringbone suits that make him look like a professor or a banker, reflect Clyde Morgan's affinity for playing a bit of a dandy when he could, no doubt another irritation for Morgan's working mother and certainly a complexity of their relationship.

The Road from Gap Creek stops before fictionalizing much of Morgan's parents' life together. It ends when Annie and Muir's first child—Angela, who represents Morgan's older sister, Evangeline—is almost a year old. It does, however, divulge the unusual circumstances of the beginning of their marriage. Fannie Levi and Clyde Morgan eloped in 1939, when she was twenty-seven and he was thirty-four, taking vows at a preacher's house with Fannie's sister and her husband as witnesses. As in the novel, Fannie convinced her husband to keep the marriage secret: they both returned to their homes after the ceremony and did not live together until Fannie found the courage, several months later, to tell her parents that they had married. In the novel, Annie admits that she enjoys her mother's dependence on her but also that she is afraid of being "in the power" of a man who will be "running his hands over" her and "having his way" (211). Sex scares Annie, a fear reflecting her culture's religiously influenced assumption that women do not enjoy sex but that "a wedding night is when the man does things" to the woman (218). Like women in Morgan's other novels, Annie soon sees that she can participate and also that the woman affects the man more than he affects her, a realization of feminine power that tempers her fear of being totally in a man's control.

Sexuality is not the only way that this novel interrogates religion. When Preacher Rice arrives to console the family about Troy's death, Annie immediately feels perturbed:

> For when a preacher comes to comfort you it always makes you feel . . . more miserable. [A] preacher's words always seem faraway. You know what he's going to say. . . . And somehow the fact that he goes ahead and says them makes you even sadder. For the preacher will say God's ways are mysterious and beyond our understanding. What seems unbearable to humans must be part of a plan. If something bad is an accident it's bad, but if it's part of a plan that's much worse. I've never understood why preachers think that is comforting. They make you feel so hopeless and stupid. For they remind you there's nothing you can do. Your suffering is all part of God's plan. (15–16)

Julie's only assertion of grief shows that she shares her daughter's exasperation. Hank once asks Preacher Rice to Sunday dinner, unable to face the reality that his wife is sick and not up to having company. Rice tells Julie that he will pray for her, that "'The Lord will look after his own.'" Julie retorts, "'The Lord didn't look after Troy. . . . I prayed every day for Troy and it didn't do no good'" (275). When a churchgoer claims that the Lord told him that Troy's death chastens Hank Richards's family's sin, Morgan uses the true-life event that hurt his loved ones in their time of sorrow. He describes in "Homecoming," a prose section of his 1978 poetry collection *Trunk and Thicket*, how a vindictive man rose during service to proclaim "that in a vision it had been revealed to him my Uncle Robert's death in Europe had been sent as punishment for family sins." [39] When the Great Depression hits, Annie surmises that only preachers could have predicted it, their constant message being that "the world was . . . coming to a terrible punishment," at that time for the "bootlegging and gangsters and wild parties in the cities, and girls that cut off nearly all their hair . . . wearing lipstick and rouge and smoking cigarettes in public" (76) during the Roaring Twenties. Clearly, Morgan draws on his frustrations with the fundamentalist intolerance and gloom he heard growing up to explain why Annie thinks for years that she "didn't want to be no preacher's wife" (117), a position she accepts with irony when Muir takes a Baptist pulpit. Yet the book's last chapter shows what John Lang eloquently argues in "Coming Out from Under Calvinism: Religious Motifs in Robert Morgan's Poetry": Morgan affirms the capacity for resurrection that is Christianity's central metaphor, seeing it particularly in nature. This motif applies to his fiction as well. As she picnics with her husband and baby near a river as butterflies dance at the end of the novel, Annie's thoughts reflect Morgan's romanticism: "The warm sunlight near the splashing water made me feel so easy I thought I could set there forever" (318). Annie renews herself from the grief of her brother's and mother's deaths not within the doctrine of Muir's conventional religion but in the consolation of the natural world.

The Great Depression that Annie says preachers' dark sermons seemed to foretell shows its effects in her southern Appalachian community. The area has enjoyed prosperity during the 1920s. People bought tractors and cars on credit as bank loans became available. With money earned building summer houses for wealthy people from Charlotte or Spartanburg, Hank has paid off the mortgage, the Model A truck, and the artesian well that Mr. McCrary from Penrose, in Transylvania County, digs after Velmer contracts typhoid from drinking contaminated spring water—details that are all drawn from Morgan's family history. But when the stock market crashes in October 1929, Hank loses the two hundred dollars he has in the bank. Both Hank and Velmer, who has quit school, are fired from their construction jobs when the house owner's invest-ments are wiped out. That man files for bankruptcy, relieving his obligation to pay debts and thus leaving Hank unable to pay his brother and brother-in-law who help him build. The cotton mill closes down. People start walking or riding horses again, and the Richards family has cornbread and cow's milk for supper. They sell eggs and muskrat skins for a little cash. Hank straightens old nails to repair fences, trying to keep busy. Annie notes her father's shame at his in-ability to provide, observing that a man with no job "won't look you in the eye" and "stays away from the house" (81). Cutting down chestnut trees killed by the 1924 blight, Hank hews railroad crossties, getting paid fifty or seventy-five cents for each. Eventually, a rumor of building and fruit-harvesting work in Florida prompts Hank and his brother Russ to head south in the Model A. Their unfortunate accident—true to Grandpa Hamp's Florida trip and re-created in the story "Crossties" from *The Blue Valleys*—enables Morgan to describe union agitators being jailed, part of the labor movement that roiled America during the 1930s. When the local store owner comes to share Hank's telephoned re-quest that Julie wire ten dollars for a car repair, the children contribute their savings to put that much cash together. When he gets home, Hank has thirty-seven cents in his pocket. He has found no work, but his role in a man's death has added to his worries.

Annie's contributions to the family finances during the 1930s comes straight from Fannie Levi's biography. With the men out of work, she puts on lipstick and lands a job as a dime store clerk, working six days a week for $1.50 a day—a weekly total of nine dollars. Rooming at a boarding house in town for five dollars and giving Mama three, Annie has one dollar of spending money each week. No wonder she is fascinated with the offer of a man claiming to be a New York talent scout looking for models to interview at the Skyland Hotel in downtown Hendersonville, where F. Scott Fitzgerald wrote his soul-searching essay "The Crack-Up" in 1935. But rumors of men enticing girls with such promises, as well as the obligation to help Julie, prevent Annie from pursu-ing the meeting. With Annie's three dollars, plus whatever cash her eggs and butter bring in, Julie buys sugar, coffee, flour, and salt. She makes dresses out of feed sacks, as most rural Southern women did. Annie sometimes helps Troy kill and sell rabbits or possums for a quarter each to cotton mill workers for their supper. As Annie lists garden vegetables, orchard fruits, hogs, chickens, and pokeweed, she emphasizes the resourcefulness that got country people through the lean years in fairly good shape.

Traveling hoboes show another facet of the Great Depression that comes to Annie's Blue Ridge home. She hears about them riding the rails and hiding in train boxcars, but she sees streams of hungry vagrants walking the road or camping along highways firsthand. Julie shares food when they ask, cornbread and garden fruits or vegetables when they're available. She watches as a destitute family steals apples, saying nothing, and does not rail when discovering they also took eggs from the henhouse, probably thinking that her family walking north from Gap Creek might have looked just as desperate. Morgan humanizes hoboes by having one tell Hank his story of losing several South Carolina jobs before deciding to walk to Asheville to live with a daughter. His talk gives Annie time to notice his bleeding feet in his too-large, cracked shoes. The stark realities of hobo life hit home when Annie finds a lone dead man in a deep gully camp. Hank has "to call the law to take the body away" (90), no doubt a recurring event around the United States during the Depression years.

Exactly as Morgan's Uncle Robert did, Troy helps the family during the Depression by joining the Civilian Conservation Corps, or CCC, earning thirty dollars a month through this program that President Roosevelt created in 1933 as part of the New Deal to give young men work on environmental and infrastructure projects, such as building bridges and roads. Except for a few dollars that were given to the boys to spend, the money went straight to their families, and the camps offered classes to help young men finish high school as well as to teach them skills such as carpentry or welding. Troy takes camp art classes from a University of North Carolina professor who had lost his job.[40] Helping to build the Blue Ridge Parkway, Troy becomes a powder man, responsible for placing and igniting dynamite that blows through rock. All these details replicate Robert Levi's years in the CCC. And interestingly, Julie saves the money from Troy's work to give to him later, while she spends what Annie makes for the family.

After his CCC stint, Troy joins his father, his brother Velmer, and his brother-in-law Muir to build military barracks at Fort Bragg, North Carolina, as officials begin to prepare for possible entry into World War II. With no jobs in Henderson County, the men travel across the state to work but come home on weekends. It is at this base in Fayetteville that Troy signs up for the United States Air Corps, starting his training at Fort Jackson, South Carolina, with the promise of mechanic school and airplane work presenting a path for military or civilian employment. Hank and Muir shift to construction work at Holly Ridge, in Onslow County near the North Carolina coast, where Camp Davis became an antiaircraft training facility in 1940, used to prepare nearby Camp Lejeune marines for World War II missions. All the men except Troy are in Green River on Sunday, December 7, 1941. When Hank turns on the radio for the bad news from Europe, North Africa, or Russia, the family hears that the Japanese have bombed Pearl Harbor, destroying the naval fleet in Hawaii. A local boy stops his car to process the shocking news coming across the airwaves. As with learning about New York's Wall Street in 1929, the small community finds itself thrust further into the outside world. Velmer, too old to fight, becomes a barber at the Columbia, South Carolina, army base while his estranged wife, their marriage crippled by their baby's death, goes to Washington, DC, with her sister to work in a government office. Coming out of the Great Depression, Green River family members find their financial prospects and worldviews expanded by the conflict that would take so many lives.

It is through Troy's death that Morgan points to the horror that World War II visits upon the world, this one person's promise erased and his loved ones' sorrow representing in some small way the worldwide despair marking the first half of the 1940s and the many years following. The presence of a non-speaking character in this novel both counters and underscores the anguish of the time. As a little boy, Troy picks out of a litter of German shepherd puppies a dog that becomes his lifelong friend, a gift from a family whose summer home Hank is building. Old Pat, the name of the dog belonging to Morgan's Uncle Robert, grows up with Troy and protects the family, warning them of a house fire and saving Annie from a tree felled by lightning. Old Pat helps in the war effort, going to Fort Bragg to be bred with another German shepherd to provide dogs for the army. Her end seems fitting. Troy has to shoot her on his last visit home, in 1942, after she grabs a Fourth of July firecracker, just as the real Old Pat did, no doubt seeing it as a thrown stick she should retrieve. Troy's act shows his grit and somehow signals the departure of his youth, the end of his Green River world of pleasant days spent swimming in the river near the family whose closeness mitigates the poverty and stresses of the time.

Morgan's decision to frame the story around the war—he has the Japanese surrender coincide with Julie's funeral on August 15, 1945, when Green River folks, meaning no disrespect, blow car horns in celebration—signals his intent to give *The Road from Gap Creek* historical significance. The Spanish flu, Locke Peace's nursing Velmer through typhoid, and men's eyes lighting up when they talk of war, even when a loved one has died fighting, provide twentieth-century context as well as age-old verities. Political divisions persist as they always do, with family men saying Roosevelt "ruined the country and got us into the war" (163) and one arguing for "Americanism," a drawing back from helping others to focus on ourselves (166). Morgan's own memories—for instance, of being startled as a toddler by the gun salute at Uncle Robert's memorial service and three years later watching an ambulance take Grandma Julia away to the Winston-Salem Baptist Hospital and then to die in Charlotte, which he describes in his unpublished memoir and his *Groundwork* poem "When the Ambulance Came"—provided images for dramas that represent personal loss and communal history. The industrialization changing the world—the radio bringing the war into homes, the cars making Annie "feel that the world is moving ahead toward the wonderful" (191), the pump lifting underground water to gurgle out of a spigot, and the store-bought casket for Julie's "undertaker funeral" (293)—generally improves people's lives. Electricity spreads across most all the Green River valley, and newspapers tout the new atomic age, predicting space travel and prosperity. But jobs supporting the war effort end, and returning soldiers add to the workforce that is seeking employment. Muir and Velmer resume farming. Annie continues working at the cotton mill—the job that replaced her clerking at the dime store—as Morgan's mother did for years. World events quickly turn from peaceful to ominous, moving to the Cold War years of Morgan's coming of age, when the possibility of fighting the Russians made him first aim for a career in aerospace engineering. Annie describes the Russians spreading communism, even in the United States. As she implies, Americans felt uneasy as newspaper, radio, and soon, television reported events that they knew, after experiencing World War II, could upend their lives.

Morgan's family novels depict a half century of change in a southern Appalachia beginning to come out of Reconstruction-era poverty, extreme isolation, and an agricultural economy into the war and industrialization that modernized America. In this liminal space, his ancestors found some stability in family connections, memories, and the ground beneath their feet. When Ginny dies in *The Road from Gap Creek*, her son Muir howls with grief before burying her in the grave she alludes to when telling him where to dig his brother Moody's resting place near the end of *This Rock*: "'Put the grave in the row with Tom and Pa and Jewel. . . . But leave a space for me.'" [41] Family burial grounds, a visual connection with the past, bring a sense of continuity and peace. Another image does as well. Beholding the steeple that Muir has finally erected atop the church he started building in *This Rock*, at the end of *The Road from Gap Creek*, Annie sees it as a symbol uniting the spiritual and the worldly: "It was the most beautiful thing, that steeple pointing straight up to heaven. It made the mountain and the valley and the whole community seem to reach up to that point of hope, far above the sinkholes and mud and confusion of the everyday things" (316). Given Annie's long resistance to being the preacher's wife she finally becomes, we might assume that her understanding of acting influences her optimistic view of such harmony. When Troy dies, she reasons that when her Aunt Lou cheerfully greets visitors, her lively demeanor must hide her true sorrow: "It come to me that most of the smart things people do are a kind of playacting. It would be awful to just act the way we feel. Better to behave for a purpose, with good sense" (165). Annie now engages with the script she earlier found disheartening, a script more open to possibilities than her mother Julie's but just as full of frustrations. Morgan's narrative cycle shows that kin on his little spot of southern Appalachian soil taught him also how to act with purpose, valuing the community across time that strengthens despite its imperfections and showing readers how to treasure it as well.

Morgan's maternal great-grandmother, Delia Johnson Capps, in 1874. Delia is the model for Julie's mother in *Gap Creek* and the subject of the poem "White Autumn." Her memories of the Civil War inspired Morgan's story in Guy Owen's creative writing class at NCSU in 1963. (Robert Morgan Family Pictures Collection)

Morgan's paternal grandmother, Sarah Matilda Pace Morgan, circa 1886, the model for Ginny in *The Truest Pleasure* and *This Rock*. (Robert Morgan Family Pictures Collection)

Morgan's paternal grandfather, John Mitchell Morgan, the model for Tom in *The Truest Pleasure*. (Robert Morgan Family Pictures Collection)

Old Morgan House, Morgan's first home. From left to right are his father Clyde, Dwight, Pearlie, grandfather John Mitchell Morgan, Mae, and great-grandfather John Benjamin Franklin (J.B.F. or Frank). Frank Pace is the model for Pa in *The Truest Pleasure* and Ben Peace in "Martha Sue." Dwight, Pearlie, and Mae are Clyde's siblings. A traveling photographer took this picture circa 1914. (Robert Morgan Family Pictures Collection)

Morgan's maternal grandfather, Robert Hampton Levi, circa 1895, the model for Hank in *Gap Creek* and *The Road from Gap Creek*. (Robert Morgan Family Pictures Collection)

Morgan's maternal grandmother, Julia Capps Levi (1883–1948), the model for Julie in *Gap Creek* and *The Road from Gap Creek*. (Robert Morgan Family Pictures Collection)

Morgan's mother, Fannie Levi Morgan, with her children, Robert and Evangeline, in 1946 by Green River near the Old Morgan House. Fannie is the model for Annie in *The Road from Gap Creek*. Clyde Morgan took this photograph, which is on the cover of *Prisoners of War*, published in 2019 on the occasion of MorganFest at Cornell University. (Robert Morgan Family Pictures Collection)

Morgan's father, Clyde Ray Morgan, in 1920, the model for Muir Powell in *This Rock* and *The Road from Gap Creek* and the subject of poems such as "Mowing" and "Working in the Rain." (Robert Morgan Family Pictures Collection

Morgan's maternal uncle, Sergeant Robert Glen Levi, in his US military uniform before his death in 1943. Robert is the model for Troy in *The Road from Gap Creek* and "The Mountains Won't Remember Us" and the subject of the poem "Uncle Robert." (Robert Morgan Family Pictures Collection)

Robert Morgan in 2018 at the rock house that his father began building when Morgan was five. Morgan grew up in this house that he now owns. (Photo by Jesse Graves)

Chapter 5

More Short Fiction: Classism, War, Machine–Age Destruction

The community that Morgan brings to life in his historical fiction and family novels precedes his own time in the Green River valley, the place whose geography and people grounded his sense of place. But in his short fiction, he gives an ongoing portrait of that place as modernity changes its landscape and inhabitants. These stories resonate with the Deep South writer whose fictional community prefigures Morgan's cultural portrait of this country's development. In his short story "Barn Burning," William Faulkner inscribes young Sarty's consciousness of the distance between a mansion and the shacks in which he has lived with his intractable sharecropping father, whose resentment of economic disparities triggers abusive retaliation against landowners as well as against his family. Morgan often inscribes a similar space, the distance between working-class Appalachians and the wealthy newcomers who are building summer homes and crowding mountain roads in their fume-releasing cars. Distances—among humans or between humans and the landscapes they ravage, especially as evolving technology enables ever-easier desecration of the supposed Edenic garden that early America claimed to be— thread through much of Morgan's short fiction. He gives no easy answers to the complex and often morally ambiguous realities that characters confront as they make their way through the decades, in stories that extend the historical fiction and family-inspired novels or portray environmental devastation or aging in the modern world.

Stereotypes and Discrimination

A story set soon after the Confederate War, as the female narrator refers to it, captures hurtful class hostility while turning a common stereotype on its head. "Dark Corner," published in *The Balm of Gilead Tree*, reverses the direction of American settlement as a poverty-stricken family of eight returns east to Asheville, North Carolina. A father moves his family to Brownsville, Texas, to escape "hardscrabble farming" and Baptist church "backbiting,"[1] a reminder of Morgan's frequent portrayal of church vexations. He sold his Asheville house, expecting to claim the square mile of land Great-Grandpappy said the Republic of Texas had granted him for helping to fight the 1846–1848 war against Mexico, a result of President James K. Polk's belief in America's manifest destiny to settle territory all the way to the Pacific. Mexico lost, ceding a third of its land to the United States. In the story, Brownsville officials have no record of that grant, and neither does Daddy. With some of the $800 left from the house sale, he buys a hundred acres and an old horse, but the dry, dead soil will not grow enough cotton or any crop to sustain the family. Mexicans get the few available jobs, and finally, the sheriff literally throws the impoverished Branch family out of their house, dumping even their clothes in a ditch. The family's trip back to North Carolina is filled with pain and tragedy, the bright spot coming from people who are least expected to extend a morally correct helping hand.

The Branches face some appalling inhumanity as they continue the trip on foot after riding trains as far as Greenville, South Carolina, where officials discover they are riding free and show how a capitalistic system puts profit before decency. The conductor calls the family "'low-down trash'" (145) before turning them over to a policeman, who throws them out into a hard rain, saying they are not worth being fed with taxpayers' money. This argument is perhaps his cover for letting them go, but if so, it's a needlessly hurtful one. Their poverty and physical misery are palpable. At a pawn shop, Daddy sells their trunk and everything in it except a family Bible and a pair of ragged pants for two dollars, using that cash for sardines and crackers at a store once they reach the countryside, glad to be away from the stares in town. As they walk mile after mile, the narrator's shoes break, causing a blister. Cold and practically starving, even before leaving Texas, the narrator twice dreams that "the world was a great breast from which [they] sucked milk and coffee" (158). They sleep inside a tiny church, where Mama boils coffee with water left in the preacher's bucket, creating a communion that temporarily lightens the family's mood. Although one lady does take them into her house for greasy biscuits and honey to help the increasingly ill father's cough, numerous people pass them without offering a wagon ride.

The irony of this saga comes in the supposed morally degenerate Dark Corner of South Carolina, whose reputation for prostitutes, liquor, and violence makes the Branch family desperate to pass it before sunset. Here, the well-dressed Zander Gosnell, who perhaps is related to Timmy Gosnell of *Gap Creek*, gives Daddy a drink of whiskey despite Mama's objections, and he offers to find the family a room. But Mama rejects his kindness out of fear, especially for her six girls. Right before Daddy dies on a ridge clearing, Gosnell shows up with a blanket and whiskey, his concern making him track the needy family in the dark. He enlists friends from Chestnut Springs to take Daddy's body up to Double Springs Cemetery. They get a preacher and give the Branch girls clothes. Looking back, the narrator says, "I don't know what we would have done without them," the "liquor people" (171). Morgan may be playing on the name Dark Corner, having shown the darkness of humanity the Branches confront before arriving at this place of ill-repute whose reality is more complex than its reputation. The now-adult narrator speaks poignantly about hiding her identity as one of those Branch girls, trying to avoid people's judgment and gossip. Mama's frequent "hush up," meant to keep her girls from complaining during that hard trip, goes beyond the expected women's silence to the place that poor people feel they inhabit in a classist society.

"Dark Corner" calls to mind another story breaking the stereotype of prostitutes. "The Sal Raeburn Gap," which appears in *The Mountains Won't Remember Us*, follows a twelve-year-old narrator as he retrieves his grandfather from Sal Raeburn's cabin because he is the only one Grandpa will listen to when a spell of drinking and running after women leads him away from home. Morgan shares the trigger for writing this particular story: "In 'The Sal Raeburn Gap' several things came together, my romantic feeling about the mountains to the west where my dad trapped and hunted when young, beyond The Big Springs. My Uncle William dug ginseng in the Long Hollow. Sal Maybin who lived there in a cabin was a well-known prostitute. And there was a story my dad hinted at, that he was once sent to find his Grandpa Pace at his mistress's house. Somehow it all seemed to fit together."[2] The terms defining women based upon sexuality, "prostitute" and "mistress," relate to the narrator's loss of innocence as he looks at pictures of naked women in discarded magazines and sees Grandpa and Sal naked through the window. Following his parents' orders not to enter Sal's house, he nonetheless eats the fried apple pie that she brings to the porch for him and notes, "The funny thing was, Sal looked just like any other woman when you seen her close up."[3] The spring rain that falls as the narrator and his energized Grandpa trek home seems baptismal, a regeneration not from sexual sin but from the wrong of defining people by one narrow trait.

Again exposing bias, *The Blue Valleys* story "Pisgah" features the gorgeous high mountains that are named for the peak from which Moses saw the Promised Land, as recorded in Deuteronomy 3:27. The Pisgah National Forest, 500,000 acres of high summits and waterfalls, lies within the Blue Ridge Mountains, with Mount Pisgah itself being near Cold Mountain, made famous by Charles Frazier's Civil War novel of that name. Morgan's story takes place right after the war, around 1870, its child protagonist now the man of the house since his father never returned from fighting. Morgan's explanation of the tale's origin attests to his familiarity with his home turf and his respect for its stories: it is "based on a story old Nelse Searcy used to tell. And the stories about him my Dad used to tell. I knew Nelse and his wife Mary when I was little. They lived in a small house up the river on the Bayne land, just beyond the Pace land. After the 1916 flood Nelse caught two sixteen-inch trout in the Lemmons Hole using grasshoppers for bait." [4] As a boy, Searcy walked from the Cradle of Forestry to Brevard, caught a deer, and sold it for coffee and meal. [5] Such images keep people alive in Morgan's memory, inspiring him to tell their truths.

Morgan calls his protagonist Nelse, a boy who uses his wits to triumph over deprivation, at least for a day. The story begins at a one-room school with a nearby outhouse and stream, from which children drink to wash down the lunches they've brought from home. Nelse and his younger sister, Mossy Bell, are new to school but stop attending after bullies kick dirt into their lunch buckets and call them "'trash from up on Pisgah.'" [6] These bullies embody humans' interminable tendency to elevate themselves by disparaging others. Walking down the mountain and along Brevard Road, with his mother's silver thimble to use as payment if the storeowner refuses to extend more credit, Nelse catches a fawn. In the store, locals convince a well-dressed salesman to increase his offer for the fawn his children might like. Seeing that nature can be a commodity, Nelse takes seven dollars for the baby deer, pays his mother's bill, and buys the goods he needs. Local men shame the storeowner into giving the boy a knife, completing the communal extension of grace that counters the young school bullies' abuse.

Adding Environmental Disasters and History

"Pisgah" sets the scene for the next story in *The Blue Valleys*, "1916 Flood," by highlighting the natural world's beauty and by introducing human intervention in it. Nelse views a pristine nineteenth-century landscape as he walks to the store after the March rains end: "The air was so clear he could see through the bare oaks and hickories down valley where poplars and locusts were already budding green. . . . [He] scanned the valley from the green at the lower end up to the lavender of the bare slopes and on up to the black of the balsam covered peaks," observing nature's gift of colors and scheduled regeneration (26–27). But in the store, Nelse encounters loggers who have been driving cut logs down the mountains with the spring freshet, beginning the environmental desecration that escalates as industry and tourism destroy forestland and compromise air quality. The loggers represent humans' culpability for disasters, such as the one that "1916 Flood" later describes.

In *Appalachian Baptism: The Asheville Flood of 1916*, Anthony Sadler explains that the great flood resulted from nature but also from the industrialization that had begun thirty years earlier, when railroads allowed timber barons to begin deforesting this region, as Ron Rash analyzes in his novel *Serena*. Large-scale logging operations destroyed root systems and thus the humus that aided the natural absorption of rain. Sadler also points to the dams that were constructed to make the Protestant Christian retreats being built in the Blue Ridge more secluded and marketable as another environmental manipulation that helped create the devastation. In 1916, two hurricanes converged, one coming up from the Gulf of Mexico early in July, filling rivers, and another arriving from the Atlantic Ocean a few weeks later. Heavy rains washed out bridges, and four earthen dams in Hendersonville, close to Morgan's home, were among the many that failed. The resulting catastrophic flood affected five states. The inundation of western North Carolina and South Carolina no doubt informed Morgan's imagining of Julie and Hank's flooded Gap Creek, and he describes the same terrifying power of raging waters in "1916 Flood," a story told from the third-person perspective of a young boy who is based upon Morgan's father.

Using the death of his grandmother, Sarah Pace Morgan, from measles in 1912 as context, and even incorporating his father's memory of crying by an apple tree when he was told she had died, Morgan creates the protagonist Raleigh, whose nightmare of floodwaters raising his mother's coffin opens the story. The boy's worry that his dream and refusal to kiss his dead mother's lips will make him responsible if the flood has indeed opened her grave stems from the fundamentalist notion of sin that has been ingrained in his psyche. On his way to church with Grandpa and the neighbors who view the flood as God's punishment for people's not "'living right,'" [7] Raleigh sees that the graveyard is intact. Buoyed by relief, he runs to ask the church folks to bring a wagon for a gray-coated corpse that is lodged against a tree, happy that his mother remains in her resting place. This short narrative merges Clyde Morgan's enduring grief over his mother's early death with the possibility that nature might intend to pay humans back for environmental destruction. Morgan's recurring personification of creeping floodwaters "eating" and "slapping" (33) makes nature's resolve palpable. His poem titled "Flood" points more directly to humans' culpability for such disasters: "we build / too close to the moving water" after stripping "forests and absorbent turfs" and "domesticating whole rivers and watersheds," [8] disrupting the nature we try to control.

Morgan returns to his mother in another story featuring disregard for the terrain. It is a story growing out of Fannie Morgan's frustration with the lack of transportation that left her feeling isolated when her husband continued to farm without a truck long after others in Green River had bought vehicles. In "The Dulcimer Maker," Morgan calls his protagonist Annie, the same name he gives to the character modeled on his mother in *The Road from Gap Creek*, but he calls her craftsman husband Frank. A consummate artist who takes time to find the perfect wood, Frank makes only a few dulcimers and refuses to sell his best instruments, an echo of the way that Morgan's father did not earn much money. Morgan avoids romanticizing the mountain folk artist by portraying Frank's human flaws. While he "caresse[s] the wood as if it was a lover's body,"[9] Frank dismisses Annie's worry about their baby's high fever. As Fannie Morgan did, Annie relies on relatives for a ride to town or walks to the bus station. Her brother-in-law, who like Frank says the baby just has whooping cough, refuses to help. Annie has to impose herself upon her temperamental brother Edward, whose inability to control his anger is attributed to his case of typhoid, the infectious disease afflicting Annie's brother Velmer in *The Road from Gap Creek*. Annie ignores Edward's fury and gets into his army surplus truck as he loads it with pole beans to take to market. After paying $1.98 for an antibiotic for the baby's pneumonia, she finds Edward at the market, mad that buyers did not pay enough for his beans, a resentment that Morgan saw his father exhibit at times. When Edward drives so recklessly on the way home that Annie gets out of the truck, she waits for a bus, relieved to have a dollar for the fare. The trash in the ditch where she waits for the bus symbolizes environmental misuse that matches the men's mistreatment of her: candy wrappers, bottles, cans, and a broken toy guitar point to the consumerism that will worsen as decades move along. Morgan leaves Annie waiting, devoting the last paragraph to Frank in his workshop, where his attention to carving his beautiful dulcimer makes his inattention to his wife and child all the more disturbing. The reader is left to navigate the ambiguity, admiring Frank's devotion to his art but lamenting his wife's need to work around the neglect and disdain of the men in her life. Morgan's compassion for Annie is clear, reflecting the impact that his mother's stories of her life had on his heart and imagination.

Fannie Morgan's great-aunt inspired the story "Death Crown," along with a bit of Appalachian folklore that also appears in Morgan's poem of the same title. Published in *The Mountains Won't Remember Us* and *The Balm of Gilead Tree*, this story memorializes Alice, the sister of his great-grandmother Delia. Alice's mental development stopped at age five or six when a boy kicked her in the shin during play, causing an infection that triggered a prolonged high fever and what the family called white swelling, tuberculosis of the bone that pushed fragments through the skin periodically and left Alice with a limp. Alice lived with her sister and Delia's unmarried daughters Rose and Corola at the homeplace on Pleasant Hill, which Delia and Fidelie Capps inherited when they moved there to care for Delia's mother Rebecca and Alice. Visiting Delia as a child, Morgan sometimes saw Alice if she came out of her room, and he remembered his mother giving her dolls or doll clothes at Christmas. As he says in his unpublished memoir, he knew the true story of a family friend sitting with Alice during her last hours and later telling his family that pillow feathers formed a crown around her head. The story thus was given to Morgan. He had only to line up the right words to reveal a theme.

Ellen, who narrates his story, is a great-niece sitting with the dying woman, and she recounts Alice's restricted life, including her father's turning away of suitors, a fact true to the biographical details of Alice's life. Ellen articulates a key point when she ponders the state of Alice's soul. Alice has been isolated, never allowed to go to school or church, and some Baptist church deacons argue that no one can enter heaven without being baptized. But Ellen is mollified by her preacher-father's assurance that no God would condemn to hell people who had no chance to become Christian, such as Chinese, Indians, or children. This part of the story reflects Morgan's worry as a young churchgoer that dooming people who never knew Christianity made no sense. He challenges that church doctrine with the Appalachian folklore belief that if feathers in the pillow on which a person dies clump themselves into a tightly woven crown, that saintly person is in heaven. Notably, this death crown of feathers connects nature to the divine, a common thread in Morgan's work. He adapts the folklore crown a bit by having the sunlight pour through a blind onto Alice's white hair, suggesting the garland to Ellen. His poem "Death Crown" also brings church and folklore together, as "saints and elders" and "Deep Water Baptists" say the feather cap was a "certain sign of another crown" in heaven. This poem's speaker no doubt represents Morgan, who discovered history and a death crown in his great-grandmother Delia's house: "I've seen one unwrapped from its / cloth in the attic, the down / woven perfect and tight for / over a century,"[10] the speaker reflects, more proof that Morgan's Blue Ridge upbringing helps him articulate humans' efforts to make sense of their lives.

The history associated with a Flat Rock antebellum mansion informs a story published in As Rain Turns to Snow. "The Wedding Party" focuses on flatlanders from Charleston who began building summer homes in Flat Rock early in the nineteenth century, as Morgan's "Poinsett's Bridge" and other stories recount. His grandfather and father helped build or maintain some of these homes, one being the Memminger house that eventually became Carl Sandburg's Connemara. This particular story, narrated by a painter who also preaches at a Holiness church, occurs during the Great Depression at Seven Oaks, a mansion owned by an Atlanta mill owner who has not visited his Flat Rock home since the stock market crash. Bowman, the mansion caretaker, provides background while telling the narrator where to check for roof leaks, mentioning the original owner, de Choiseul. In fact, Xavier de Choiseul, French consul in Charleston from 1831 to 1856, did build the Castle in Flat Rock in 1831, and Morgan's description of Seven Oaks matches that mansion's appearance. The tale is that the house is haunted by the ghost of the Frenchman's bride, who was twenty years younger than he and who disappeared on the wedding night while playing hide-and-seek with guests. Morgan fills the story with suspense. When the narrator opens an old trunk in the attic and discovers bones partly covered in lace, his detective work tells him that neither the body nor the tracks on the dusty floor can be a hundred years old. He knows that he has discovered Bowman's wife, who supposedly left him five years earlier. "It was rumored Bowman was glad to get rid of her," he thinks.[11] This murder mystery effectively weaves the parallel stories of Bowman and the teenaged bride's disappearance into a tale that also turns on a conflict between the working class and the wealthy that runs through so much of Morgan's fiction. It also recalls his own years of painting houses before his move to Ithaca, a time when he too sometimes felt the sting of being poor.

War and Other Wounds of Machine-Age Change

Morgan's World War II–era stories achieve several goals, focusing on soldiers but also on changes of the time period that bring longstanding conflicts into the 1940s. These changes often center on industrialization's effects on the landscape, reflecting Morgan's consistent concern about environmental degradation.

The very short "War Story" seems to gather some aspects of Morgan's family story that are recounted in *The Road from Gap Creek*. Doug, home on leave, drives Troy's Dodge into South Carolina to marry his girl, whose references to her cotton mill job and her mother's displeasure with her marriage reflect Fannie Morgan's elopement. Grandpa Harm, a variation on Grandpa Hamp, and Grandma discuss letters, whose lines are mostly blacked out, from Troy in East Anglia. This story's description of 1940s gas pumps as "skinny robots,"[12] and its details of men sitting on bottle crates outside filling stations, paint the changing rural landscape of the era. The preacher who marries the couple on Caesar's Head, oblivious at the end to the lightning "reaching out a delicate wand to touch the mountaintop" (72), shows a distance from the natural world that all Morgan's work seeks to connect to spirituality. This early story combines themes that his later work continues to explore.

"Caretakers" is set at the end of World War II, with honking cars repeating the celebrations that interrupted Julie's funeral in *The Road from Gap Creek*.

The first-person narrator looks forward to construction supplies again being available for the house she dreams of building on the fourteen acres her father has deeded to her. The crux of "Caretakers" lies in upper-class dismissal of employees' humanity. The Mountain Manor owners see Willa and her husband Roy simply as hired help, although Mrs. Swain pretends to care about their two-month-old baby, Sarah, who stays alone except for her parents' periodic checks on her. The Swains drive the telltale Cadillac indicative of Florida people who flaunt the wealth that allowed them to come to the North Carolina mountains in Morgan's fiction, while Roy has a brown Chevrolet Roadster with one black door he put on after an accident. Sharing details of his childhood with his friend, the poet Jeff Daniel Marion, Morgan reflects on the "sense of inferiority" that tourists made Blue Ridge mountain people feel: "In my county this [sense] was heightened by the presence of many wealthy lowlanders in the nearby Flat Rock area, going back to the 1820s, who summered in the mountains and sometimes hired my relatives for menial jobs. And in my time by the thousands of tourists that drove in from Florida and the rest of the Deep South. Nothing can make you feel more backward than hundreds of Miami Cadillacs among the pickups of your hometown."[13] In Morgan's life and in his writing, those Cadillacs represented the materialism and snobbery symbolized by Jay Gatsby's Rolls-Royce in Fitzgerald's novel *The Great Gatsby*.

The class conflict the cars represent comes to a head when Willa finds the burned remains of a picture of Sarah that Mrs. Swain requested in a fireplace. Willa immediately calls the bank to learn that the loan she and Roy applied for has been approved. She then gives their notice, quickly responding to Mrs. Swain's warning that she will not rehire them: "'We won't be coming back.'"[14] This working woman is strong in her convictions, sensitive to the slight of doing more work for no more salary but able to play the deferential role that's necessary to keep her job. Even when a guest, Mr. Fuller, pats her backside, Willa says nothing. Another lodger giving her terrier "'a little toddy'" (108) encapsulates the distance between well-to-do travelers and working locals, as shown earlier when the lodger seems oblivious to the fact that her dog has rolled in carrion, a detail too earthy for this rich woman, who is far removed from the realities of dogs' and laborers' lives.

"The Welcome" brings Blue Ridge soldiers home at the end of World War II, and it is one of several stories exploring an ironic reality that Hemingway reinforced, as Morgan explains in his Air Force Academy address: while the soldier longs for home, he may be unhappy when he arrives there, finding home different from his memories of it.[15] Appearing in *The Balm of Gilead Tree*, in its proper chronological sequence between two other stories of the conflict, "Murals" and "Tailgunner," "The Welcome" again echoes the horn-tooting during Julie Richards's funeral near the end of *The Road from Gap Creek*. Dutch returns from a Nazi prisoner of war camp where he spent time after parachuting into a German cabbage patch. The community's car parade and outdoor feast overwhelm Dutch, who is emotionally deadened by war and unable to be the person his community remembers. Firecrackers make him jump, and he wants desperately to walk alone in the woods, seeking nature's solace. In fact, the hogpen stench strengthens Dutch when he feels nauseated. Buddies help him escape on a truck ride, all of them drinking rye whiskey and moonshine, and the liquor connects him to his old life. They dig up rocks, a destructive act that seems out of character for a man soothed by the natural world until we learn that the lake they roll the rocks into was built by the "new Florida people," an understated reference to locals' resentment of wealthy outsiders. Dutch calls clearing the mountaintop of rocks "putting the world in order," [16] a momentary catharsis from prison camp angst that he barely mentions to friends or family. Like other young men in Morgan's work who are going to or returning from war, Dutch feels unsure about his feelings for a girl, Lena, who waited for him. Critic Larry Grimes's superb comparison of this story to Hemingway's "Soldier's Home," including the repetition of phrases that creates the almost hypnotic voice, argues that Dutch does not agree to live the lie that Krebs, who is pretending to fit into civilian life, resigns himself to. He also sees that when Dutch looks beyond the horizon, his gaze signals possibilities for his future away from the "arrested development" of his friends who did not go to war.[17] The soldier's repeated wishing at the end, including his wish not to have to go back to his parents and Lena, seems to hold some promise that counters his lethargy. But the Asheville smokestack's "black scrawl" (226) across the sky communicates a disturbing message, warning of the degradation of both the landscape and the human spirit by war and mechanization.

Following Dutch's homecoming in *The Balm of Gilead Tree*, "Tailgunner" continues to show Hemingway's influence as Morgan explores a returning soldier who does, as Grimes says, live the lie that Krebs chooses. Morgan's story is inspired by the death of his cousin, Norman Capps, in World War II,[18] but he imagines that the soldier survives and comes to a discontented end. "Tailgunner" opens and concludes with Cyrus Jones from Henderson County, born in 1924, being thrown from an exploding plane in Germany, his friends' body parts vividly etched in his memory. Like Dutch in "The Welcome," he parachutes into a cabbage patch and ends up in a prison camp. Shifting back and forth among three war flashbacks and scenes from Cyrus's later life with his wife Lorna, the third-person narrator reveals that marital distance intensifies Cyrus's loneliness: he has feigned devotion to the woman he weds when he was too disoriented to resist, and he sinks deeper into the "emotional disengagement and self-bifurcation" that Hemingway's war veterans suffer.[19] The couple leaves Cyrus's childhood farm for Spartanburg and then Sumter, South Carolina, to be close to their only daughter, Alva, who now wants to build a summer home at the farm. Cyrus cannot make himself give her permission to do that, even though she will inherit the place. He still feels tied to that land, and he misses the pasture hills and broom sedge. In South Carolina, he stands under pine trees to feel "closer to a self he had lost in the war and never recovered."[20] Besides his unlucky marriage, urbanization and technological progress also increase Cyrus's alienation. Fields have been bulldozed into lots to be sold. People watch news instead of praying. And Alva, detached from her father over the summer home, takes her children to McDonald's after church instead of eating Sunday dinner with her parents. After working thirty years in construction, which has changed from skilled work to "just knock[ing] together sections already assembled at a factory," Cyrus suffers a heart attack. In retirement, he admits that he "had not been happy since he quit working with his hands" (231), a sign of the ways that industrial advancements usurp pride in work well done. Like Morgan's other veterans, Cyrus kept his war experiences to himself, finding that nobody wanted to hear about them when he wanted to talk decades later. Now, he feels too disillusioned to attend a military reunion. As the story ends, we see him again parachute out of the damaged plane as pressure in his chest signals a second heart attack. The sensory details escorting his descent ground him not just in the explosion in Germany but in the sights and smells of his childhood, as Grandma's front room, schoolhouse glue, and his river baptism signal his return to that home and the self he has been seeking since the war.

"Murals" comments on the conflict between art and industrialization as the United States moves into World War II. Occurring on December 8, 1941, it traces the despair of a Works Progress Administration (WPA) artist named Gardner, who is trying to finish a post office mural as funding stops so that the money can go toward the war effort following Japan's bombing of Pearl Harbor. This story is partly inspired by Morgan's father's helping to sponsor a muralist's work at the Flat Rock Post Office in the 1980s, even though his family needed those dollars. Gardner's work in the Jackson County town of Webster is totally funded by the Federal Art Project, a venture that brings art to everyday people while also putting money into artists' pockets during the Great Depression. Prior to this job, before and during art school in Chicago, Gardner mainly painted human figures and the natural world, a subject suggested by his agronomy-related name. But now he feels pressured to draw machines to keep up with the times: "Most of Gardner's friends had no trouble executing something futuristic, or celebrating cars and cotton mills, assembly lines and bulldozers, the energy of the industrial sublime." Gardner notes that "machines were much of the power of Rivera's murals,"[21] referencing the famous Mexican artist Diego Rivera, who was commissioned in 1932 to paint large-scale public art in Detroit after popularizing murals in the 1920s following the Mexican Revolution. Rivera's notion that artists served the community influenced Roosevelt's decision to create the Federal Art Project as part of the Works Progress Administration. Rivera painted murals that captured the industrial age while highlighting the duality of nature and machines. He admired American industrial might, but in his murals, he showed workers sacrificing themselves to industry, to mechanical gods.

Gardner's WPA supervisor had assisted Rivera on murals in Detroit but seems oblivious to the ambiguity that the muralist incorporated into his depiction of the human-machine relationship. He tells Gardner that "'the future is with machines. . . . Machines are our friends, machines are the allies of the common people. Only machines will get rid of poverty and discrimination.'" Gardner knows that he must paint his combine "as heroic helpmeet to the common man" to please his boss. But his description of the harvester in a letter to his girlfriend implies deeper thinking about the changing nature of agricultural work and the way machines are taking humans' jobs: "'Not only does the machine combine several functions different men used to do, cutting, gathering, threshing, bagging. It connects man and earth, present and future, steel and muscle'" (191). The detailed description of his mural reveals an awareness of technology's complex place in the universal scheme:

> The wheel loomed up against the sky and touched the outline of the cloud. It turned like a great ferris wheel in the carnival of work and the men were turning with it, pitching straw, lifting sacks of grain, spinning the wheels of tractors and trucks. The sky was one long curving wheel of clouds and blue implying the pageant of the seasons and the orbit of the planet around the sun (189).

And earlier:

> The wheat reached like hands and flames through the turning blades. [Gardner plans to include] [m]en and women . . . advancing around the combine as though pulling themselves up out of the earth . . . [as if they are] fighting with, and along with, nature for a decent community, for dignity. (187–88)

Both nature and humans battle the machine, a telling description of its power.

Gardner's belief in the power and permanence of art, his hope that people will look up at his combine years later, might seem naive in the face of the "euphoria [that sweeps] through the town" when military conflict erupts. Children shoot toy guns, World War I veterans march, and men line up to enlist. Someone attacks a Japanese stranger in Charlotte in retribution for the Pearl Harbor attack. Gardner sees the power of war to inspire, to bring people together in common purpose as no art, not even "guitar playing," can (190). Forced to abandon his project, he plans to join the military, leading critic Harriet Buchanan to argue that he has "resolved his ambivalence about the war." [22] But his capitulation shows resignation more than resolve. As the story ends, a crowd cheers boys boarding army buses. "No one noticed Gardner with his paint smudged hands and face" (203), suggesting that Americans prone to empty gestures of patriotism will ignore his imaginative take on mechanization.

Gardner's artistic philosophy shows a reconciliation of opposites, such as these different responses to war and art. These lines represent Morgan's own duality of vision, his reliance on concrete, touchable objects in his poetry and prose, and they also reflect a twenty-first century opposition related to technology, the conflict between the real and the virtual:

> When he was a boy, Gardner tried to imagine the relationships between specific things out in the woods and fields, a rock, a particular tree, a spring hidden in the cedars, with the great world in general, the government, the mass of people, things in books, in history. And he wondered which was truer for him, the smell of the cow stalls where he milked, or the discussions of milk and dairy products and a proper diet in his health book.
>
> Gardner remembered the exact date, when he was in art school, when he realized that he needed both kinds of perceptions to be who he was. He could draw and paint the isolated, tattered cornstalks, the hidden alcove in the pines, but in doing so he had to be conscious of the world in general, all kinds of people, even the course of history. He could not have one without the other. (197–98)

This merging of dualities supports the role serious art plays in a world marked by technological change, a dichotomy connecting to the last story in Morgan's first collection, *The Blue Valleys*.

"Blinding Daylight" presents Morgan's most serious study of technology's effect on the world. As his protagonist, David, a college art professor, sits in blinding sunlight at the story's end, the "separate shapes [of trees and barns] and distances . . . merging in a flood" create "a storm advancing over him."[23] This imagery suggests either that David will commit suicide, as planned, or that he foresees chaos. The ambiguity connects perfectly to David's paintings of the dichotomy between the natural world and machines, seen in the context of Henry Adams's contemplation of technology at the turn of the twentieth century.

David twice finds subject matter for his art during walks in his native Blue Ridge woods. In graduate school, "distraught" with worry that he will be drafted for the Vietnam War, he goes home to "[walk] out his frustration in the mountains" (160) and finds inspiration in "ridges cresting one behind the other." His "Ocean of Mountains" series jumpstarts his career, as the many boys in his county who had not gone to college or even high school "were available for Vietnam" (161), a critique of the United States war machine. On a subsequent trip home, David contemplates suicide to escape his quandary of being in love with a woman who is not his wife. But seeking the proper place to shoot himself, he comes across a rusty, abandoned Ford in a vacant field. The next day, he begins a series of paintings, the first

> a wide painting of a wheatfield with a stock car hovering over it. The field was a million candles of fountaining light, each painted distinctly, and the race car a rush of thunder. Later he realized the secret inspiration must have come from Dali's "Last Supper," as well as the field at the edge of the Flat Woods. The first articles written about him were on the wheatfield and race car paintings. . . . One critic said the power was in the contrast between the ancient and the modern, and quoted Henry Adams from "The Dynamo and the Virgin." Another saw evidence of a schizoid attraction to both gentleness and violence at once. Only the columnist for the Atlanta paper saw a feeling for the miraculous, a retelling of the Ascension, power transcendent to nature. (161–162)

Both the Adams and Dali allusions point to Morgan's theme.

The grandson of John Quincy Adams and the great-grandson of John Adams, Henry Adams (1838–1918) had an intellectual interest in contrasts and unity. His studies of the Abbey at Mont-Saint Michel and Chartres Cathedral led him to see the remarkable social impact of medieval Christianity, as humans built lofty edifices to steer their thoughts heavenward, similar to Muir's church in *This Rock*, a novel that also references Adams. Seeing the Virgin Mary icon as a unifying spiritual force that drove an architectural revolution, Adams began to look at history in relation to fixed points in time, an organizing principle for *The Education of Henry Adams*, which was first printed privately in 1907, though it went on to win the Pulitzer Prize in 1919. Adams wrote "The Dynamo and the Virgin" chapter of this influential book after visiting the Great Exposition of 1900 in Paris, where the "forces" hall exhibited huge dynamos, generators running continuously to produce electrical energy from mechanical energy, or mechanical energy from electrical energy. Adams describes his response: "he began to feel the forty-foot dynamos as a moral force, much as the early Christians felt the Cross. The planet itself seemed less impressive, in its old-fashioned, deliberate, annual or daily revolution, than this huge wheel . . . scarcely humming an audible warning to stand a hair's-breadth further for respect of power. . . . [O]ne began to pray to it," prayer being an instinctive response to "infinite force."[24] Twentieth-century mechanization will replace religion, Adams predicts. In a 1953 essay titled "The Frontier versus Europe: A Question of Values," Walter Blair and Randall Stewart explain Adams's argument that "the dynamo was obviously a force, but neither spiritual nor unifying. As religion decayed, enormous, incalculable forces unleashed by science—steam power, electricity, radioactivity—threatened to destroy mankind. It was a serious question, Adams thought in the *Education*, whether there was enough intelligence and moral character in the world to control these new forces and use them for man's welfare."[25] Adams saw that humanity's inability to manage a technologically driven world might result from denying the mystery that both religion and science reveal, a concern that Morgan shares. His painter David channels this concern in noting Dali's "Last Supper" as inspiration.

All of these artists—Dali, Adams, Morgan, David—seek to straddle the divide between religion and science. Dali's 1955 surrealist painting *The Sacrament of the Last Supper* features a mystical Christ sitting with the twelve disciples, sunlight pouring through windowpanes, and a giant torso, presumably God, hovering over the center. Dali responded to criticism of his portrayal of Christ's body by saying it represents the scientific fact that all things, even bodies, are not solid but made of energy, moving molecules, as Morgan suggests in poems such as "Dark Energy," the title poem of his 2015 collection that portrays the movement and mystery of matter and space. As Adams sees "a revelation of mysterious energy like that of the Cross" in scientific rays,[26] Morgan sees divinity in soil, in human bodies, in dark energy, in the sunlight at the end of "Blinding Daylight" that merges shapes, polishing trees and barns and luring yellow jackets from mulch. John Lang's claim that Morgan really is trying "to transcend the very dichotomy implicit in the terms 'sacred and secular'"[27] applies to David's paintings as well as to Gardner's work in "Murals." Their images of machines dominating a natural landscape ask viewers to consider the relationship of the spiritual, physical, and mechanical worlds, to be alert to changing dynamics that might lead to the dangerous veneration of technological marvels.

Morgan continues to explore this very risk in numerous stories taking place in the 1970s, an era when southern Appalachia moved even more into modernity's consumer culture. "Let No Man," for instance, creates a desecrated landscape that matches human disappointments. Everything about this story seems arid and tainted, with even Josie's poor eyesight, caused by childhood poisoning, signaling her blindness to the marriage she enters into in her thirties. Traveling to their honeymoon in South Carolina's Myrtle Beach, a symbol of commercialism signified in the hotel's vibrating bed, Nathan and Josie drive past factories, mills, shopping malls, and filling stations surrounded by rusted, wrecked cars sitting in weeds. Restaurants, Cokes, and professional wedding photographers also signal a world far removed from Julie Harmon Richards's life in Gap Creek. Stultifying heat makes the roads ripple in a "pollution-purple haze"[28] that foreshadows trouble. After Nathan's Trans Am overheats, they finally make it to the hotel, where Nathan shares that he never developed sexually, adding that he lied to the doctor, saying that he had told his fiancée of his condition. Josie resigns herself to thwarted expectations, thinking that at least she will avoid worries other women have, presumably adultery or pregnancy or the burden of raising children. The irony that Nathan drives a macho sports car, showing how commercialized America's marketing has achieved its goal, reminds us that Morgan consistently matches cars to characters and themes.

Vehicles play a minor role in a late 1960s or early 1970s story in *The Blue Valleys*, where Morgan teaches some southern Appalachian history. The title, "The Lost State of Franklin," refers to land west of the Appalachians, in present-day eastern Tennessee, that North Carolina offered to Congress in 1784 to help the fledgling nation pay Revolutionary War debts. Never admitted as a state, the short-lived Franklin was the birthplace of Davy Crockett, as Morgan mentions in his *Lions of the West* portrait of that legendary figure. In the story, it is a visitor who knows the history of this place, a Vietnam veteran whose great-great-great-grandfather lived here: John Peter Corn, a real Revolutionary War soldier buried in the Ebenezer Baptist Church cemetery in Hendersonville. This grounding in history makes the "lost" of the title more suggestive: the contemporary husband and wife in the story are lost in their marriage, their visitor gets lost for two days in the jungle of Vietnam during America's never-declared war, and even his words get "lost in puffs of vapor" as he tries to introduce himself to the couple he visits.[29] Morgan forms this pair based upon the life of his Uncle Robert's fiancée, mined in *The Road from Gap Creek* and "The Mountains Won't Remember Us." Susan's husband Doug died in Vietnam, so she married John, who "'can't compete with a dead man'" (96), and he confronts his wife about Doug's letters and picture, like Sharon's husband in the novel and no-vella. Doug's army buddy Richard visits to fulfill his promise to Doug to visit his wife, reminiscent of Woodruff's delivering the watch of John Powell, the Civil War prisoner, to his widow at the end of "A Brightness New and Welcoming." Feeling threatened by the past, John turns up the television volume to dis-rupt Susan's conversation, and he retrieves his gun to intimidate Richard. His battered pickup, looking unsightly beside Richard's shiny red Barracuda, and the repossessed trailer he bought with Doug's insurance money signal John's ineptness. Pepsi cans and pizza boxes cluttering the trailer add to the sense of decay, making Susan feel guilty that she does not garden like her mother. In fact, guilt centers Susan in her fragile world, and like other unhappy women in Morgan's contemporary stories, she seems to decide to make a change, to start a journey even though she cannot clearly see all its steps. Her positive memories of Hendersonville and a desire to be alone suggest a possible return to find herself in the place of her roots.

"Frog Level" is another story that depicts a Vietnam veteran's problems as well as car culture's influence on individuals and the environment. The story, named for a mountain community buried under an interstate, opens with the female narrator, Rachel Lessing, thinking she sees her husband's truck at the new Biltmore Mall near Asheville, although she cannot be sure since "There must be a hundred red 4x4's with oversize tires in Western North Carolina." With air-conditioned buildings that look like "cathedrals and palaces" as well as a parking lot the size of Asheville's downtown,[30] the shopping center is a testa-ment to the worship of commercialism defining 1970s and 1980s America. This story also portrays women's growing independence, as Rachel eventually takes action against the male-dominated, money-centered real estate development world as well as against her philandering husband.

Rachel makes her husband, Fielding, flee during a raucous, dangerous car chase that she instigates after spying him with a girlfriend, her rage at his infidelity matching her anger at overdevelopment. Her Maverick—the car name signals her refusal to conform any longer to the good little wife image she's maintained for fifteen unhappy years—keeps up with Fielding's four-wheel-drive truck for a good while. They screech tires, cut into traffic, and run over curbs, reflector poles, shopping cart railings, and picnic tables, their wild choreography filling eleven pages and reminding readers of Muir's escape from officers in the Model T in *This Rock*. Rachel and Fielding drive on the CCC road that Troy Richards in *The Road from Gap Creek* (and Morgan's Uncle Robert) helped to build in the 1930s, bringing the past and the chain-store present together when they drive by a Walmart. In town, traffic is "bumper to bumper, as it always is in August. . . . The Cadillacs from Florida, the BMWs and

Mercedeses of tourists, were gridlocked with the pickups and local hotrods" (122). These high-end car drivers spur overdevelopment. Black Construction Company, owned by a man from Connecticut, has bulldozed mountaintops to build homes on ridges, cutting roads and opening gullies that send mud washing over Rachel's ancestral family home: "The yard in front of the house looked like somebody had poured tons of mud over the boxwoods. Mud had spilled into the toolshed, covering up the plows and rusty hoes. . . . The spring below the house was buried in mud" (115–16). The "golf course and condominiums and rich-man's houses along King Creek" (123) signal the outsiders' intrusions. Mr. Black accuses mountain people of being backwards, preferring to keep their land "'in corn patches and moonshine stills'" (117). But Rachel's community college course in ecology and land use has given her confidence to stand up to Black, who cleans up and erects erosion barriers when another resident calls the State Environmental Agency before she does. Appalachian natives must challenge corner-cutting developers who are concerned only with financial gain, Morgan implies, before the investors buy all the family land to sell for millions in profit, as Rachel sees they are doing.

Rachel's schooling gives her confidence to leave Fielding as well, but Morgan complicates her thinking about her marriage. After Fielding finally evades Rachel in the car pursuit, she demolishes their mobile home, proving that "women will commit violence," although men think they "will put up with anything" (128). She loads up her Maverick, reflecting on the influence automobiles have had on her life: "I suppose every wife wonders from time to time why she ever married her husband," Rachel muses. "But I remember all too clearly what attracted me to Fielding. It was his Jeep" (119). She married to escape the poverty of the fruit stand, where Fielding delivered his daddy's homemade liquor for her daddy to sell in the years before marijuana became the most lucrative mountain cash crop. His Jeep, on which he takes Rachel to Ann Mountain, where Moody Powell dies in *This Rock*, represents the getaway that cars have signified since their creation. Rachel sees Fielding's current vehicle as a symbol of their incompatibility: "The way the 4x4 had climbed up the mountain reminded me how crude he was. He could go where I couldn't because he was so big and rough. He had gotten away with everything all his life because he was so crude" (127). But remembering Fielding's story of being the only survivor of a Vietnam War calamity, when he faked injury to avoid rescuing pilots from a downed bomber that he expected would explode, Rachel confronts the complexities that shape people's character and behavior and that often make their lives incredibly hard.

Following "Frog Level" in *The Mountain's Won't Remember Us and Other Stories*, "Cracklin' Bread," which again features a military veteran, presents a changing economy that shifts family land from subsistence farming to the consumer-driven nursery business that's suitable to the mountain climate. The aging narrator and his wife move into a trailer behind the old family home that his son, Everett, and his bride move into following his stint in Vietnam. Rather than appreciating that generosity, Everett arrogantly assumes owner-ship, leading the men's clashing worldviews to erupt in a physical altercation. While the father values the work that is central to Morgan's philosophy of a life well-lived, Everett considers money to be the end goal. He sees only "'money in this ground,'" taking no pride in the way his ancestors made a living on it for two centuries.[31] Growing landscaping plants for businesses and suburban homes in Atlanta and Charlotte, Everett works all the family members into the night. His father worries about raping the land, sending mountain topsoil to yards in South Carolina, a reality that Morgan describes in his poem "Atomic Age," where mountain loam goes with trees and shrubs to cities, suburbs, and interstate medians, thinning the topsoil in the coves, the "savings of centuries of leaf rot" sold.[32] Everett derisively comments that they can grow more soil. Building a three-story house and buying lots of machinery, he loses all sense of family, neglecting to take his own son hunting, destroying his mother's garden, pushing his wife, and deciding on his own to tear down the old house that his great-great-grandfather built after the Civil War. Everett's total devotion to mammon makes him ignore his father's advice to "'leave a margin at the edge of the field'" for nesting birds, rabbits, and spiders, the "ecological insurance" of diversity that he hears a radio show endorse (131). The son dismisses this border between woods and field, symbolic in Morgan's work as a place where wilderness and civilization collide.

Such a periphery allows a two-way view, something the father under-stands, though Everett does not. Everett cares only about the present and in-sults his father's love of cracklin' bread as a tie to the past, when people killed hogs at home. "'The world's moving on'" and "'there'll be no more . . . cracklin' bread'" (142), he threatens, not analyzing the meaning of time's movement as deeply as his father does. The older man knows that Everett disparages his reluctance to put money in the bank because he did not live through the Great Depression. He admits that he remodeled his own father's house when he and Mildred moved into it despite seeing that Pa "didn't cotton to so much fixing up and changing around" (144). He wonders whether Vietnam affected Everett negatively, making him change over time. The older man is aware that the modern world is altering his pleasure of sitting quietly in the woods. But easing into the Jacuzzi that Everett installs to help his father heal from a stroke triggered by their physical fight, the elder man accepts the machine that is replacing the woods as a place of regeneration, as the waters of this newfangled pool warm his muscles. Readers respect the way he adapts to change while worrying about the long-term effects of a culture that privileges machines over nature.

Older characters adapting to technology in "The Half Nelson" seem more blind to its effects than Everett's father. This story of a changing United States, where Charles flies from California across the country for a business meeting in Atlanta and visits his mother while he's near his Blue Ridge childhood home, addresses technology's interventions in human community. Charles and his mother, who thinks he should move back to Appalachia, visit neighbors living in a trailer that "smell[s] of hot electric circuits and plastic."[33] Liddy, with a history of high blood pressure and a stroke, is glued to a televised wrestling match, watching with her husband Alvin with only the flickering screen illuminating the dark room. Unable to take her eyes from the screen, Liddy barely glances at Charles and seems oblivious to the sport's fakeness, emphasized by wrestlers' wigs and masks. One of the performers, Cherokee McGee, wears a feather and does a war dance, surely Morgan's comment on the commodification of Indian culture. Liddy and Alvin feel disappointed when their favored team loses, as though they have wound their own identity into the caricatured entertainment. Wrestling's artificiality counters the reality of another neighbor's recent death from emphysema after two years of suffering, about which Alvin says, "'I'm sure the Lord knows what he's doing'" (129). It's not quite a dismissal of a friend's pain but a mollifying line common in fundamentalist religious circles. One wonders whether the television's draw kept people from visiting this man as he lingered with bedsores. Through a window, Charles sees a subtle warning of the collapse in values brought about by technology: heat lightning, actually a reflection of distant lightning on high clouds, appears as a flash of light near the horizon, signaling a distant storm far enough away that people cannot hear the thunder. Katydids join the heat lightning to impart a message, as Charles thinks that their "dialogue sounded vivid enough to be translated, if one knew the terms." Walking home with his mother in the dark, he delivers an ominous last line: "'Our eyes will be adjusted to the dark soon'" (132), adjusted and therefore oblivious to the mechanized world's threats. The symbolism of light, lightning, and seeing seems supported by the wrestlers' half-nelson hold. A half-nelson is less dangerous than a full nelson but still implies that we are strangling ourselves. This simple but powerful story suggests that we will save ourselves only if we heed nature's warnings.

The changing world that "Cracklin' Bread" and "The Half Nelson" showcase includes conflicts concerning family and land, of course, that Morgan saw in his home community. In fact, his story "Family Land," published in *The Blue Valleys*, presents a female narrator who learns about its value. Television, phones, and

consumerism—symbolized by shopping at Woolworth's—has led to a frag-
mentation of family here, sadly enhanced by the narrator's marriage to Clint,
who first attracts her for the way he thwarts traditions like church. Her father
has deeded the family land to her and her husband, and Clint wants to sell it
as needed to buy a sauna or build another garage for the boats and sports cars
that he values above everything else. While they have the biggest house in the
valley, when Clint ruins the clutch on his truck by pulling an oversized boat, he
does not have enough money to repair it. Such modern values are passed down
to the children, who ignore their grandfather when he brings fresh blackber-
ries to them. The little girl stays glued to the television, eating an ice cream
sandwich for breakfast while blatantly ignoring her mother's directions to eat
the hot cereal she has cooked. The narrator works a word-processing job to
pay bills, leaving no time to care for her mother, now in a rest home, and her
father visits only when he knows Clint is away. Similar to Rachel's epiphany
in "Frog Level," the narrator's fifteen-year-long bad marriage leads her to act
when a lawyer calls to say that she may have to take a lien on their house to
post bail for Clint, who gets arrested for molesting a nine-year-old girl. She
decides that she will not pay, that she will not sell a foot of land to help him
out of legal troubles. Earlier, the narrator had vowed to shoot Clint when he hit
her one year into the marriage, indicating a degree of inner strength that she
let materialism overcome. She seems to resurrect that self-respect when she
finally rethinks her relationship to her family and the land.

Another story in Morgan's first collection exposes encroaching industrial-
age concerns through the widower Will Vance, the defensive man who narrates "The Pickup," telling about his thwarted efforts to remarry after his wife
dies of cancer. The husband of the woman he is attracted to, Nettie, has also
died of cancer after working at the Enka chemical plant (a Dutch company
established outside Asheville in 1928), leading Will to note that "most people
that ever worked in chemicals got cancer."[34] This line echoes Fannie Morgan
telling her son that a cemetery outside Hendersonville held many people who
ingested chemicals at the local cigarette paper plant. As in other stories, farm
homeplaces have been sold and turned into trailer parks, and spring water is
muddy from bulldozing. This particular narrator is less sympathetic than most
of Morgan's characters who resent the derision from the wealthier classes. In
fact, Will, in his constant feeling of victimization, resembles Faulkner's Snopes
clan. He harbors anger at the hypocrites who did not serve time for moonshining, as his daddy did, and he still begrudges the Cantrells, whom he sued over a
land boundary. Marrying Nettie would be a move up for him, and her deceased
husband's GMC pickup and farm add to the appeal of Nettie's well-preserved
looks. But when her son explains that his father lost money in the 1987 stock

market crash and that the farm and truck will be sold but will not cover all the medical bills, Will's dashed hopes send him running from the marriage commitment, furious at what he sees as Nettie's deception. He denies that he ever pushed Nettie, and his repeated claims that people treat him unfairly seem suspect. When he thinks of turning his own land into a trailer park, Will reminds readers of Morgan's less-than-admirable characters who ravage acreage for these factory-made dwellings. This story also critiques the extravagant cost of modern medicine, quite advanced from the little medical assistance available to Ginny and Julie in the family novels but also so expensive that it can ruin people's financial stability. Changing times in "The Pickup" bring county-sponsored meals to senior citizens but no easy answers for life's difficulties.

In "The Bullnoser," Morgan explicitly contrasts the industrial defilement of family land with the old ways that a deceased grandfather once lived. The narrator, fired from his cotton mill job after a back injury, lives and drinks with his drug-addicted, alcoholic mother whom he calls Carlie, suggesting a degraded parent-child relationship. They live in a trailer on her father-in-law's land, now being developed after she sold it to T. J., the man her husband had borrowed money from before he died. Discovering that T. J. is burying oil drums and paint cans for Republic Industries, illegally poisoning the ground, the narrator threatens to alert authorities but then considers just blackmailing T. J. into repairing his pickup and keeping him in cigarettes and beer. Settling for hush money counters the narrator's own nostalgia for his grandpa, leaving readers saddened that commercialism's values may have won.

The narrator refers frequently to his grandfather's place as an Edenic garden, with apple orchards, mowed grass, and a hard-working man who orders that pleasant world. The story is as much about Grandpa as it is about the mechanical bullnoser that buries poisons and knocks down trees to make way for T. J. "to grow trailer sites . . . [in] the old pasture."[35] Morgan's similes contrast the old world and new: "oil tanks on their stands stood like steel cows behind every trailer, and off on the side of each one a satellite dish tilted like a big white flower" (157). Decades earlier, when the grandson lets a bull escape, Grandpa snaps a chain into the bull's nose ring, calmly leading him back home as the natural bullnoser. Neighbors helping to corral the bull comment on Grandpa's son bringing "cotton mill trash" into Riley's family when he marries Carlie: "'Got to keep your breeding stock up, otherwise a family will run to ruin in two generations,'" one declares (155). This metaphor makes the narrator's decision even more crucial. The story ends with his memory of Grandpa showing him where he started hiding his tools when the altered world made theft more likely. He trusted his grandson to cherish the old-time, manual instruments. But the encroaching values of industry—with land developers being higher on the social scale than cotton mill workers, and with mill work inhibiting people's relationship with the land—endanger the narrator's ability to act on environmental desecration. As the superhighway obscures the view of the valley, and as kudzu hangs mournfully as it smothers native plants—perhaps knowing that its invasion of the South will lead to increased herbicide spraying—we can only hope that the confidence a cold beer gives the narrator will spur action that honors Grandpa and saves the soil he loved.

Morgan's gaze at a changing world in "The Bullnoser" centers mostly on land, but it also notably shows that modern times have brought women into the traditionally male world of drinking, a point he emphasizes in a story published in *The Balm of Gilead Tree: New and Selected Stories*. "A Taxpayer and a Citizen" features a female narrator, Sallie, who drinks too much wine to ease her anxiety about serving papers on her husband, who has left her for a young country singer. Driving drunk, she gets stopped by a policeman, who twice has to chase her when she tries to escape. When neither her feminine wiles nor her demands as "a taxpayer and a citizen" convince the policeman to let her go, the narrator loses control, becoming a humorous but sad resister who shows the effects of too much alcohol. Sallie also reflects a breakdown of the traditional family portrayed in Morgan's novels set before mid-twentieth century, when characters stay in imperfect marriages, waiting for time to lessen their anger and hurt. Sallie's vomiting by the side of the road evokes our sympathy as she tries "to heave out all the poison and pain, . . . the confusion and frustration, the humiliation [her husband] had given" her.[36] Under arrest, Sallie feels paralyzed as she faces divorce and an uncertain future. Her anxiety parallels the disquiet that Morgan's fiction conveys about the way humans are handling much about the contemporary world. Highways and driving play emblematic roles as part of the machine age's taint of spiritual harmony, reflecting the opening of the mountains that had begun in "Poinsett's Bridge" and in *The Hinterlands*, with "The Trace" and "The Road."

In another story in Morgan's third collection, driving on the superhighway turns into a hellish scene. In "The Ratchet," both a logging truck and tourists mark the intrusion of the machine into the garden, to appropriate Leo Marx's metaphor for technology's disruption of the pastoral ideal. Sightseers pull off the road at fruit stands that offer cigarettes and handmade crafts, marking the commodification of mountain culture and the locals' economic dependence upon outsiders who pollute the mountain air. A horrific accident that Morgan remembers happening near his home, as he explains in his unpublished memoir, informs this nail-biting narrative. Two brothers rush to reach the sawmill with their overloaded logging truck on a steamy summer Friday afternoon, hoping to get to the bank to cash checks, one to buy an air-conditioner for his trailer, the other to escape mountain congestion by driving to Myrtle Beach. The truck's brakes fail because in their rush to cut more trees to make money, on land whose timber rights were bought from the old Lewis place heirs, neither of them has checked the master cylinder lately. A mile-long line of cars, many of them Cadillacs driven by out-of-state tourists, stretches in front of the logging truck when the brakes stop working. As Fred and Albert careen down the mountain and see an eighteen-wheeler "barreling" toward them "like a bull with its head lowered," they face the ethical quandary that out-of-control vehicles bring: "it was better to shove into a car or pickup truck on the right than hit the transfer head-on." [37] But when a pickup edges to the right shoulder and the transfer truck swerves, Albert maneuvers the logging truck between them, prolonging the agony for the brothers and readers alike. The brothers wish for nature to save them—"If only there was a field or a hillside to turn onto"—but the yard of the filling station they see at the bottom of the hill is "cluttered with cars and trucks. There [is] no room to pull off" (271). When a chain snaps and logs begin to roll off, the truck swings and plunges into a river. Fred wakes to muddy water swirling around the cab, unable to move his neck and wondering if Albert is still breathing. Consumerism, greed, environmental destruction, and the brothers' heated arguing coalesce to portray an industrialized world out of control in this disturbing story.

The collision of mechanization, the natural world, and ethics transforms another Edenic landscape in "The Balm of Gilead Tree" when Morgan brings to the page the true midair crash of a Cessna 310 and a Boeing 727 near Hendersonville in July 1967, with the horror of falling bodies intensified by looters scurrying to steal cash and valuables from the corpses before the police arrive. Driving to the scene, Morgan's narrator notes that roadwork makes the new road look like "bomb craters" or a "shelled zone," his Vietnam experience providing metaphors for land development[38] and no doubt contributing to his moral confusion. Dashing from body to body to hunt for wallets, the narrator justifies his theft, telling himself that someone else would take the money if he does not, that surviving relatives will get insurance money, that he needs cash to build his girlfriend a hair salon. Brawling with a bread truck driver as they try to shake the same body from a tree, he knocks his competitor unconscious and pockets his stolen money. When he takes wads of cash from a Florida woman's purse, we sense it is an act of revenge against the infiltration by wealthy outsiders that he's noted earlier: "The mountains had been overrun by retirees from south Florida ever since I was a kid. They filled up the streets and highways with their long Cadillacs" (334). With his remaining (superficial) shame, he hopes not to see anyone he knows, and he shuns naked bodies because they embarrass him. While all Morgan's narratives describing veterans' dysfunction and anxieties are subtle anti-war stories, this one seems explicitly so. The narrator sees the crash scene as a battlefield: "at no time in Nam had I seen this many bodies" (331), or "Nothing I had glimpsed in the infantry was more sickening" (335). But his point that just surviving is a fight—for instance, against drought or plant disease or falling planes that wipe out crops—complicates this story's portrayal of a world gone awry.

The story's title, "The Balm of Gilead Tree," compels a reading of its spiritual wilderness and paradoxes in terms of biblical allusion. Hiding and scavenging in an apple orchard, the narrator chews on a Balm of Gilead tree twig, tasting the spicy, physically curative salve that the biblical book of Jeremiah presents as spiritual medicine. But spiritual healing does not come. The narrator ultimately crawls through a muddy ditch contaminated by the chemicals that have been sprayed on the apple trees, accompanied by a snake that has entered the garden along with burnt fuel, corpses, and greed. Crossing the edge of the orchard boundary to get to the smoky scene where the main plane parts fell, this panicked protagonist "wills himself out of the orchard"[39] and slithers on the ground, losing his humanity in the pursuit of cash. He is not unlike other characters in the collection whose pursuit of gain or errors in judgment represent a fall from innocence. From "The Tracks of Chief de Soto," which opens the collection, to this last story's horrific crash scene, characters show a lack of compassion for others and for the environment. Grimes rightly calls *The Balm of Gilead Tree: New and Selected Stories* Morgan's "jeremiad against the ever-encroaching materialism of American life into the Eden that was once Appalachia" as he points again to Hemingway-influenced stylistic devices such as repetition and irony.[40] Part of the irony in "The Balm of Gilead"—the story, the story collection, and the African American spiritual that shares the same title—is that Jeremiah 46:11 says that "in vain" will the balm be used, "for thou shalt not be cured" (KJV). We are left wondering what will make the wounded whole. And yet, this story closes with the narrator expecting to be "home free" once he reaches the new road; human resilience presents the possibility of hope in our fallen world.[41]

Two stories in Morgan's fourth collection, *As Rain Turns to Snow and Other Stories*, however, give no indication that human beings are learning to control the machine age's threats. "The Cliff" is an action-filled industrial-age tale following a runaway bulldozer through a mountain town, with the unsolved mystery of who started the unmanned machine on its way. The huge Caterpillar leaves its interstate construction site during lunch hour, when its driver takes his buddies to play video games on his truck computer. The possible culprits tell the tale of development: maybe one of the many local people upset that the new highway is taking their land started the machine and jumped off; maybe an environmental activist trying to stop development did it; or maybe, if the driver failed to turn the machine off, it takes off on its own, a possibility meshing with Morgan's personification of the big Cat that revs its own engine to maintain forward momentum. Crawling over cars, buildings, and walls, the machine almost kills a baby, explodes gas tanks, and destroys shiny new Buicks as well as a bank building and safe, leading horrified bystanders to find their wits enough to dive for bills and coins, similar to the way people steal from the crash victims in "The Balm of Gilead Tree." When the narrator, who had experience driving tanks during the Vietnam War, finally jumps into the cab, he faces near death from an oncoming train and a fall over a cliff that the dozer lumbers down before he gets it stopped in a hayfield, proud that his heroism impresses his girlfriend. Morgan's title implies that humans may be throwing themselves off a cliff with uncontrolled mechanization. We almost have a sense of dark humor here, with a policeman trying to shoot the Cat's controls, and the gawking crowds running behind and away from the giant machine, unthinking victims of technological advance.

A related story features several layers of collapse. A breakdown of marriage appears again in "Bird Wars," though here, it is a possible reason a teenaged culprit, angry that his mother has left, taunts his great aunt and uncle not only by shooting birds but also by running his loud motorcycle, another machine in the garden that the small mountain farm used to be. The narrator, Matty, no longer understands this changing world that has lost "ties of fellowship and work." [42] Kinship bonds are gone despite her efforts to excuse her sister's grandson for his destruction and despite her repeated mantra that he is family. Willard's father also shows weakened familial loyalty, ignoring Matty's pleas that he control the boy's destructive behavior and accusing her and Art of hurting his son when they stand by their chicken house and cause him to skid during a motorcycle rampage. Matty's world has been moving into modernity for decades. She stopped cracking walnuts for homemade cakes when she went to work at an instrument plant. She laments that pesticides being sprayed on crops are killing wildlife and that acid rain is killing balsams. A major tie to her past, the birds serenading in the mingled mulberry and walnut trees in the old chicken yard bring her special pleasure and symbolize her passion for nature. When Willard shoots these birds, his action signifies his disrespect for the older generation as well as his disregard for the ecosystem that chemical makers display on a larger scale. Matty's observation that the many species of birds vying for the same rich harvest in entwined tree leaves seem to be at war, as though they have "chosen sides according to their different colors" (50), articulates the sad irony that living things seem disposed to fight. After Matty discovers that Willard has shot hundreds of those beautiful singers and stacked their bodies like wood, she perhaps now wonders whether Art's assessment of Willard's abnormality might be correct. Even so, Morgan has made his point about painful family conflict and the harmful, unnecessary demolition of the natural world.

Aging in an Industrialized World

While Morgan's stories progressively portray aging characters like Matty, his first collection also reflects his childhood intimacy with older generations. In "Night Thoughts," Lily is stuck in a nursing home, a sign of cultural change noted in her thinking that she "wanted to die at home" like her parents and sister[43] rather than in a facility with bland food and pills to keep the patients quiet. Convinced that the night staff tries to kill her by setting fire to and bulldozing the building, Lily thinks of the hell preachers described as she imagines the loud machine crashing through the walls. Her memories paint a modest early twentieth-century life, including a suitor who is torn between her and her sister (though neither of them ever married) and a life in poverty that includes trapping birds for food. Lily remembers once tricking her sister into eating a rat she pretended was a bird, and she reviews a long list of other wrongdoings that she thinks her present predicament is punishment for, including breaking up couples and faking an acceptance of Jesus. Her visions of the nursing home staff crawling through flames add to the story's critique of religious teachings' psychological effects, as Lily projects hellfire onto those she sees as enemies. But her thoughts about her nephew George are equally significant: with his power of attorney and right to sell the homeplace, Lily is certain that he wants her to die before she uses up all the money. Her surety that the machine is coming for her and that no neighborhood residents will hear the commotion because they are inside their houses watching television offers a sad statement about aging and dying in the modern world. This story seems to connect to Morgan's Aunt Wessie's experiences in a nursing home near Hendersonville. Explaining his poem "Wise Virgin" to interviewer Robert West, Morgan says that Wessie—who kept him when he was small after the death of his grandmother, Julia—once doused her roommate with a pitcher of water, thinking she was extinguishing a fire.[44]

Some older characters do find a bit of delight in the world changing around them, such as the father in "Cracklin' Bread" and other characters in Morgan's second story collection. The narrator of "Mack" is another of these types of senior citizens. This story perhaps grew out of the decline of Morgan's own father. Clyde Morgan died of congestive heart failure in 1991, two weeks after turning eighty-six. The narrator, who is eighty-five, mimics Clyde's affinity for

Scotland and meditates on the solace his dog offers during lonely days that are marked by a shortness of breath and the worry that his heart could stop at any moment. And when the narrator describes Mack peacefully lying at his feet, musing, "If only I could be that much at home in the world,"[45] he certainly reflects Morgan's observation that his own father seemed to be an anachronism in modern society.

Overall, "Mack" is an affirmative story, although it is rife with sadness, too. It establishes basic human solitude, and the narrator's interiority contrasts his feelings with others' views of him. Even his wife Annie, the name Morgan gives his mother in *The Road from Gap Creek*, tires of her husband's care and, like Lorna in "Tailgunner," she seems oblivious to how curt she often sounds. The narrator's border collie, by contrast, treats him kindly and gives him purpose. In fact, the retired narrator, who still needs satisfying work, muses that he and Mack have become each other's employment. Morgan once told Jeff Daniel Marion that he tries "to create verbal spaces in which other *things* and animals, not just people, can be heard,"[46] and this story approaches that goal as the narrator articulates what humans can learn from dogs. They hold no grudges, for instance, and do not put on airs—traits humans might well emulate. Mack encourages the speaker not to give in yet to his depression and impending death, suggesting that he get up and move since he will have plenty of time later to "become the elements" in his grave (172), a hint that human bodies become compost like everything else. Similar to the speaker in "Cracklin' Bread," this man notes that connection requires slowing down, and in this story, automobiles symbolize the way that the modern world has replaced kindness with speed. As the speaker and Mack cross lanes of heavy traffic on daily walks, drivers often yell obscenities and insults, making the one driver who stops traffic for them stand out, a representation of hope that compassion has not gone extinct. Another writing goal that Morgan shared with Marion seems to guide his creation of this speaker: "My prime obligation is to communicate that surge of feeling that comes when the ordinary stuff . . . is seen anew."[47] Morgan does that through this sometimes tearful man whose despair about waning breath eases as he learns from Mack that life is "a dance that takes [us] forward . . . along the surface of the earth" (171). His breath—his spirit—flows a little more smoothly as he sees the world from Mack's point of view.

In Morgan's second story collection, "Mack" leads into "The Mountains Won't Remember Us." The novella marks the first time Morgan wrote in a woman's voice, after reading Wolfe's *The Web of Earth*, and its female narrator, Sharon, gave Morgan his breakthrough in fiction. In a nursing home recuperating from a foot and lower leg amputation, Sharon, Troy's fiancée in *The Road from Gap Creek*, finds her own voice as she remembers two marriages and, most importantly, her feelings about losing Troy forty-seven years earlier in a plane crash, an accident based upon the death of Morgan's Uncle Robert in England in November 1943. With her determination to walk on her prosthesis mirroring her resolve to come to terms with her past, Sharon moves back and forth between 1990 and scenes she remembers from the past, essentially narrating herself into selfhood by exploring the relationships that defined her. As she analyzes decisions and feelings, she concludes that recalling her past will allow her to forget its pain, thus allowing her to find peace in her final years.

As in *The Road from Gap Creek* and the related story "The Lost State of Franklin," Sharon's quick marriage after her fiancé's death in World War II promptly turns sour. Her husband's jealousy of a dead man makes him destroy Troy's arrowhead collection and paintings, and his anger leaves her unable to act in her own defense. Looking back, Sharon sees that she was "stupid with confusion"[48] when she gives in to Charles's hostility. Paralyzed, she stays in the miserable marriage for fifteen years until Charles leaves her for another woman. That stasis echoes her bewilderment when Troy was killed. His death left her at nineteen with no plan for the future, not unusual for an Appalachian girl in the 1940s who did not have any models for attending college or going elsewhere to find a job. She accepts advice to get on with her life, defined as falling in love with another man. Similar to the army buddy's visit in "The Lost State of Franklin," Troy's friend Robert Trammel visits, but again the jealous husband runs him away before he can talk to Sharon. Trammel's visit gives Sharon her first epiphany—she and Charles will never like each other—but she fails to act on that realization, remaining compliant to social expectations by having two boys. They later turn to criminal behavior and desert their mother.

Tellingly, Sharon realizes that she has sublimated her feelings over the decades and in fact describes her confusion about Troy as "all inside [her], waiting to be pulled out" (197), a line that connects to Troy's search for Indian arrowheads, a detail Morgan mentions in every narrative describing his Uncle Robert and a metaphor for mining the cultural or personal past. This readiness to confront her deep past comes after her second husband, Bill, dies a few short years into the happy union they enter into in their midfifties, evidence that living actively into older age is possible. This unhappily married man divorces to be with Sharon, giving our protagonist another chance to analyze herself as she decides that her life is her own business, despite what gossipers think. Another small epiphany comes when Sharon, before she meets Bill, is fired from her dime store job, a victim of ageism when the managers decide she is too old, in her fifties, to make the sales they expect. Sitting on a bench while dreading the next job interview, she lets the spring sun and robins lull her into ease with her gray hair and her ungrateful, problematic children. She goes home to slice seed potatoes, following the season's call to garden. Again, nature grounds a troubled female character, bringing awareness of what matters in the moment, a step toward understanding past motivations and mistakes.

Between Bill's death and her amputation, Sharon begins an active search for details of Troy's death. The narrative leaves those details murky, just as they were to Morgan's family at the time of Uncle Robert's death. Sharon's research follows Morgan's own process of learning why his Uncle Robert was on the B-17. She even thinks about visiting England, as Morgan did in 1986, when he stood at the crash site and talked to a farmer who witnessed the explosion. In the novella, Sharon's research contributes to her blooming independence and intellectual fulfillment, as she gets a university library pass and writes letters to the National Archives, piecing together bits of information to solve the mystery. Her contacts find Robert Trammel, but he never responds to Sharon's letters. That frustration contrasts with Morgan's ultimate discovery of Uncle Robert's buddy Frank O. Conwell, who contacted Morgan from Arizona in 2012, explaining much of what Morgan had been trying to learn and sharing that he saw Robert's plane explode.[49] Writing the novella before talking to Conwell, Morgan uses what he knew at the time in a seven-page shift to limited omniscient narration that follows Troy in Alconbury, England, as he practices bombing missions with the Eighth Air Force. Morgan blends historical details with Troy's thoughts of Sharon, whose face he often cannot remember. This traumatic section ends with Troy "asleep behind his oxygen mask" after a dropping of incendiary bombs (247). Imagery of smoky mountains back in North Carolina ties that interlude to the main narrative, where Troy's silent ghost appears to Sharon in the nursing home.

The short last section brings Sharon's final self-confrontation and epiphany. Weeping in a catharsis of her resentments, she is surprised to hear anger as she questions the ghost about his and his family's attitude toward her. "'I realize now I was intimidated, and too young and foolish to know it,'" she admits as she recalls Troy's talents that attracted her. Spent, she laughs as she realizes, "The only thing alive is me," before she predicts a soothing sleep that will rejuvenate her for her trip home, compliments of Troy's sister Annie, with whom she has reconnected. The powerful last lines speak not only to Sharon's mining of her past but to the movement of time and the natural world's ultimate endurance that so much of Morgan's prose and poetry portray: "I think what a privilege forgetting is. The fields where we work, and the mountains we look at, even the people coming after us, won't remember us at all. And it's better that way" (250). In this story inspired by Wolfe's female narrative voice, it is worth noting Wolfe's similar lines in "The Four Lost Men," where he imagines presidents Garfield, Arthur, Harrison, and Hayes surveying Civil War battlefield corpses, "knowing the fields will steep to silence after us, the slant light deepen on the slopes, and peace and evening will come back again."[50] Sharon plans to use her newfound peace about this universal order to continue research into Troy's military experiences and to work in her garden. Emblematic of Morgan's characters' solitary contemplation of their place in the world and their mature realization that that place is less important than they first assumed, in her final thoughts Sharon also exudes hope that the earth will survive the damage it incurs from humans' disregard.

In his 2017 collection *As Rain Turns to Snow and Other Stories*, Morgan continues to explore aging as he blends some historically oriented narratives with contemporary pieces set in retirement homes or rehabilitation centers. The transformation suggested by the title runs as a theme through the stories collected here, and some new narrative approaches and subject matter show Morgan's continuing growth into new literary places.

The opening story marks a departure in narrative style. Going beyond the plain prose he has used from the beginning of his career, in "The Burning Chair" Morgan tackles the objective point of view of many Hemingway stories, reminding us of his attraction to Hemingway when he began his writing career. The story emulates stage directions, with no narrative consciousness interpreting the scene. We get a description of what appears in a room, with a little dialogue added six pages in. In a bungalow in the woods, an intoxicated man, Elmer, sleeps as a fire that was started by his cigarette begins slowly creeping along the arm of his chair. Liquor bottles, magazines, prescription bottles, and opened mail clutter the floor and nightstand. The contrast of the stationary man with the flickering fire and the sounds of rain, wind, and a periodically ringing telephone creates an ominous atmosphere. Books, pictures, and mail give the background information. Paperbacks such as *Patton* and *The Great Schweinfurt Raid* suggest a connection to World War II, an association verified by a soldier's photograph featuring Dachau and Berlin directional signs. Pictures of children who favor the soldier and the woman's voice we hear when he finally knocks the ringing phone off its hook tell of a veteran now addicted to pills and alcohol, his family estranged. Unable to get out of the chair, he is barely able to say "fire" into the phone. Understanding that he is in danger, the woman arrives to help. She crawls through a window, beats the flames with magazines, and pours cold water on Elmer before kissing his head and wrapping him in a blanket. Morgan's experiment with language in "The Burning Chair," making the narrative voice removed from the scene, reflects his dive into playwriting with *Homemade Yankees*. With little action except the flame and the woman's entrance, the story works through suggestiveness, making us imagine a wife frustrated with a husband's pain and a miserable man trying to medicate himself with booze, cigarettes, and other chemicals, unable to face the subpoena that lies on the floor. We see the result of his transformation from soldier and father to debilitated, isolated sufferer, a portrait suggesting Hemingway's returning soldiers. Morgan's Air Force Academy comments on Hemingway's understatement resonate with this story's achievement. He lauded the way Hemingway applied Imagism's tenets to his fiction, recounting the "direct treatment of the 'thing'" while also describing the "photographic quality of the writing, even the cinematic quality of it."[51] "The Burning Chair" has that cinematic appeal.

Several stories in Morgan's 2017 collection emphasize sex, which is also a part of Sharon's description of her older-age marriage in "The Mountains Won't Remember Us." The title story, "As Rain Turns to Snow," again seems a bit experimental, with its unexpected plot taking us into dark humor with a first-person, detached narrator. One of three men accompanying a local doctor to his home to catch his wife in the act of adultery, the narrator seems to regret blindly following Dr. Lewis, who has given him work as a handyman in Flat Rock. There is something comical about four men sneaking through rainy woods to do Dr. Lewis's mysterious bidding. When the doctor flings open the bedroom door to expose his wife and a lawyer naked, the narrator joins the laughter. But reading the humiliated man's and Mrs. Lewis's eyes, the narrator obviously feels some sympathy for them. The telling detail comes when he fails to recognize himself in a mirror and then turns away from his image on a second glance, mortified that he participated in this shaming. After Mrs. Lewis dresses and leaves, the narrator listens for a car or horsehoof beats but hears nothing. Then he sees the rain turning to snow, a transformation leaving the woman in the cold. That the narrator reports but does not comment upon seeing Mrs. Lewis leave home for hours when doing work at their house keeps the narration mostly objective. We are left to decide whether we agree with Mrs. Lewis and her lover that Dr. Lewis is indeed a pig and not a cuckold who deserves revenge.

In "Halcyon Days," sex serves the purpose of showing older people accepting change as they get on with life after the death of their spouses. The narrator, Raymond, a widower in a Florida retirement home, lets himself be seduced by an attractive sixty-eight- or seventy-year-old widow as he grieves his wife's death. Their relationship is an affirmation, and it leads to Raymond sleeping better, working out, and playing golf again as he forms friendships and enjoys life. Not romanticizing old age, however, Morgan includes details about a resident dying of a heart attack as the story ends, giving Raymond's friends at the retirement home a chance to come to the new widow's side during and after the crisis, providing the comforting community that Morgan touts in all of his work.

The natural world counters aging's downside in "Dans Les Hautes Montagnes," where the eighty-five-year-old narrator, Raymond Morris, lives miserably in a medical facility, paralyzed by a stroke he experienced more than a year earlier. Even more so than "Night Thoughts," this story comments on the modern world's medical-industrial complex and seems influenced by Morgan's own experiences with his father's years of ill health and perhaps his mother's as well. Raymond thinks that the medical attendants are pretending that they can help him walk again in order to get the $1,500 he pays weekly. The story reflects the outrageous cost and sterile environment of medical service in a time when doctors can keep people alive perhaps too long, as Raymond says, with "fuss and torture."[52] He contemplates suicide, with pills that nurses will not bring or by electrocution with lamp wires and a pan of water. But he is stuck in his bed, dependent upon his pain pill schedule and the orderly who cleans him while wearing earphones that keep people from listening to each other. Raymond's isolation has been worsened by the heart attack of the woman he married just a year before his stroke. His daughter, like his bride's sons, did not approve of that old-age marriage, so he is now estranged from the daughter who should be visiting him. In every way, Raymond's situation is terribly sad, with therapists and nurses shaming him for screaming in pain, often when he is unaware that he is yelling. His only pleasure is coffee, the drink that soothes many Morgan characters in various works of fiction that cover centuries of time.

Raymond's memories and associations with nature provide a counterpoint. The story's title refers to the French botanist Andre Michaux's late eighteenth-century exploration of North American flora. In southern Appalachia, he found the flower *shortia galacifolia* and wrote underneath the specimen in a Paris museum, "Dans les hautes montagnes de Caroline"—"in the high mountains of Carolina." A century later, the assistants of the American botanist Asa Gray searched the high mountains but finally discovered it, the flower locals knew as Oconee Bell, in lower elevations, history that Morgan recounts in his poem "Lost Flower" from *Groundwork*. This misconception parallels the medical staff's failure to understand what Raymond tries to convey. He stops talking, but his brain continues to make connections. Reflecting that *shortia galacifolia* is related only to a flower in China's mountains, and remembering hunting for ginseng, which Michaux taught locals the Chinese would buy, Raymond teaches readers how southern Appalachian natural history relates to the larger world. His reveries on Michaux, the woods, enclosed spaces, and his changing view of death—from a fear of preachers' hellfire to a belief that we "just slip inside the here, out of the now" (91)—distract him from the intense suffering his aged body now endures. His knowledge of his world and his acceptance of mystery suggest that he can exit with a satisfied soul, if only doctors and nurses will stop their charade. Watching Raymond, we think of Morgan's "Go Gentle," a poem he composed after seeing his father angrily resist his end. Countering Dylan Thomas's famous villanelle "Do Not Go Gentle into That Good Night," Morgan's elegy argues for "the right / and gentle passage to that night"[53] when the body's transience takes hold.

In "The Calm," a son deals directly with an ailing father, this time an arthritic and alcoholic father wielding a .44 magnum in his bed, threatening the preacher who wants to pray for him as well as the son who is trying to help. That this fictional father is argumentative perhaps stems from Clyde Morgan's difficult personality after his open heart surgery and the raging that "Go Gentle" describes. Time and again during Clyde Morgan's years of decline, Morgan's mother asked her son to come home to handle his father. He did, of course. In the story, set around Hendersonville, the narrator's mother leaves the husband, who is abusive in his drunken rages. She and her children go to her parents' home in Tryon, thus marking another broken marriage in *As Rain Turns to Snow*. The tense scenes end calmly. When the son finally decides to take the gun away, acting on his moral duty to save his dad, he finds him peacefully passed away. The son's open struggle with obligation in the face of his father's threatening to "'blow [his] damn college brains out,'"[54] seemingly a reference to Morgan's education, articulates the Cornell professor's dilemma of trying to meet obligations in places hundreds of miles apart.

His mother's fretful transition to death sparks "Happy Valley," a story based upon Fannie Morgan's anger at her son for putting her into a rehabilitation and nursing home when he and his sister Evangeline could no longer care for her after she broke a hip. Told from the fictionally named Annie's point of view, the story includes her return to facts that are recorded in the family-based novels: she expects her husband Muir to be waiting in his pickup when she escapes the home but once remembers that he died twenty years earlier, at age eight-six—definite references to Clyde Morgan. Part of Annie's resentment stems from the fact that she quit work to care for her mother through her brain tumor illness, as described in *The Road from Gap Creek*, so she never accepts her son's reasoning that he cannot miss any more work. Morgan made many trips from Ithaca to Green River to care for his mother but did reach a point where he needed to cover classes at Cornell. During her third attempt to escape in the story, Annie slips her wheelchair into a darkened room to hide from employees. She thinks that the body they roll into the room on a gurney is her mother, coming out of brain surgery in Charlotte. Trying to take her mother home with her, Annie pulls the corpse off onto her own body. This incredibly sad story ends ambiguously, similar to "Blinding Daylight," with the blinding light suggesting either the electric lights the attendants turn on or possibly Annie's death. The ironically named Happy Valley Rehab Center and Nursing Home reinforces the theme from "Dans Les Hautes Montagnes," that the modern medical world obscures but cannot erase the ordeals of old age and disease. Writing this story hopefully brought some catharsis of the angst Morgan's mother's admonishment caused him during her last years, and his candid narrative prepares readers to face similar hard times.

Transitioning Religion and Another Portrait of the Artist

Two stories in *As Rain Turns to Snow and Other Stories* take a changing culture into contemporary times by looking at religion and recent technology, exploring the state of affairs in present-day southern Appalachia, where many visitors who drove big automobiles into the mountains in the mid-twentieth century decided to stay and where people now communicate with computers and cell phones. These narratives both revisit and rewrite themes from the earlier stories as well as their reflections on communal ties.

Morgan takes account of a changing Blue Ridge religious culture in "The Church of the Ascension," presenting a sometimes humorous look at the recurring collision between insiders and outsiders as he brings a nudist colony and a female religious leader—an impossibility in the world of Ginny Powell or Julie Richards—into an Episcopal church setting. This story brings earlier religious conflicts into modern times, with the strong female narrator, an Episcopal priest, clothing thirty nudists with choir robes, curtains, and Christmas pageant costumes when they seek refuge from a Baptist and Pentecostal mob whose prayer meeting outside the Rainbow Acres locked enclave turns violent. Some Episcopal congregants have cut ties with the church for allowing a female in the pulpit, and the mob represents the strict, uncompromising religion that Morgan saw in childhood, with its surety that both aging nudists and the priest who protects them are devilish sinners. But the narrator acts on her conviction that she must minister to all people, even when the nudists put her into the category of "'religious people . . . responsible for this kind of hate.'" [55] They too seem biased even though they are correct that not all law enforcement in this "'hick county'" (42) will pursue justice after they were attacked on private property. As the church sustains physical damage from Molotov cocktails thrown through windows, and as a nudist woman dies from a heart attack, the priest uses communion wine, the symbolic blood of Christ, to put out the fire. She willingly transforms her rituals to meet present needs, following her mentor's teaching that the church is not a refuge from the world but is in the world.

Again, Morgan dissolves the boundary between the sacred and the secular, this time in a traditional sacred space rather than in the natural world.

In fact, this open-minded Episcopal priest considers the riot a moment of self-discovery and knows that ministering will continue that journey of growth. Referencing some of Morgan's favorite church reformers, such as Thomas Cranmer, the compiler of liturgies for *The Book of Common Prayer* and a man who was also important to John Trethman, the preacher in *Brave Enemies*, she represents the importance of scholarly study of the past. Yet she envies the preaching talents of Preacher Pritchard, the Green River Cove Full Gospel Tabernacle leader and radio preacher guiding the mob. She urges him to see that Christians should love all people and does not respond to his insults, as she earlier made the most of the personal crisis she faced when her husband unexpectedly left her. Including *Ascension* in the church name, Morgan gives hope and direction for religious institutions and all people to improve their sense of community, bringing sacred and secular outlooks into a common purpose.

Morgan's contemplation of national circumstances, aging, and his own literary legacy seems a probable context for a university professor's pondering the insufficiencies of technology for a satisfactory life of the mind in "Big Words and Fame." As he turns fifty, the history professor at the center of this story looks for a new project examining the relationship of eras, similar to the book he wrote comparing 1960s radicalism to nineteenth-century utopian communities such as Brook Farm, inspired by the Transcendentalists important to Morgan's spiritualism and poetry. The narrator had expected a revolution to follow the idealism of the 1960s, similar to the way the Civil War reacted to the utopian thought of the 1830s and 1840s. But "the only revolution that had occurred since the 1960s was technological," he observes, adding that email, cell phones, and personal computers have given us "radical means of communication, and nothing much to communicate." Morgan adds a critique of modern America: "Congress was more lethargic than ever, the administration more petty and timid and confused, the press more tabloid, and special interests owned government more completely than at any time since the presidency of Grant."[56] Leaving Washington, DC, the site of his supposed sabbatical research, the disaffected narrator goes hiking in North Carolina's Blue Ridge Mountains, where his discovery of a writer from an earlier generation, Stephen Evans, leads to smelly old newsprint and conversations with living humans, his favorite kind of research. As usual in Morgan's work, a connection with the past transforms perspective, as the scholar realizes that his own frustrations pale in comparison to those faced by a hermit little appreciated by his contemporaneous world.

Stephen Evans, whose deserted cabin the narrator encounters on the hiking trail, shares many of Morgan's values. Newspapers from the 1930s feature Evans's poems on nature as well as his articles on nineteenth-century customs and Civil War times. In the 1950s, Evans complained about paper mills' pollution and about retirees and tourists building on mountaintops. His sister says that Evans doubted that time exists and that when he talked against war and said Americans should not hate the Japanese because "'all people was the same race,'" his neighbors turned against him, especially after local boys started dying in World War II. These were "'crazy ideas,'" his sister Maude believes (157), and she offers her assessment that her brother's constant reading marked him as lazy, a complaint that many intellectuals and writers endure. Locals' aversion to Evans's views led teenaged boys to play a cruel trick on him, adding further physical debilitation to a crippling spinal nerve injury. An eccentric whose self-education people failed to understand or respect, Evans wrote for decades, and his now ruined pages are scattered around the cabin the park service owns. Even his family did not want his writings or his books when he died. This mountain man—whom his niece called "Big Words" because he used an extensive vocabulary and "'read books all the time,'" part of what made him "'weird'" (150)—gained no fame for his forward thought or his verbal art. Pondering this fellow artist's struggles against an indifferent world energizes the historian word-craftsman to follow his passions in research yet to stop judging what he sees as his failures.

The three artists here—Evans, the scholar, and Morgan—create layers wherein we find Morgan pondering not just a changing world where technology may be analogous to the "'strange beings . . . controlling people's minds'" in Evans's story but also what of his own work future generations will find meaningful. The narrator decides that Evans "had looked for an explanation for the craziness of human behavior" (159), a mystery that Morgan, like many writers, explores. This portrait of an artist, like those in "Murals" and "Blinding Light," reveals a writer explaining his urge to research the past, to articulate insights and probe possible meanings of events, to share with readers the role of the arts in a world often blind to their worth. The historian also captures the focused work ethic that fashioned Robert Morgan's prolific literary output: "I would rather be going *toward* something than merely walking," the scholar says (137), a desire that has directed Morgan since his childhood days.

Chapter 6

Poetry's Place: Memory, Nature, Science, Resurrection

Robert Morgan launched his productive literary career as a poet, crafting lines rooted in the soil, people, flora, and fauna of the Blue Ridge Mountains, elucidating the workings of nature with a scientific perspective and metaphoric language that conveys its transcendent mysteries. He established his reputation with eight volumes of poetry before publishing his first story collection, and he turned out poetry books at a steady pace even as his prose publications flourished. Asked about keeping a number of genres going at once, Morgan offers a unified vision:

> Working alternately on poetry and prose has helped sustain me as a writer. When I have finished a project in one genre, or just run out of steam, I have switched to the other form and moved on. But most of my poems and prose are cut from the same cloth, the same preoccupations with memory, family, history, the natural world. While researching history for nonfiction I seem to stumble on many good ideas for poems. Poetry has given me opportunities to explore my interests in science and technology, tools, and the history of science.[1]

His poetry indeed complements his prose, unlocking sacredness in the ordinary—in the same way his fiction opens everyday people's lives—and appreciating the universe's complex design.

Poetry's Take on History, Family, Fictional Themes

"Mound Builders," the poem that ends his collection *Terroir*, provides an example of themes that cross genres to reveal the wholeness of Morgan's vision. Here, he invites United States citizens to confront the colonialism of our founding. The poem explores how Georgia's Creek Indians built flood refuge mounds from corpses and relics signifying tribal beliefs. As the Creeks "deposited their dead, their kin, / in ceremonial heaps," so too must we "[stand] atop" the "sacred dirt" of our own past, his speaker implores: "all of us rely, and must, / on our traditions and the deep / ancestral memories and ways / to bear us up and get us through / the deadly and uncertain days, / sustaining breath and sight and hope / on residue and legacy / of those beloved who came before / and watch us from the glittering stars." [2] Beyond a plea to discover blood-related predecessors, implicit in these lines are the national erasure of Indigenous people's cultures—accentuated in *Terroir*'s "Land Stealer," the Shawnee term for a surveyor's compass used to mark boundaries of land for settlers' claims—and, in "uncertain days," the risks of destroying the earth's balance. Stars sheltering souls as well as tangible remains of ancestors signal the unity of history, spirituality, and science that Morgan conveys with ease.

Numerous poems capture Morgan's own ancestral memories, paying tribute to individual family members who are important to his fiction. His father, for instance, is the subject of "Working in the Rain" and "Mowing," *Topsoil Road* poems featuring Clyde Morgan engaged in two of his favorite activities; both show his penchant for isolating himself from family and a capitalistic world. *Dark Energy*'s "Heaven's Gate" captures his mother's fortitude that Morgan ascribes to her fictional counterpart, Annie Richards Powell. *Sigodlin*'s "Sunday Keeping" features Uncle William, William Velmer in *The Road from Gap Creek*, inspecting crops on Sunday afternoons, keeping close to the land. "White Autumn" describes Great-Grandmother Delia, in her old age in her home that taught Morgan much history, reading and drinking coffee as "she ruled a tiny kingdom" of family.[3] In "Chant Royal," published in *At the Edge of the Orchard Country*, Morgan applies this old French form to the life of Grandpa Hamp Levi, Hank of *Gap Creek*. Critic P. H. Liotta lauds Morgan's execution of this difficult form, its play with sound meeting all the rhyming and repetition requirements. In this poem, Hamp meets Julia Capps as she cuts wood with her mother, just as *Gap Creek* describes, and the same collection's "Bare Yard" shows Grandma Julia sweeping with broom sedge, as rural women did before readily available mowers made lawns the trend. And as earlier chapters reveal, poems to Uncle Robert and to Frank Pace's Civil War experiences complement Morgan's fictional portrayals of those relatives' engagement in the country's military conflicts.

The impact of religion extends from fiction to poetry as well. The experiences Morgan's grandmother Sarah had speaking in tongues (translated to Ginny's experiences in *The Truest Pleasure*) become the subject of *October Crossing*'s "The Holy Laugh," named for the phenomenon that sometimes accompanies Pentecostal worshippers' dancing and speaking in tongues. "Holy Cussing," also in *October Crossing*, describes transported believers' cascade of profanity, a shocking expression of holy spirit. Morgan explores his thinking about these practices more personally in "The Gift of Tongues," a poem he finally wrote at age forty to describe his unease with his father's breaking into that unknown language. His speaker remembers "savoring the gift of silence," once escaping the church to stand under soothing pines.[4] This poem shows Morgan following his own advice to "'write where the pain is,'" as his former student Jesse Graves says Morgan suggests.[5] For Morgan, poverty, mountain diction and idioms that he stopped using when formally educated, and certainly the embarrassment of Pentecostal services that he felt as a child, provide opportunities to embrace what he once found discomforting. Resolving mixed emotions about his past surely connects to his feeling that the Appalachian material chose him.

Another motif tying Morgan's poetry to his fiction is the physical work defining his ancestors' lives. "Carpet Tacking" (from *Dark Energy*), "Cleaning Off the Cemetery," "Harrow," "Hay Scuttle" (from *At the Edge of the Orchard Country*), "Canning Time," "Burning the Hornet's Nest," "Burnoff" (from *Groundwork*), "Polishing the Silver," "Sharpening a Saw" (from *Topsoil Road*), "Moving the Bees" (from *Sigodlin*), and "Turpentine the Dog" (from *Land Diving*) explain processes that generation taught generation. In these poems, Morgan commends his ancestors' self-sufficiency and skill. As critics have pointed out, building is a specific type of masculine work Morgan explores in both genres. Randall Wilhelm's "Bricking the Text: The Builder in Robert Morgan's Mountain World" elucidates constructed spaces and structures— hogpens, smokehouses, potato holes—as metaphysical and creative expressions, where laboring hands fit human existence into a given landscape. Morgan clearly sees rural craftsmen as artists, and he often employs the language of building for his work with words. Pondering glaciers, extinct animals, Cherokees, frontier settlers—all the earth's past that haunts its current state—he describes his writing as building new wholes from disjointed remains: "All is in fragments, and the recognition and gathering of those shards inspire the cubism of memory and imagination that implies the whole. All the best poetry is fragments joined in new ways, the broken edges sharp enough to cut as well as refract light and attention," he says.[6] The poet works like Muir and Hank as they fit rocks together to build the church in *This Rock*, or like skilled carpenters in "Sigodlin," whose "erect and sure" angles, joists, and studs show the poet the proper technique to create his own "place in creation's / fabric."[7] Morgan emphasizes that the ancestors often worked communally, lending a hand to family or neighbors to can summer fruits, brick a church, or cut encroaching trees from graveyard margins. Volunteering or swapping labor created a sense of cooperation and shared humanity that also prompted people to congregate for release from physical work. Morgan reveals such merriment in "Clogging," where participles—"turning," "stamping," "hammering," "trampling," "nailing," "stepping," "cooling," "stomping," "summoning," and "raising"—convey an energetic, rhythmic reviving of body and soul in a traditional Appalachian dance.[8]

Elegiac poems honoring nonfamily historical figures expand Morgan's regional portrait. *At the Edge of the Orchard Country* opens with "Horace Kephart," depicting that writer in his Great Smoky Mountains camp working on *Our Southern Highlanders: A Narrative of Adventure in the Southern Appalachians and a Study of Life among the Mountaineers*, his influential book, first published in 1913, on rural Appalachian geography and culture. *Sigodlin* offers "The Body of Elisha Mitchell," recounting that geologist's 1857 deadly fall near the mountain named in his honor after he identified it as the highest peak east of the Mississippi River. *Sigodlin* also shares that a well-known Georgia poet and musician died about twenty miles from Morgan's Zirconia home. "Sidney Lanier Dies at Tryon 1881" mentions Lanier's Confederate army service but focuses on his flute-playing, his "notes and language," the "pause / and the continuing line" with which his later fellow poet connects.[9] Also amplifying the area's history is "Looking Homeward," Morgan's homage in *At the Edge of the Orchard Country* to the Blue Ridge artist who was most critical for inspiring his own career. A second poem on that famous writer follows his trips to the West in the 1930s. Morgan composed "Ancient Talk" to accompany his keynote address at the 2013 Thomas Wolfe Society meeting in Boise, Idaho. In these lines, he interprets Wolfe's awe at the sequoias and the majestic Rockies as a "suggestion that we find our own / communion with the noble trees / and rocks and diamond peaks, and pause / to see and listen to the whisper / of our now fragile hemisphere."[10] As he links Wolfe's life in the twentieth century's first three decades to our twenty-first century as well as to geological formation, Morgan evokes the sense of community spanning time and space that is essential to people's acting for planetary health.

Many poems point to human culpability for ecological wounds. "Topsoil Road" evokes Solomon and David's roadbuilding in *The Hinterlands* as settlers trek into the hills:

> Wheels sliced
> into leaves and tore the humus,
> banged on roots and rocks and ground
> the topsoil in the rush toward

the horizon, to step into
the future the West pulled them to.
No creek or rocky shelf could stall
such exhilaration. Their passion
poured in floods along the ruts as
oxen bawled and stabbed the dirt with
hooves and horses tamped the gravel.
When it rained every track became
a runnel, became a run or
ditch becoming a gully in
yellow clay and red, the wash burned
deep in wet weather reaching to
bedrock and subsoil and making
new horizons in dust as traffic
plowed and plowed again thaw furrows
and puddle holes, until the road
was more pit than passageway, more
obstacle than access, and yet
another must be found to soothe
the unbearable urge to stride
beyond and back, as eros fed
erosion and wander vision
vanished quick as snow in May.[11]

Lengthy sentences running from line to line suggest the motion of wagons
and animals on the arduous journey of opening the mountains to opportunity
but also to ruin, such as the slaughter Morgan laments in "Passenger Pigeons"
in *At the Edge of the Orchard Country*. Morgan's play on etymology—the Greek
"eros," signifying desire, feeding "erosion," whose Latin root *erodere* means "to
gnaw away"—goes to the heart of human shortsightedness. "Big Bone Lick,"
charting a transformation mentioned in *Boone*, also declares humanity's deleterious effect. In what is now Boone County, Kentucky, Daniel Boone came
across sulfur and salt licks in the early 1770s, a site from the Pleistocene era
that drew mammoths, who found themselves trapped in marshy soil around
springs. The poem describes explorers finding mammoth and sloth ribs and
mastodon tusks: "they saw the ruins of a world / survived by its diminutives,
/ where Eden once gave way and shrank / to just a regular promised land / to
fit our deadly, human scale."[12] Morgan reproves humans' failure to be good
stewards of creation, but his words also hold hope.

Resurrection in Soil and Science, Ambivalence about Technology

Intimating that respect for the natural world begins with understanding its basic processes, many poems scrutinizing Morgan's family homestead turn the repulsive—bejeweled by honest language, cadence, and metaphor—into beautiful renewal. "Manure Pile," for instance, shows a "gold and powerful" decomposition that feeds butterflies before they "shiver off into the sky / where carillons of convection ring."[13] Besides "Manure Pile," *At the Edge of the Orchard Country* gives us two more poems on dung, "Sunday Toilet" and "Earth Closet." The latter helps non-initiates experience the inside of an outhouse, and the former describes Daddy's sprinkling lime to cut the odor in a hog pen, chicken yard, and toilet, transforming feces into talc that flies use as ink for writing on the screen door. "Dung Frolic," in *Sigodlin*, describes community men working together to transfer excrement from livestock stalls to fields as natural fertilizer. Decay and regeneration, the essential Christian trope, are basic to many Morgan poems, such as "Loaves and Fishes," where each atom of a deer carcass is "identified and sorted, hauled / away by scavenging coyotes, / by maggots, worms, bacteria, / each bite sent to its proper place / to feed the needy multitude."[14] One thinks of Whitman's "This Compost," a poem that glorifies soil's ability to transform diseased bodies into fruits and grasses, working its chemistry to turn putrefaction into new life.

Whitman is one of the poets important to Morgan's development in the Romantic tradition, an affinity growing organically from his intimacy with the natural world and its constant renewal. In "The Cubist of Memory," Morgan speaks to the regeneration Whitman describes, connecting earthly processes, the "promise of resurrection" that hymns and church taught, and language's possibilities for recovering or even rectifying the past: "The stuff of poetry is compost, human as well as vegetable, verbal and cultural; but it is the prospect of rising from the rot and ruin that empowers the statement and embodiment of the words."[15] The Romantics' erasure of divisions between the earthly and the spiritual, signified in Emerson's contention that "nature's noblest ministry is to serve as an apparition of God,"[16] gave Morgan perspective on the Baptist and Pentecostal emphasis on otherworldliness. The Romantics' attitude toward science also matched his own. Reflecting on fundamentalism's rejection of scientific learning, Morgan recalls that his early observations of the physical world and his elementary study of Darwin convinced him that "all was in a state of continuous evolution, and nothing was static, not even the stones and mountains." These insights made him welcome science as an "exhilarating" way to understand the world, as British and American Romantics did as well.[17]

Morgan follows these earlier poets in celebrating science, plying its truths, its uncertainties, and its language to explore time, space, and the material world's profundities.

Many poems illustrate how science enhances perception, offering a way to read experience that Morgan practiced in college before turning to creative writing. "Lightning Bug" shows that science and a sense of the divine are not mutually exclusive approaches. It begins with a metaphor extolling the insect as "carat of the first radiance," sending "morse code" that bewilders the speaker, who wonders, "What instrument / panel is on?" Scientific diction describes nature's mechanisms while language such as the Greek *nous*, representing mind or divine reason, evokes its concomitant mystery: "Your noctilucent syllables / sing in the millennium of / the southern night with star-talking / dew, like the thinker sending nous / into the outerstillness from / the edge of the orchard country."[18] The speaker marvels at nature's communication, avowing a theme that directs Morgan's poetic career. In the early collection *Red Owl*, "Cedar" exalts the melodic language of fragrant wood used for chests: "Smell the recorders buried here. / Music lies in the wood / . . . still giving / its breath, radioactive—releasing / a subtle verb for years."[19] Morgan's next volume, *Land Diving*, continues the trope, as "Witch Hazel" describes the plant that Realus gives Petal to end her section of *The Hinterlands*. This shrub waits to flower in autumn (when "cornfields stink / scatologically") to provide bees a place for orgies, "corrupting the / grammar of the seasons for / a mardi gras."[20] These poems reflect ideas about reading the world that Morgan recorded in journal notes in the 1970s: "Science is our new language for talking about experience. The scope of its challenge to a poet could be frightening, except that science is just vocabulary. It is our job to discover its human grammar."[21] Nature's correspondence forms the crux of "Writing Spider," where Grandpa's belief that "the writing spider's runes could spell / a message to the world"[22] connects to the same metaphor in "Ancient Script," where "crows in fields of snowy drifts / resemble black cuneiform, / perhaps a poem from the time / of Sumer or Akkad, a song / of winter's promised passing."[23] Such poems imply that nature's exquisite syntax should spur us to slow our erasure of it.

Nature's cycles embody time, another scientific concept long occupying Morgan's imagination. In his fiction, time's passing directs intergenerational relationships, changes in landscape and culture, and memories. His poetry treats these concerns and often depicts relics of times past, such as hatpins in "Grandma's Bureau," churns and crocks in "Jugs in the Smokehouse" (from *Sigodlin*), or pages recording names and dates in "Family Bible" (from *Topsoil Road*). But his poetry also examines the deep time of astronomy or mineralogy, such as zircons' emergence at earth's dawn. Contemplation of the planet's origins stretches to envisioning a distant future in "Milkomeda," a poem describing the Milky Way's crashing into Andromeda "just several billion years from now," triggering a dance into new planetary schemes, "enhancing possibilities for life / and extra-heavy elements, / restructuring the zodiacs,"[24] birthing a fresh world to continue long after the Anthropocene epoch fades. "Milkomeda" again construes resurrection scientifically, this time welcoming remote cosmic booms. Conscious of his obsession with time, Morgan explains that in one poem, "the future, looking ahead, is seen also as a way of looking back." In ten lines, "Rearview Mirror" describes car drivers looking back as they move forward, metaphorically representing Morgan's rationale for studying history and writing about the past. The "trees and highway, bank and fields" wane as they "split on the present then merge in / stretched perspective, radiant in / reverse, the wide world guttering / back to one lit point, as our way / weeps away to the horizon / in this eye where the past flies ahead."[25] We can assume that Morgan's own interpretation of "Rearview Mirror" conveys his belief about time: "We can only visualize the future in terms of the past."[26]

As Morgan probes the intricacies of natural phenomena, his urge to see correspondences clearly equals his curiosity about the science itself. "Inertia," for instance, explores the paradox of matter's "soaring in its stasis," resisting as "Electrons spin and molecules / twitch." But it also suggests human inertia, our reluctance to reflect or change. We think not just of mass but of people "remaining undisturbed, by poise / of precedence, occupation, / reluctant as a bear to wake / from the immanence and ponder." Etymology again shapes meaning in the last line, "the gravity of mere artlessness."[27] The word *inertia* derives from terms meaning "without art," as Morgan clarifies before concluding that art thus signifies "that which changes." This poem implicitly defends art itself and its ability to advance humans' cognizance. Translating another scientific phenomenon into language, *Sigodlin*'s "Radiation Pressure" moves from a description of photons surging to a clarification that on the earth, "we feel / only slightest pressure, a kiss, / a breath come across the mighty / distances to urge away, while / we're stayed by our very sadness,"[28] correlating the resistance of mass to the weight of human despondency. Among *Dark Energy*'s celebrations of physics is "Neutrino," a twenty-seven-line sentence pondering humans' urge to examine this subatomic particle with the lowest known mass, similar to settlers' compulsion to discover unknown geographical landscapes. Astrophysics comes into play as "Parhelion" describes refractions of sunlight through ice crystals, creating dazzling spots beside the sun that make us question our perceptions, and as "Coriolis Effect" explores the deviation caused by planetary spinning that makes directly reaching our goal impossible. The "swerving routes, and twisting paths" represent life's struggles as well as astrophysical deviations.[29] These poems explaining the workings of the universe give us, as "Dark Matter" makes plain, "honest awe / and curiosity, / and lesson of humility" as we recognize that "what we know is just / a fraction of what is."[30] Speaking of the connection of science and poetry, Morgan refers to several scholars who point out that both embrace uncertainty. Poets and scientists operate with openness to possibilities, and Morgan, seeing science as "a tool for both the imagination and memory,"[31] plies it to deepen his analyses of a fascinatingly complex and often mystifying world.

Bringing scientific scrutiny to the machine age, Morgan tends to admit the ambiguity of industrialization's effects. "Man and Machine" describes his cousin Luther's passion for driving his tractor, riding it like a "smelly beast" as he jams its brakes and blasts across fields. Not working except with a machine, Luther comes to define himself by a motor's power, reminding us of the dynamo's dominance in stories such as "Murals" or "Blinding Daylight," although Luther's transformation productively makes the fields "new" after he plows all night.[32] This machine-obsessed farmer might have been on Morgan's mind as he composed "Engine," appearing in *Dark Energy*'s last section, devoted to mysterious forces that energize our bodies, our galaxies, and our imagination. The poem depicts humans' reliance on machines and disquiet about our devotion to their power: "A motor is a kind of god / with blood of grease and oil upon / its altar."[33] Religious diction throughout this poem exposes our pledge to and reverence for technology's seemingly supernatural capabilities, illustrating Morgan's belief that in the twentieth century, science replaced traditional religion as "the most essential authority."[34] Another poem presents the logic of that veneration. "MRI" describes the magnetic resonance imaging medical machine that has improved health care, relating sounds the patient hears inside the metaphorically termed "white crypt" to birdsong and insect calls,[35] describing the potentially life-saving machine in both negative and positive terms. In these and other poems, Morgan's explorations of technology's secrets parallel his descriptions of the essential workings of natural phenomena, such as rotting wood in "Nurse Log" or dying in "Cry Naked," two poems in *Terroir*. His scrutiny of technology also resonates with his view that nature and past civilizations have left their mark: "Our language and age are writing us, in ways we can't always see,"[36] he says. As the machine age evolves, he records the ways it also scripts our lives.

Poetic Forms, Music's Place, Sacredness in the Ordinary

This fascination with language fed Morgan's intensifying interest in prosody and form. From early imagistic, compressed lines, he experimented briefly with incantatory poetry in the 1970s, influenced by Christopher Smart's *Jubilate Agno* ("Rejoice the Lamb") as well as his rereading of the Bible and his memories of prophesying sermons.[37] In *Iron Mountain Review*, fellow Appalachian poet Michael McFee notes that the incantatory *Mockingbird*, which appears first in *Trunk and Thicket* and later as a standalone book, encapsulates qualities and themes that are central to Morgan's poetic career as it also shows his willingness to let a speaker reveal a connection to place and people. Many lines signify Morgan's coming fully to his southern Appalachian subject: "Create brief / Yoknapatawphas . . . . Take Saluda River / and Shoestring Gap . . . Don't cringe at / the thought of Grandma with her birch toothbrush. . . . / Reject the dryhides and / take the holy dance." The chanting voice convinces the poet to embrace his Green River world, to find "[his] own resurrection"[38] in this landscape urging him to fashion lines that reflect its truths.

Complex forms allow Morgan to play with the carefully measured line that becomes a hallmark of his poetry. He creates a villanelle in "Subduction," a poem published in the early collection *Green River* that conveys earth's geological transformations in five tercets and a final quatrain whose eight-syllable lines exude an ease that counters the hills' and river's constant movement. Eventually, the eight-syllable line emerges as a favorite form, enabling him "to free the voice of the poems" as he concentrates on sentences. In fact, Morgan maintains that adding "the arbitrary mathematical element to poems was a breakthrough," teaching him that "there is, in fact, no necessary connection between content and form" but that any subject fits any form. A poem's pleasure, he contends, comes partly "from the way the natural cadence of a sentence can contrast with the arbitrary form it passes through."[39] Morgan weds his eight-syllable line to Shakespearean-sonnet rhyme in three quatrains and a couplet to describe his father's blowing breath to cool hot cereal in "Care" (from *Topsoil Road*). Another form that he seems to enjoy is the pantoum, its required pattern of repeated lines challenging him to match meaning to form. Successful pantoums include "Mica Country," where Morgan weaves repeated lines to describe "the glare of blinding poverty / reflected in the luminous soil / here in the poorest mine country" and contrasts the riches of manure, dirt, and minerals with the economic poverty of his southern Appalachian place.[40] In the pantoums "Hearth" (from *Topsoil Road*) and "Audubon's Flute" (from *Sigodlin*), the consistency of an eight-syllable line again echoes the meditative mood that repeated lines create, and in the latter poem, that repetition contributes to an incantatory musicality that simulates Audubon's flute, enchanting readers as the bird lover's music charms deer and heron.

One of many poems honoring naturalists important to Morgan's worldview, "Audubon's Flute" proclaims the significant role that music plays in

Morgan's poetry, not just in cadence and sound but in subject matter as well. *Land Diving*, for instance, includes "Concert," featuring Aunt Wessie playing a pump organ, the one that her father Hamp Levi buys for eighty bushels of sweet potatoes in *Sigodlin*'s "New Organ," a poem that connects the physical work of growing sweet potatoes to Wessie's pumping organ peddles to transmute farming labor into a hymn.[41] *Topsoil Road* juxtaposes a quartet of poems that showcase instruments and their builders. Fiddle and dulcimer makers look for aged timbers that create "sweeter, more / mellow sounds" in "History's Madrigal," while in "Tail Music," those craftsmen place a snake rattle inside the box "to swell / the resonance" of the "devil's instrument," the name the church leaders gave the fiddle for the way it inspired sinful, all-night dancing.[42] The speaker of "Mountain Dulcimer" marvels at the aching sadness the wood and strings create, the instrument lying on a woman's lap evoking the Pietà lamenting the crucified Christ. Still centering on mountain music, "The Grain of Sound" lauds a banjo maker's skillful search for the right wood grain to achieve the desired sound, the tree singing again through the hide of a cow, skunk, or cat that is stretched to enhance the sad twang. An intriguing poem highlighting Morgan's attention to music, mathematics, and science is "Music of the Spheres," also in *Topsoil Road*. Its title alludes to the mathematician Pythagoras, who is credited with discovering that the universe is based on numbers, even musical harmony intervals and heavenly bodies whose mathematical relationship produces the famed "music of the spheres." Many poems illustrate Morgan's ability to hear that music everywhere, even in power lines, as he shows us in "Even Me" and "High-Tension Lines," both appearing in *Dark Energy*. That he began composing music in his head early in life, creating a "musical correlative" for all his experiences,[43] helps to explain the way he links science, history, music, and nature so tightly in his poetic lines. Sensing this correlation freed him to explore the secret essence of the most mundane objects in his poetry.

Language's musicality plays a role in a series of anagrams that form one of Morgan's most lauded poems, one that Bhisham Bherwani calls his "ars poetica."[44] "Mountain Graveyard" taps a core of Morgan's literary themes in transposed letters arranged to evoke a tombstone's shape. Here is the poem in its entirety:

stone   notes
slate   tales
sacred   cedars
heart   earth
asleep   please
hated   death.[45]

"Notes," "slate," and "tales" connote writing and storytelling, while "sacred cedars" encapsulate Morgan's tenet about the natural world. We sense his attachment to buried ancestors as "please" conjures Morgan's aching need to dig deep into the past and into the earth itself, the art of poetry, of prose, and of living requiring attention to the mysteries there revealed. Collection titles such as *Land Diving* and *Groundwork* signify this desire to get inside the earth, and numerous poems, such as "Cellar" (from *Red Owl*) or "Earth Closet" and "Potato Hole" (from *At the Edge of the Orchard Country*), penetrate its secrets in enclosed spaces redolent of graves. Morgan's extensive search into family and national stories as well as into geological history reverberates through this ars poetica that speaks with the decorum and subtlety of all his work. "Mountain Graveyard" connects to many other poems, including his early "Mound Builders," published in *Red Owl*. That poem's metaphoric ending line, "The dirt is our ancestors," suggests soil's sacred, transforming work as well as the connection between past and present that all Morgan's work extols.

Morgan returns to the restfulness of the simple yet complex "Mountain Graveyard" in a later cemetery evocation that counters burial's supposed stasis with vertical motion. "Living Tree" taps science in a contented statement about humans' relationship to nature as the speaker explains that ancestors planted junipers in cemeteries "to soak up spirits of the dead / through roots into the growing wood." Here, a first-person speaker wishes to be part of a juniper's composition, not of his own accord but from nature's resolve: "I like to think / that when I'm gone the chemicals / and yes the spirit that was me / might be searched out by subtle roots / and raised with sap through capillaries / into an upright, fragrant trunk." [46] Nature is the speaker's ideal for a useful, concrete afterlife. These lines, unusual in Morgan's poetic oeuvre in presenting a first-person speaker, again confirm the resurrection inherent in the tangible world that we take for granted. The sacredness in the ordinary could not be clearer.

Chapter 7

Final Words: The Morgenland Elohist

I n 1998, Robert Morgan delivered a lecture at Cornell University titled "Nature is a Stranger Yet," a reference to a line from Emily Dickinson he cherishes. A later Dickinson passage elucidates the metaphor: "That those who know her know her less / the nearer her they get." The paradox that studying nature, or any subject, makes it more enigmatic seems foundational to Morgan's literary career, as his comments about his writing about southern Appalachia make clear:

> Paradoxically, the more we study a place, the longer we know a place, the more mysterious it becomes. The more we respond to experience, the more we discover there is to respond to. . . . I wrote hundreds of poems and dozens of stories where I tried to communicate the mystery and fear, the terror and resentment, the harshness and futility, the contradictions and cruelties, as well as the loyalties and kinships and beauties, of the world I had grown up in. I was never interested in portraying a pastoral world, a simpler world, but in dramatizing the complexities of the seemingly plain, the sharpness of the everyday, the cruelties of the conventional, the isolation of the rural. I wanted to show the thresholds of the theatrical in the ordinary.

He reflects, too, on the effect that moving to Ithaca had on his writing:

> The more I walked among the red pines and battlement-like gorges of Treman Park, in awe of the drama of that landscape, the more I wrote about Green River, about the speech of the Southern highlands. Cornell gave me a perspective from which to see and explore the world I had grown up in. The more I resolved to write about the North the more I could only write about the South. And the more I wrote about family history and folklore, the more I discovered there was to write. The more I resisted those subjects, the more they claimed and possessed me. The

poetry of the Blue Ridge stuck to me like an infection I could not shake off. I could only cool my fever by writing more and more.[1]

Morgan goes on in this lecture to confess that looking back at a quarter-century of work, he saw that he had failed to seize that Green River world in language, at least to his own satisfaction. But he deemed that recognition a gift, and he saw his writing up to that point as a necessary preparation for going forward. He continued to follow his memory and research into the physical work and spiritual lives of his family as he also charted the changing landscape of his Mountain South. As his understanding of universal order evolved, he coupled mathematical and scientific precision with his insider's knowledge of southern Appalachian culture and land to become an essential poet and master storyteller, making his own art from the poetry embodied by his rural highlands.

Daniel Boone, Robert Morgan, and Appalachian Mythos

In his biography of Daniel Boone, Morgan offers a metaphor that resonates with his own life and literary career. The idea for the metaphor comes from Annette Kolodny's study of American women's writing about westward expansion, *The Land Before Her* (1984), a book that *Boone* cites several times. Kolodny argues that frontiersmen saw the wilderness in sexual terms, as virgin land to be taken, while frontier women saw it in nurturing terms, as a fertile garden to be cultivated and preserved for sustenance. Explaining that Daniel Boone spent summers as a boy in a cabin in the woods with his mother, tending cattle and sheep about five miles from their homestead in Oley, Pennsylvania, Morgan names that forest Boone's "mother world, a place of shadows and mystery, infinite diversions and pleasure."[2] Boone, he says, remained closer to that mother world than to the masculine, father world of trade, business, and authority. We see Kolodny's elevation of women's role in exploration and settlement in Morgan's portrayal of Boone's wife, Rebecca, as a bold, strong worker in her own right, as well as in his portraits of Petal Jarvis in *The Hinterlands* and other women in his fiction. We might also see that Morgan's attraction to Kolodny's contention stems from personal experiences: his own mother teaching him the intimate details of the natural world and her will to prevail, even in the secondary role she played as a woman; his affinity for Romanticism's understanding of nature; even his father's draw to the wilderness, perhaps an instinctive attempt to reconnect with his own mother, Sarah, who died when he was seven, leaving him distant from the masculine world of commerce that flummoxed him for the rest of his life.

Kolodny's discussion of the landscape as symbolic of humans' worldview seems pertinent as well. Seeing landscape as territory to be dominated means that we treat it harshly, whereas seeing landscape for its sustaining qualities leads us to cherish it, a distinction underlying Morgan's poetry and fiction that calls attention to the natural world's beauty or our failure to consider its health. Morgan's Blue Ridge farm became his mother world, a garden that he could not escape cultivating through language despite wanting to escape the hard work and poverty he knew there.

But Morgan's focus on the place where he grew up does not narrow his view or make him *just* an Appalachian writer. He connects the specific place to larger themes and concerns at every turn, giving portraits of war veterans' alienation, class prejudice, poverty, ingenuity, gender discrimination, or humans' deleterious effects on the environment. In the last chapter of *Boone*, he explicitly examines the reciprocal relationship of literature and history, one of his significant contributions not just to southern Appalachian studies but to literature itself. Early on, the Boone legend personified "America's ideal of itself," he declares,[3] and it became part of the national consciousness that influenced the country's first writers: James Fenimore Cooper, Ralph Waldo Emerson, Henry David Thoreau, Walt Whitman. He adds that even British Romantics such as Samuel Taylor Coleridge and William Wordsworth knew the legend of Boone and read William Bartram's *Travels*, a record of the naturalist's exploration of the American South in the mid-1770s, with scientific descriptions of flora and fauna as well as sympathetic descriptions of the Indian tribes he encountered. Morgan mentions Bartram in his fiction as well as in his poems commenting on early Appalachia or the later loss of plants and animals that the naturalist depicted. Proving that notions of Americans' independence and resourcefulness were born out of Boone's living the romantic ideal, Morgan quotes long sections of Whitman's poetry. He ties young Boone's discovery of the wilderness as he summered with his mother to Whitman's "There Was a Child Went Forth" and the adult, noble figure of Boone to "I Sing the Body Electric." Contextualizing the poetry, Morgan elevates literature for people who are not conversant with it. As he breaches divisions between history and the arts, these connections also illustrate his cohesive vision and sense of community. Simultaneously, he promotes the reality of Appalachia's central place in the American story.

Boone's appeal for Morgan includes more than the heroic figure's romanticism. The two sides that he sees in this frontiersman create another point of common identity. For as the biography explains, Boone lived in the middle ground between white settlers and Indians, between his family community and his long treks alone in the wilderness. Morgan likewise has lived on the edge between contradictory worlds. Comments in "The Transfigured Body: Notes on Poetry from a Journal" credit the geology of his home landscape with inspiring a double vision. He explains that his southern Blue Ridge is "a kind of island of foreign soil floating on the continent," not part of the original continental plate but pushed up and "pinched off by the Atlantic crust." He sees the physical appearance of these rugged mountains as "unsettled and unsettling," a perfect place to birth a poet's images and ideas. He goes on to claim that "in the backwardness and isolation a piece of the American innocence was kept alive," illustrating the paradox that "the marginal and chaotic" can promote solidity and permanence.[4] Ultimately, he found his stability on the fringes that he claims in this essay as his place, borders that he began to sense as a youth witnessing the "contrast of sophistication and poverty" that rich tourists coming to the Blue Ridge made clear. That he "never felt quite at home in Zirconia, even as a child"[5] made his move to New York a relief, but one that paradoxically did not alleviate the yearning for home that his father, who also was never fully comfortable in his twentieth-century southern Appalachian world, always answered. Whereas his father returned after foiled attempts to make his way beyond Zirconia, Morgan stayed the course at Cornell, feeding his longing for home with words. Grounded in a southern Appalachian agrarian space but flourishing at a northern Appalachian elite educational institution, Morgan lives out the two-sidedness he describes in his poem "Double Springs." "I've had one foot in one kind of world . . . and the other in another," he claims. "I've emerged from . . . a virtually nineteenth-century world of small farms, subsistence farming, literally a one-horse farm, water from a spring, light from a kerosene lamp—to a world of electronics, and that gives me a double perspective which is an advantage to a writer."[6] With double perspective as a guide, he creates colloquial fictional voices and formal lyric poetry, women characters whose inner strength outshines the boundaries imposed by their time and place, and fiction and poetry that moves beyond the heroism of settlement, expansion, and war to capture injustices toward Indians, Blacks, the poor, and the earth itself. As he conveys the *outsideness* that many people think he exaggerates about his Blue Ridge home,[7] he erases the significance of that isolation by making readers identity with people whose work and worldview, pain and triumphs he preserves.

Morgan's success in lifting the Appalachian South into the national story relies partly on his choice of narrative voice and tone. When he turned to fiction in the 1980s, Morgan eschewed the sometimes sarcastic portraits of the doleful mountain people that Thomas Wolfe created before him, using the perspective of distance and time to understand those people and let them tell their own stories, as he explains in his essay "Appalachia." He respects his Blue

Ridge ancestors and, in a notable comment revealing his open-minded perceptions, he credits their fierce religious doctrinal debates with training him to be a student of Appalachia and the larger world: "These were intellectual arguments: they were quoting scripture, and arguing about this passage meaning one thing and this another—explication, real hermeneutics—a scholarly tradition."[8] Such validation shows us how to see beyond stereotypes that still plague the nation's view of Appalachia. It also explains how Morgan goes so effectively into his memory of the place where he lived his first sixteen years.

When he directs himself, in those early journal notes on poetry from the 1970s published as "The Transfigured Body," to be "the poet of informed humility, the elohist of topsoil,"[9] Morgan alludes to another binary related to his grounding in biblical texts during a childhood spent in church. As John Lang explains in "Coming Out from under Calvinism," *Elohim* is the Hebrew word referring to "God's role as creator and ruler of all." It is opposed to *Yahweh*, the Hebrew word referring to "the God who enters into a covenant with a chosen people."[10] Morgan's choice of the term *elohist* marks a step in his finding a comfortable place outside the Baptist and Pentecostal fundamentalism of his upbringing. He rejects the notion of chosen people in favor of inclusivity and attention to all creation. Twenty years after his move to the North, Mary C. Williams takes a look at Morgan's poetry collections through *At the Edge of the Orchard Country*, published in 1987, sixteen years after he relocated to New York. She argues that the sense of isolation and loneliness evident in his early books begins dissolving in *Groundwork* (1979) and vanishes in the 1987 collection, where the poems reveal a creator at ease with going back to his home country (only) through language, at ease with exploring what he finds buried there. As *elohist*, Morgan recreates, creates, and connects the southern Appalachian mythos to the country and the world, sometimes implying that past Appalachian values seem superior to a spiritually bankrupt contemporary world, sometimes taking our vision to the mysterious dark matter of astrophysics, and always urging us to examine our place in universal space and time.

Morgan ends his essay "Appalachia" with a suggestion that we all seek knowledge of our past, our home, and our community through time: "The blue valleys, the fog-haunted coves, the tireless milky waterfalls, are still there, but the people, the people with wisdom in their hands and humility in their hearts, have slipped away forever, unless we find them in our own words, and in our own hands and hearts." Chronicling legends, history, and underrepresented voices, he captures the beautiful topography evoked here but also describes a landscape transformed by the consumer-driven, mechanical age that has altered the Blue Ridge community he knew as a child, showing that chemical sprays and bulldozers blind humans to the sacredness of the land as their work distances them from it. Not arguing for a return to the poverty and isolation of the southern Appalachia he knew—he celebrates the jobs, cultural events, schools, and diversity of the region that modernization has brought—he yet wants to preserve the past in cultural memory so that future generations can know the Cherokees and their hunting ranges, the wild turkeys and panthers, the vistas seen by people whose grit and blemishes moved our world forward through time.[11] Preserving Appalachian distinctiveness in an America becoming rather homogenized through commercialization and the influence of technology, his work conveys with clear-eyed affection the geography, people, and happenings of the morgenland that make it always his home.

Notes

PREFACE

1. Morgan, "Literary North Carolina."

CHAPTER 1

1. Wright, "Interview: Robert Morgan," 185.
2. Anderson, "A Conversation with Robert Morgan," 34.
3. Marion, "Interview with Robert Morgan," 4–5.
4. Morgan, "Zircon," *Dark Energy*, 72.
5. Ballard, "Interview with Robert Morgan," 119.
6. Roberts, "'Wonderfully Simple,'" 12.
7. Faulkner used this phrase in a 1956 interview, published in *The Paris Review Interviews*, vol. II, Picador, 2005, 57.
8. Morgan's 2005 Ehle tribute comments appear in Roberts, "'Wonderfully Simple,'" 21.
9. Email to author, February 14, 2016.
10. Morgan, "Wilma Dykeman," 276.
11. Morgan, "Writing the Living Voice," 182.
12. Morgan, "Fred Chappell's *Midquest*," *Good Measure*, 94–95.
13. Morgan, "Hemingway," 140–41.
14. Booker, "Interview with Robert Morgan," 18.
15. Lang, "Coming Out," 262.
16. Morgan, *Mountains, Machines, and Memory*, 197.
17. Morgan, *Mountains, Machines, and Memory*, 204.
18. Morgan, "Work and Poetry," 174.
19. Email to author, December 22, 2010.
20. Email to author, August 30, 2012.
21. Bizzaro and Bizzaro, "The Poetics of Work," 97.
22. Harmon, "Imagination, Memory, and Region," 29.
23. Marion, "Interview with Robert Morgan," 4.
24. Miller, "Appalachian Literature at Home," 21.
25. Morgan, "Double Springs," *Land Diving*, 5.
26. Morgan, "Field Theory," *At the Edge of the Orchard Country*, 68.

CHAPTER 2

1. Welty, "Place in Fiction," 130, 128.

2.   Booker, "Interview with Robert Morgan," 18.
3.   Morgan, "The Cubist of Memory," *Good Measure*, 10.
4.   In a June 3, 2021, email to the author, Morgan explains that he recently learned that his ancestors hailed from North Wales.
5.   Anderson, "A Conversation with Robert Morgan," 34–35.
6.   Morgan, "Frank Pace."
7.   Morgan, "Ninety-Six Line," *Sigodlin*, 40. "Attakullakulla Goes to London" appears in *Topsoil Road*.
8.   Walt Whitman's *Memoranda During the War* (ed. Peter Coviello, Oxford UP, 2004) notes the Confederate Army deception. On February 28, 1865, in Washington, DC, one Confederate escapee from North Carolina shared that he was "first conscripted for two years" but then kept arbitrarily in the ranks. The escapee explained that many in the Secession army were thus fooled and so felt no shame in walking away from the battlefield (74).
9.   Morgan, "Frank Pace" and *Mountains, Machines, and Memory*, 189.
10. Morgan discusses Delia's Civil War memories in Bizzaro and Bizzaro, "The Poetics of Work," 106–107.
11. Morgan, *Mountains, Machines, and Memory*, 171.
12. Morgan, "White Autumn," *At the Edge of the Orchard Country*, 13. His poem "Death Crown" appears in *Groundwork*.
13. Morgan mentioned these writers during a personal interview with the author on October 13, 2012.
14. Morgan, "Work and Poetry," 171.
15. Morgan, *Mountains, Machines, and Memory*, 17.
16. Morgan, *Mountains, Machines, and Memory*, 148.
17. Morgan, *Mountains, Machines, and Memory*, 222.
18. Morgan, "Coccidiosis," *At the Edge of the Orchard Country*, 40.
19. Morgan, *Mountains, Machines, and Memory*, 230.
20. Bizzaro and Bizzaro, "The Poetics of Work," 109.
21. Email to author, February 7, 2018.
22. Morgan, "Sigodlin," *Sigodlin*, 3.
23. Morgan, *Mountains, Machines, and Memory*, 142.
24. Morgan, *Mountains, Machines, and Memory*, 230–31.
25. West, "To Connect," 200.
26. Morgan, "Work and Poetry," 174, explains his changing view of his father; letters to Matthews and Banks are in the North Carolina Collection, Wilson Library, University of North Carolina at Chapel Hill.
27. Morgan, *Mountains, Machines, and Memory*, 213.
28. Morgan, *Mountains, Machines, and Memory*, 235.
29. Morgan, *Mountains, Machines, and Memory*, 215.
30. Morgan, *Mountains, Machines, and Memory*, 232.
31. Morgan, *Mountains, Machines, and Memory*, 241.
32. Morgan, *Mountains, Machines, and Memory*, 243.
33. Morgan, "Purple Hands," *Terroir*, 43.
34. Morgan, *Mountains, Machines, and Memory*, 73.
35. Morgan, "O Lost," 3.
36. Donald, *Look Homeward*, 9.
37. Marion, "Interview with Robert Morgan," 3–4.
38. Morgan, "O Lost," 5.

39. Morgan, "Discovery of Poetry," 19.
40. Morgan shared some details about Wildacres in emails to the author on June 5 and July 12, 2015. He also shared with the author an unpublished essay titled "Wildacres."
41. Bizzaro and Bizzaro, "The Poetics of Work," 112–113.
42. Personal interview with author, December 12, 2012.
43. Email to author, July 26, 2020.
44. Bizzaro and Bizzaro, "The Poetics of Work," 113.
45. Booker, "Interview with Robert Morgan," 10.
46. Interview emailed to author, June 12, 2014.
47. Morgan, "Fertile North Carolina," 16. In Anderson, "A Conversation with Robert Morgan," Morgan names that story as "Sunday Afternoon" and says that he published a revised version in the late 1960s but does not name the publication source (32).
48. Morgan, "11/22/13," *Dark Energy*, 29.
49. Morgan made these comments about Western writers in his speech honoring Dr. Joseph Flora at the annual South Atlantic Modern Language Association meeting in Research Triangle Park, North Carolina, November 2012.
50. Morgan, "Fertile North Carolina," 17.
51. Wright, "Interview: Robert Morgan," 182–83.
52. West, "The Art of Far and Near," 67.
53. Morgan, "Nostalgia May Not Be the Right Word" interview with Lirette. Morgan also discusses here his early thinking about how to match language to things—for instance, to the land.
54. Ravenel, Comments on Robert Morgan, North Carolina Writers Conference.
55. Ravenel accepted "The Trace" and asked for two more novellas to complete the volume that Algonquin published as *The Hinterlands*. Email to author, June 4, 2021.
56. Interview emailed to author, June 12, 2014.
57. Smith, "Going Back to the Mountains," 57.
58. Interview emailed to author, June 12, 2014.
59. Smith, "Going Back to the Mountains," 57.
60. Interview emailed to author, June 12, 2014.
61. Morgan comments on the lack of writing time in a May 12, 1969, letter to Russell Banks, archived in the North Carolina Collection, Wilson Library, University of North Carolina at Chapel Hill.
62. A February 1967 letter to Banks and Matthews in the North Carolina Collection mentions a comic novel. On May 30, 1967, Morgan writes to Matthews that he's sent a draft to an agent, adding, "Fiction is neither my forte nor passion and I'm glad to have it off my hands." His early novel was rejected, but parts of it appeared in stories, he shared with the author.
63. Email to author, July 20, 2016.
64. Morgan shared with the author an unpublished essay titled "Leo's House" that includes these details.
65. Email to author, October 15, 2016.
66. Interview emailed to author, June 12, 2014.
67. "James McConkey and the Quest for the Sacred," posted September 14, 2010. Accessed April 2, 2018, at www.cornell.edu/video/robert-morgan-on-james-mcconkey.

68. West, "To Connect," 208.

CHAPTER 3

1. Morgan, "O Lost," 7.
2. Morgan, "O Lost," 7.
3. Wolfe, "Letter to Julian Meade," *The Letters*, 339. The comment identifying Meade appears in *The Letters*, 319.
4. Morgan, "O Lost," 8.
5. Email to author, December 15, 2010.
6. Graves, "The More Mysterious," 156.
7. Wolfe, *The Web of Earth*, 214.
8. Morgan, *The Hinterlands*, 4. In the rest of the chapter, quotations from this book are cited parenthetically.
9. Johnson, "Eliza Gant's Web," 43, 44.
10. Wolfe, *The Web of Earth*, 223.
11. Guzi, "Weaving as Metaphor," 46.
12. Wolfe, *The Web of Earth*, 301.
13. Morgan, "Autobiographical Essay," 261.
14. Eads, "Feminist Forgiveness," 160.
15. Morgan, "The Tracks of Chief de Soto," *The Balm of Gilead Tree*, 6. In the rest of the chapter, quotations from this story are cited parenthetically.
16. Morgan, "The Distant Blue Hills," *As Rain Turns to Snow*, 79–80.
17. Morgan, "Wild Peavines," *Topsoil Road*, 7.
18. Conway, "Robert Morgan's Mountain Voice," 284.
19. Email to author, July 20, 2014.
20. Email to author, December 21, 2018.
21. Morgan, "Poinsett's Bridge," *The Mountains Won't Remember Us*, 1. In the rest of the chapter, quotations from this story are cited parenthetically.
22. Morgan, "Watershed," *The Mountains Won't Remember Us*, 27. In the rest of the chapter, quotations from this story are cited parenthetically.
23. Morgan, "A Noble," 5.
24. Schürer, "An Interview with Robert Morgan," 259.
25. In an email to the author on May 24, 2012, Morgan says that people still dig along the branch near Carl Sandburg's home, looking for gold.
26. Godwin, "After the Fighting," 172.
27. Morgan, *Brave Enemies*, 33. In the rest of the chapter, quotations from this book are cited parenthetically.
28. Perry, "Becoming America," 276–77.
29. Godwin, "After the Fighting," 174.
30. Godwin, "After the Fighting," 171.
31. Morgan, "The Jaguar," *As Rain Turns to Snow*, 174.
32. Morgan, "Jaguar," *Dark Energy*, 5.
33. Anderson, "A Conversation with Robert Morgan," 43.
34. Morgan, "Martha Sue," *The Mountains Won't Remember Us*, 72. In the rest of the chapter, quotations from this story are cited parenthetically.
35. Douglass, *Narrative of the Life of Frederick Douglass*, 41.
36. Morgan, *Chasing the North Star*, 1. In the rest of the chapter, quotations from this book are cited parenthetically.

37. Jacobs, *Incidents in the Life of a Slave Girl*, 1.
38. Camp, "The Pleasures of Resistance," 543–44.
39. Jones-Rogers, "Rethinking Sexual Violence," 113.
40. Camp discusses enslaved persons' finding "transcendence" in their bodies (540).
41. Jacobs, *Incidents in the Life of a Slave Girl*, 56.
42. Robinson, "Why *Does* the Slave Ever Love?" 39–41.
43. Camp, "The Pleasures of Resistance," 562.
44. Morgan, *Lions of the West*, xix.

CHAPTER 4

1. Bizzaro and Bizzaro, "The Poetics of Work," 105–107.
2. Morgan, *The Truest Pleasure*, 16. In the rest of the chapter, references to specifics and quotations from this book are cited parenthetically.
3. Morgan, "Work and Poetry," 165–66.
4. Morgan, "Work and Poetry," 166–67.
5. Drewitt-Crockett, "Authority, Details, and Intimacy," 121–22.
6. Morgan explains the Hard-Shells in "Work and Poetry," 165.
7. Morgan, "Zircon," *Dark Energy*, 72.
8. Morgan, "The Medicine Rock," 36.
9. Ballard, "Interview with Robert Morgan," 125.
10. Morgan, *This Rock*, 72. In the rest of the chapter, quotations from this book are cited parenthetically.
11. Personal interview with author, March 10, 2012.
12. Graves, "The More Mysterious," 166.
13. Morgan, "A Noble," 4–5.
14. Morgan, "A Noble," 5.
15. Hovis, "Ten North Carolina Stories," 146.
16. Other writers have referred to this elephant hanging, including Sharyn McCrumb in *She Walks These Hills*.
17. Morgan, *Mountains, Machines, and Memory*, 149.
18. Ballard, "Interview with Robert Morgan," 124.
19. Miller, "Appalachian Literature at Home in This World," 13.
20. Schürer, "An Interview with Robert Morgan," 256.
21. In "Mountain Bride," Morgan follows the storyline appearing in an 1881 novel published in Raleigh, North Carolina, *The Heirs of St. Kilda: A Story of the Southern Past*, by John Wheeler Moore. Appalachian writer and historian George Ellison discovered this book in an excerpt printed in an "All-Appalachian Issue" of *North Carolina Folklore* (16, no. 3 [1968]) edited by Guy Owen and Richard Walser. In this version, the bridegroom dies, leaving the bride hovering under quilts to escape the fangs until neighbors find her. See Ellison for more details.
22. Morgan, *Gap Creek*, 15. In the rest of the chapter, quotations from this book are cited parenthetically.
23. Morgan, comments at the Upcountry Literary Festival in Union, South Carolina, March 23, 2013.
24. Morgan, comments at Country Bookstore, Southern Pines, North Carolina, April 2, 2014.
25. Morgan, comments at the Winston-Salem Literary Festival in Winston-Salem, North Carolina, September 6, 2014.

26. Email to author, May 14, 2020.
27. Marion, "Interview with Robert Morgan," 4.
28. Morgan, "Cowbedding," *At the Edge of the Orchard Country*, 35.
29. Morgan, "Time's Music," *The Strange Attractor*, 13.
30. Drewitz-Crockett, "Authority, Details, and Intimacy," 118.
31. Morgan, comments at Country Bookstore, Southern Pines, North Carolina, April 2, 2014.
32. Graves, "The More Mysterious," 157.
33. Morgan, *The Road from Gap Creek*, 3. In the rest of the chapter, quotations from this book are cited parenthetically.
34. Godwin, "After the Fighting," 177. "Uncle Robert" appears in *At the Edge of the Orchard Country*, 44–47.
35. Godwin, "After the Fighting," 178.
36. Morgan, "Uncle Robert," *At the Edge of the Orchard Country*, 46.
37. Email to author, December 14, 2010.
38. Godwin, "After the Fighting," 179.
39. Morgan, "Homecoming," *Trunk and Thicket*, 30.
40. Morgan uses Troy's painting skills to develop the tale of Mrs. Anhalt in the novel, based on the true report of a woman's keeping preserved corpses of her husband and sister in her house south of Ithaca. E-mail to author, June 24, 2012.
41. Morgan, *This Rock*, 304.

CHAPTER 5

1. Morgan, "Dark Corner," *The Balm of Gilead* Tree, 151. In the rest of the chapter, quotations from this story are cited parenthetically.
2. Email to author, August 6, 2019.
3. Morgan, "The Sal Raeburn Gap," *The Mountains Won't Remember Us*, 50.
4. Email to author, September 1, 2014.
5. Personal interview, March 13, 2011.
6. Morgan, "Pisgah," *The Blue Valleys*, 23. In the rest of the chapter, quotations from this story are cited parenthetically.
7. Morgan, "1916 Flood," *The Blue Valleys*, 40. In the rest of the chapter, quotations from this story are cited parenthetically.
8. Morgan, "Flood," *Land Diving*, 25.
9. Morgan, "The Dulcimer Maker," *As Rain Turns to Snow*, 62.
10. Morgan, "Death Crown," *Groundwork*, 19.
11. Morgan, "The Wedding Party," *As Rain Turns to Snow*, 95.
12. Morgan, "War Story," *The Blue Valleys*, 66. In the rest of the chapter, quotations from this story are cited parenthetically.
13. Marion, "Interview with Robert Morgan," 5.
14. Morgan, "Caretakers," *The Mountains Won't Remember Us*, 107. In the rest of the chapter, quotations from this story are cited parenthetically.
15. Morgan, "Hemingway," 151.
16. Morgan, "The Welcome," *The Balm of Gilead* Tree, 223–24. In the rest of the chapter, quotations from this story are cited parenthetically.
17. Grimes, "Echoes and Influences," 106.
18. Email to author, June 7, 2012. Morgan adds in the email that "Tailgunner" is "one of the stories that got [him] going in the 1980s" as he wrote many of the stories

that became *The Blue Valleys*. He first read the story at the Air Force Academy in Colorado, where it was well received.

19. Grimes, "Echoes and Influences," 106.
20. Morgan, "Tailgunner," *The Balm of Gilead Tree*, 232–33. In the rest of the chapter, quotations from this story are cited parenthetically.
21. Morgan, "Murals," *The Balm of Gilead Tree*, 187. In the rest of the chapter, quotations from this story are cited parenthetically.
22. Buchanan, "Changing Contexts, Changing Textures," 30.
23. Morgan, "Blinding Daylight," *The Blue Valleys*, 168. In the rest of the chapter, quotations from this story are cited parenthetically.
24. Adams, "The Dynamo and the Virgin," 380.
25. Stewart and Blair, "The Frontier versus Europe," 15.
26. Adams, "The Dynamo and the Virgin," 383.
27. Lang, "Coming Out," 263.
28. Morgan, "Let No Man," *The Blue Valleys*, 76.
29. Morgan, "The Lost State of Franklin," *The Blue Valleys*, 93. In the rest of the chapter, quotations from this story are cited parenthetically.
30. Morgan, "Frog Level," *The Mountains Won't Remember Us*, 109. In the rest of the chapter, quotations from this story are cited parenthetically.
31. Morgan, "Cracklin' Bread," *The Mountains Won't Remember Us*, 134. In the rest of the chapter, quotations from this story are cited parenthetically.
32. Morgan, "Atomic Age," *Topsoil Road*, 17.
33. Morgan, "The Half Nelson," *The Blue Valleys*, 128. In the rest of the chapter, quotations from this story are cited parenthetically.
34. Morgan, "The Pickup," *The Blue Valleys*, 149.
35. Morgan, "The Bullnoser," *The Mountains Won't Remember Us*, 156. In the rest of the chapter, quotations from this story are cited parenthetically.
36. Morgan, "A Taxpayer and a Citizen," *The Balm of Gilead Tree*, 318.
37. Morgan, "The Ratchet," *The Balm of Gilead Tree*, 270. In the rest of the chapter, quotations from this story are cited parenthetically.
38. Morgan, "The Balm of Gilead Tree," *The Balm of Gilead Tree*, 326. In the rest of the chapter, quotations from this story are cited parenthetically.
39. Grimes, "Echoes and Influences," 111.
40. Grimes, "Echoes and Influences," 113–14.
41. Gina Herring's "Climbing Paradox Mountain: The Stories of Robert Morgan," *Appalachian Journal* 27, no. 3 (2000): 260–71 presents a useful exploration of this collection's themes and its comments on American history.
42. Morgan, "Bird Wars," *As Rain Turns to Snow*, 57. In the rest of the chapter, quotations from this story are cited parenthetically.
43. Morgan, "Night Thoughts," *The Blue Valleys*, 144.
44. West, "To Connect," 204.
45. Morgan, "Mack," *The Mountains Won't Remember Us*, 173. In the rest of the chapter, quotations from this story are cited parenthetically.
46. Marion, "Interview with Robert Morgan," 6.
47. Marion, "Interview with Robert Morgan," 6.
48. Morgan, "The Mountains Won't Remember Us," *The Mountains Won't Remember Us*, 189. In the rest of the chapter, quotations from this novella are cited parenthetically.
49. Godwin, "After the Fighting," 178.

50. Wolfe, "The Four Lost Men," *From Death to Morning*, 125.
51. Morgan, "Hemingway," 144.
52. Morgan, "Dans Les Hautes Montagnes," *As Rain Turns to Snow*, 89. In the rest of the chapter, quotations from this story are cited parenthetically.
53. Morgan, "Go Gentle," *Terroir*, 45.
54. Morgan, "The Calm," *As Rain Turns to Snow*, 164.
55. Morgan, "The Church of the Ascension," *As Rain Turns to Snow*, 38. In the rest of the chapter, quotations from this story are cited parenthetically.
56. Morgan, "Big Words and Fame," *As Rain Turns to Snow*, 128. In the rest of the chapter, quotations from this story are cited parenthetically.

CHAPTER 6

1.   Godwin, "'Music of the Spheres,'" 192.
2.   Morgan, "Mound Builders," *Terroir*, 92–93.
3.   Morgan, "White Autumn," *At the Edge of the Orchard Country*, 14.
4.   Morgan, "The Gift of Tongues," *At the Edge of the Orchard Country*, 29.
5.   Graves, "The More Mysterious," 165.
6.   Morgan, "The Cubist of Memory," *Good Measure*, 10.
7.   Morgan, "Sigodlin," *Sigodlin*, 3.
8.   Morgan, "Clogging," *October Crossing*, 1.
9.   Morgan, "Sidney Lanier Dies at Tryon 1881," *Sigodlin*, 33–34.
10. Morgan, "Ancient Talk," *Dark Energy*, 7.
11. Morgan, "Topsoil Road," *Topsoil Road*, 3.
12. Morgan, "Big Bone Lick," *Dark Energy*, 4.
13. Morgan, "Manure Pile," *At the Edge of the Orchard Country*, 21.
14. Morgan, "Loaves and Fishes," *Terroir*, 11.
15. Morgan, "The Cubist of Memory," *Good Measure*, 10.
16. Booker-Canfield, "The 'Rush toward the Horizon,'" 37.
17. In an unpublished essay shared with the author on June 26, 2021, tentatively titled "Science and Poetry: The Flesh Made Word," Morgan discusses his Blue Ridge fundamentalist community's distrust of science, the Romantics' embrace of it, and the role of science in his own poetry.
18. Morgan, "Lightning Bug," *At The Edge of the Orchard Country*, 24.
19. Morgan, "Cedar," *Red Owl*, 39.
20. Morgan, *Land Diving*, 59.
21. Morgan, "The Transfigured Body: Notes from a Journal," *Good Measure*, 111.
22. Morgan, "Writing Spider," *Sigodlin*, 49.
23. Morgan, "Ancient Script," *Dark Energy*, 58.
24. Morgan, "Milkomeda," *Dark Energy*, 71.
25. Morgan, "Rearview Mirror," *Sigodlin*, 21.
26. Morgan, "Rearview Mirror," *Sigodlin*, 21. His two comments on "Rearview Mirror" quoted in this paragraph appear in "Science and Poetry: The Flesh Made Word," shared with the author on June 26, 2021.
27. Morgan, "Inertia," *Sigodlin* 8. His comments about the word "inertia" cited in this paragraph appear in "Science and Poetry: The Flesh Made Word," shared with the author on June 26, 2021.
28. Morgan, "Radiation Pressure," *Sigodlin*, 19.
29. Morgan, "Coriolis Effect," *Dark Energy*, 75.

30. Morgan, "Dark Matter," *Dark Energy*, 67.
31. Morgan, "Science and Poetry: The Flesh Made Word," shared with the author on June 26, 2021.
32. Morgan, "Man and Machine," *At the Edge of the Orchard Country*, 50, 51.
33. Morgan, "Engine," *Dark Energy*, 74.
34. Morgan, "Science and Poetry: The Flesh Made Word," shared with the author on June 26, 2021.
35. Morgan, "MRI," *Dark Energy*, 76.
36. Morgan, "The Cubist of Memory," *Good Measure*, 10–11.
37. Booker, "Interview with Robert Morgan," 12, 14.
38. Morgan, *Mockingbird*, 16–17, 9.
39. Godwin, "'Music of the Spheres,'" 192.
40. Morgan, "Mica Country," *Sigodlin*. 53.
41. In an email to the author on June 7, 2021, Morgan identifies "he" in "New Organ" as Hamp Levi.
42. Morgan, "History's Madrigal" and "Tail Music," *Topsoil Road*, 48, 49.
43. Booker, "Interview with Robert Morgan," 13.
44. Bherwani, "The Elegiac Strain," 83.
45. Morgan, "Mountain Graveyard," *Sigodlin*, 27.
46. Morgan, "Living Tree," *Dark Energy*, 46.

CHAPTER 7

1. Morgan, "Nature is a Stranger Yet," robert-morgan.com/essays.
2. Morgan, *Boone*, 10.
3. Morgan, *Boone*, 446.
4. Morgan, "The Transfigured Body," *Good Measure*, 110.
5. Booker, "Interview with Robert Morgan," 7.
6. Anderson, "A Conversation with Robert Morgan," 48.
7. Booker, "Interview with Robert Morgan," 8.
8. Anderson, "A Conversation with Robert Morgan," 41.
9. Morgan, "The Transfigured Body," *Good Measure*, 114.
10. Lang, "Coming Out from under Calvinism," 269–70.
11. Morgan discusses his views of a changing Henderson County in West, "To Connect," 207.

Bibliography

Adams, Henry. "The Dynamo and the Virgin." *The Education of Henry Adams*. The Modern Library (Random House), 1931 (1918 by Massachusetts Historical Society), 379–90.

Anderson, Donald. "A Conversation with Robert Morgan." *Xavier Review* 12 (1992): 17–38. Rpt. in *Conversations with Robert Morgan*, edited by Randall Wilhelm and Jesse Graves. University Press of Mississippi, 2019, 32–49.

Ballard, Sandra. "Interview with Robert Morgan." *Appalachian Journal* 29, no. 4 (2002): 494–504. Rpt. in *Conversations with Robert Morgan*, edited by Randall Wilhelm and Jesse Graves. University Press of Mississippi, 2019, 117–29.

Banks, Russell. "Bob Morgan at Chapel Hill." *Pembroke Magazine* 35 (2003): 82–84.

Bherwani, Bhisham. "The Elegiac Strain in Robert Morgan's Poetry." *Yale Review* 105, no. 1 (2017): 80–106.

Bizzaro, Patrick and Resa Crane Bizzaro. "The Poetics of Work: An Interview with Robert Morgan." *North Carolina Literary Review*, no. 10 (2001): 173–90. Rpt. in *Conversations with Robert Morgan*, edited by Randall Wilhelm and Jesse Graves. University Press of Mississippi, 2019, 96–116.

Booker, Suzanne. "Interview with Robert Morgan." *Carolina Quarterly* 37, no. 3 (1985): 13–22. Rpt. in *Conversations with Robert Morgan*, edited by Randall Wilhelm and Jesse Graves. University Press of Mississippi, 2019, 7–19.

Booker-Canfield, Suzanne. "The 'Rush Toward the Horizon': The Geography of Land and Language in Robert Morgan's Recent Poetry." *Southern Quarterly* 47, no. 3 (2010): 36–44.

Buchanan, Harriet. "Changing Contexts, Changing Textures: Robert Morgan's 'Murals' over Its Publication History." *Pembroke Magazine* 35 (2003): 28–36.

Camp, Stephanie M. H. "The Pleasures of Resistance: Enslaved Women and Body Politics in the Plantation South, 1830–1861." *Journal of Southern History* 68, no. 3 (2002): 533–72. *ProQuest*. Accessed March 20, 2021.

Conway, Cecelia. "Robert Morgan's Mountain Voice and Lucid Prose." *Appalachian Journal* 29 (2001–2002): 180–99. Rpt. in different form in *An American Vein: Critical Readings in Appalachian Literature*, edited by Danny L. Miller, Sharon Hatfield, and Gurney Norman. Ohio University Press, 2005, 275–95.

Donald, David Herbert. *Look Homeward: A Life of Thomas Wolfe*. Little, Brown, 1987.

Douglass, Frederick. *Narrative of the Life of Frederick Douglass, An American Slave, Written by Himself*. 2nd edition, edited and with an introduction by David. W. Blight. Bedford-St. Martin's, 2003.

Drewitz-Crockett, Nicole. "Authority, Details, and Intimacy: Southern Appalachian Women in Robert Morgan's Family Novels." *Southern Quarterly* 47, no. 3 (2010): 117–28.

Eads, Martha Green. "Feminist Forgiveness in Robert Morgan's 'The Trace.'" *Southern Quarterly* 47, no. 3 (2010): 151–61.

Ellison, George. "Nature Journal: A Mountain Folk Tale of Deadly Snakes on a Wedding Night." *Citizen Times*, Dec. 5, 2018. www.citizen-times.com. Accessed July 29, 2019.

Godwin, Rebecca. "'After the Fighting, the Scars Remain': An Interview with Robert Morgan on His War Literature." *North Carolina Literary Review* 23 (2014): 6–17. Rpt. in *Conversations with Robert Morgan*, edited by Randall Wilhelm and Jesse Graves. University Press of Mississippi, 2019, 169–80.

———. "'Music of the Spheres' Heard as 'World Opening onto World': An Interview with Robert Morgan. *North Carolina Literary Review Online* (2017). Rpt. in *Conversations with Robert Morgan*, edited by Randall Wilhelm and Jesse Graves. University Press of Mississippi, 2019, 191–97.

Graves, Jesse. "The More Mysterious: An Interview with Robert Morgan." *Georgia Review* 66, no. 1 (2012): 65–87. Rpt. in *Conversations with Robert Morgan*, edited by Randall Wilhelm and Jesse Graves. University Press of Mississippi, 2019, 148–68.

Grimes, Larry. "Echoes and Influences: A Comparative Study of Short Fiction by Ernest Hemingway and Robert Morgan." *Southern Quarterly* 47, no. 3 (2010): 98–116.

Guzi, Gloria. "Weaving as Metaphor in Thomas Wolfe's *The Web of Earth*." *Thomas Wolfe Review* 7, no. 2 (1983): 44–47.

Harmon, William. "Imagination, Memory, and Region: A Conversation." *Iron Mountain Review*, vol. 6 (1990): 11–16. Rpt. in *Conversations with Robert Morgan*, edited by Randall Wilhelm and Jesse Graves. University Press of Mississippi, 2019, 20–31.

Hovis, George. "Ten North Carolina Stories that Ought to be Films." *North Carolina Literary Review*, no. 21 (2012): 145–58.

Jacobs, Harriet A. *Incidents in the Life of a Slave Girl, Written by Herself.* Edited and with an introduction by Jean Fagin Yellin. Harvard University Press, 2000.

Johnson, Douglas. "Eliza Gant's Web: Her Role as Earth Mother and Moral Hub in *The Web of Earth*." *Thomas Wolfe Review* 18, no. 1 (1994): 42–47.

Jones-Rogers, Stephanie. "Rethinking Sexual Violence and the Marketplace of Slavery: White Women, the Slave Market, and Enslaved People's Sexualized Bodies in the Nineteenth-Century South." *Sexuality and Slavery: Reclaiming Intimate Histories in the Americas*, edited by Daina Ramey Berry and Leslie M. Harries. University of Georgia Press, 2018, 109–123. *eBook Academic Collection*. Accessed November 21, 2020.

Justus, Michelle. "*Gap Creek*'s Celebration of Women's Subjugation." *Journal of Appalachian Studies* 23, no. 1 (2017): 99–113. *Academic Search Complete*. Accessed August 20, 2020.

Lang, John. "Coming Out from under Calvinism: Religious Motifs in Robert Morgan's Poetry." *Shenandoah* 42, no. 2 (1992): 46–60. Rpt. in *American Vein: Critical Readings in Appalachian Literature*, edited by Danny L. Miller, Sharon Hatfield, and Gurney Norman. Ohio University Press, 2005, 261–74.

———. "Speaking Charmed Syllables: The Two-Fold Vision of *Topsoil Road*." *Pembroke Magazine* 35 (2003): 16–21.

Liotta, P. H. "Pieces of the Morgenland: The Recent Achievements in Robert Morgan's Poetry." *Southern Literary Journal* 22, no. 1 (1989): 32–40. *ProQuest*. Accessed July 10, 2019.

Marion, Jeff Daniel. "Interview with Robert Morgan." *Small Farm*, no. 3 (1976): 40–43. Rpt. in *Conversations with Robert Morgan*, edited by Randall Wilhelm and Jesse Graves. University Press of Mississippi, 2019, 3–6.

McFee, Michael. "'The Witness of Many Writings': Robert Morgan's Poetic Career." *Iron Mountain Review* 6 (1990): 17–23.

Miller, Jim Wayne. "Appalachian Literature at Home in This World." *Iron Mountain Review* 2 (1984): 23–28. Rpt. in *American Vein: Critical Readings in Appalachian Literature*, edited by Danny L. Miller, Sharon Hatfield, and Gurney Norman. Ohio University Press, 2005, 13–24.

Morgan, Robert. "Appalachia." www.robert-morgan.com/essays. Accessed September 3, 2018.

———. *As Rain Turns to Snow and Other Stories*. Broadstone Books, 2017.

———. *At The Edge of the Orchard Country*. Wesleyan University Press, 1987.

———. "Autobiographical Essay." *Contemporary Authors: A Bio-Bibliographical Guide to Current Writers in Fiction, General Nonfiction, Poetry, Journalism, Drama, Motion Pictures, Television, and Other Fields*, edited by Scot Peacock, vol. 20. Gale, 2002, 258–86.

———. *The Balm of Gilead Tree: New and Selected Stories*. Gnomon Press, 1999.

———. *The Blue Valleys: A Collection of Stories*. Peachtree Publishers, 1989.

———. *Boone: A Biography*. Algonquin Books of Chapel Hill, 2007.

———. *Brave Enemies: A Novel of the American Revolution*. Algonquin Books of Chapel Hill, 2003.

———. *Chasing the North Star*. Algonquin Books of Chapel Hill, 2016.

———. "The Cubist of Memory." *Good Measure*, 8–11.

———. *Dark Energy*. Penguin Books, 2015.

———. "Discovery of Poetry." Unpublished essay shared with author.

———. "Fertile North Carolina." *Amazing Place: What North Carolina Means to Authors*, edited by Marianne Gingher. University of North Carolina Press, 2015, 11–18.

———. "Frank Pace 1838–1918." Comments presented at Green River Baptist Church on September 17, 2006, on the occasion of the Frank Pace plaque dedication honoring his donation of land for the church in 1890. Plaque donated by Fannie L. Morgan. Comments shared with the author.

———. "Fred Chappell's *Midquest*." *American Poetry Review* 11 (1982): 45–47. Rpt. in *Good Measure*, 94–105.

———. *Gap Creek: The Story of a Marriage*. Algonquin Books of Chapel Hill, 1999.

———. *Good Measure: Essays, Interviews, and Notes on Poetry*. Louisiana State University Press, 1993.

———. *Groundwork*. Gnomon Press, 1979.

———. "Hemingway and the True Poetry of War." *War, Literature, and the Arts: An International Journal of the Humanities* 12, no. 1 (2000): 136–56. *Academic Search Complete*. Accessed May 17, 2016.

———. *The Hinterlands*: Algonquin Books of Chapel Hill, 1994. John F. Blair, 1999.

———. *Land Diving*. Louisiana State University Press, 1976.

———. "Leo's House." Unpublished autobiographical essay sent to author in June 2020.

———. *Lions of the West: Heroes and Villains of the Westward Expansion*. Algonquin Books of Chapel Hill, 2011.

———. "Literary North Carolina: Robert Morgan on North Carolina's Hospitality Toward Writers." October 17, 2010, www.nclhof.org/inductees/2010-2-robert -morgan. Accessed June 19, 2019.

———. "Little Willie and the Blue Jacket." *Algonquin Reader* 5, no. 1 (2015): 40–42.

———. *Mountains, Machines, and Memory.* Unpublished memoir shared with author.

———. *The Mountains Won't Remember Us and Other Stories.* Peachtree Publishers, 1992.

———. "The Medicine Rock." *Algonkian*, New Series no. 8 (1998): 36–37.

———. "Nature Is a Stranger Yet." www.robert-morgan.com/essays. Accessed July 2, 2021.

———. "A Noble and Dangerous Tradition." *Algonkian*, New Series no. 14 (2001): 4–5.

———. *NC Bookwatch* interview by D. G. Martin. July 14, 2016. Episode 1821, www .unctw.org/video/ncbookwatch. Accessed March 12, 2020.

———. "Nostalgia May Not Be the Right Word." Interview by Christopher Lirette. *Southern Spaces*, December 11, 2013, www.southernspaces.org. Accessed June 7, 2019.

———. "O Lost, and Found." *Thomas Wolfe Review* 24, no. 2 (2000): 3–9.

———. *October Crossing.* Broadstone Books, 2009.

———. *Red Owl.* W. W. Norton, 1972.

———. *The Road from Gap Creek.* Algonquin Books of Chapel Hill, 2013.

———. "The Transfigured Body: Notes from a Journal." In *Good Measure*, 109–18.

———. *Trunk & Thicket.* L'Epervier Press, 1978.

———. *Sigodlin.* Wesleyan University Press, 1990.

———. *The Strange Attractor: New and Selected Poems.* Louisiana State University Press, 2004.

———. *Terroir.* Penguin Poets, 2011.

———. *The Road from Gap Creek.* Algonquin Books of Chapel Hill, 2013.

———. *This Rock.* Algonquin Books of Chapel Hill, 2001.

———. *Topsoil Road: Poems.* Louisiana State University Press, 2000.

———. *The Truest Pleasure.* Algonquin Books of Chapel Hill, 1995.

———. "Wilma Dykeman: A Good Spring is Mighty Hard to Find." *Appalachian Journal* 34, no. 3–4: 276–77.

———. "Work and Poetry, the Father Tongue." *Southern Review* 31, no. 1 (1995): 161–79.

———. "Writing the Living Voice: The Achievement of Lee Smith." *Pembroke Magazine* 33 (2001): 182.

Perry, Lori A. Davis. "Becoming America." *War, Literature, and the Arts: An International Journal of the Humanities* 16, no. 1–2 (2004): 275–80. *Academic Search Complete.* Accessed June 08, 2017.

Ravenel, Shannon. Comments Honoring Robert Morgan. North Carolina Writers Conference. Winston-Salem, North Carolina, July 27, 2013.

Roberts, Terry. "'Wonderfully Simple, Yet Complex': The Mountain Novels of John Ehle." *North Carolina Literary Review* 19 (2010): 11–23.

Robinson, Angelo Rich. "'Why *Does* the Slave Ever Love?': The Subject of Romance Revisited in the Neoslave Narrative." *Southern Literary Journal* 40, no. 1 (2007): 39–57. *ProQuest.* Accessed April 28, 2020.

Sadler, Anthony. *Appalachian Baptism: The Asheville Flood of 1916.* Master's Thesis. Appalachian State University, 2016. Available through NC Docks (Digital Online Collection of Knowledge and Scholarship), posted as PDF February 17, 2017. https:// libres.uncg.edu/ir/asu/listing.aspx?id=21526. Accessed March 02, 2018.

Schürer, Norbert. "An Interview with Robert Morgan." *Pembroke Magazine* 36 (2004): 252–60.

Smith, Newton. "Going Back to the Mountains from 'Topsoil Road': A Retrospective Look at Robert Morgan's Poetry." *Pembroke Magazine* 35 (2003): 55–63.

Stewart, Randall and Walter Blair. "The Frontier versus Europe: A Question of Values." *The Literature of the United States: An Anthology and History from the Civil War to the Present*, edited by Walter Blair et al. 1953. Scott, Foresman, 1970, 12–22.

Welty, Eudora. "Place in Fiction." *The Eye of the Story: Selected Essays and Reviews.* Virago Press, 1979, 116–33.

West, Robert. "The Art of Far and Near: An Interview with Robert Morgan." *Carolina Quarterly* 40, no. 3 (1997): 46–68. Rpt. in *Conversations with Robert Morgan*, edited by Randall Wilhelm and Jesse Graves. University Press of Mississippi, 2019, 67–82.

———. "To Connect with That Beyond Ourselves: An Interview with Robert Morgan." *Appalachian Journal* 44, no. 102 (2017): 132–41. Rpt. in *Conversations with Robert Morgan*, edited by Randall Wilhelm and Jesse Graves. University Press of Mississippi, 2019, 198–208.

Wilhelm, Randall. "Bricking the Text: The Builder in Robert Morgan's Mountain World." *Southern Quarterly* 47, no. 3 (2010): 142–50.

Williams, Mary C. "Inside-Outside in Robert Morgan's Poetry." *The Poetics of Appalachian Space*, edited by Lanier Parks Jr. University of Tennessee Press, 1991, 149–60. Rpt. in *Poetry Criticism*, edited by Jonathan Vereeke, vol. 213, 2019. *Gale Literature Resource*. GALE|H1420126508. Accessed June 04, 2020.

Wolfe, Thomas. "The Four Lost Men." *From Death to Morning*. Scribner's, 1935, 114–33.

———. "Letter to Julian Meade," 21 Apr. 1932. *The Letters of Thomas* Wolfe, edited by Elizabeth Nowell. Scribner's, 1956.

———. *The Web of Earth. From Death to Morning*. Scribner's, 1935, 212–304.

Wolfram, Walt and Donna Christian. *Appalachian Speech.* Center for Applied Linguistics, 1976.

Wright, William. "Interview: Robert Morgan." *Oxford American*, 82 (2013): 34–39. Rpt. in *Conversations with Robert Morgan*, edited by Randall Wilhelm and Jesse Graves, University Press of Mississippi, 2019, 181–90.

Index

Note: "RM" stands for Robert Morgan. Page numbers in italics refer to illustrations.